HELP

A Handbook for
Working Mothers

HELP

A Handbook for Working Mothers

Barbara Kaye Greenleaf
with Lewis A. Schaffer, M.D.

Thomas Y. Crowell, Publishers
Established 1834   New York

HELP: A HANDBOOK FOR WORKING MOTHERS. Copyright © 1978 by Barbara Kaye Greenleaf and Lewis A. Schaffer. All rights reserved. Printed in the United States of America. No part of this book may be used or reproduced in any manner whatsoever without written permission except in the case of brief quotations embodied in critical articles and reviews. For information address Thomas Y. Crowell, Publishers, 10 East 53rd Street, New York, N.Y. 10022. Published simultaneously in Canada by Fitzhenry & Whiteside Limited, Toronto.

FIRST EDITION

Designed by Janice Stern

Library of Congress Cataloging in Publication Data

Greenleaf, Barbara Kaye.
  Help.
  Bibliography: p.
  Includes index.
  1. Mothers—Employment—Handbooks, manuals,
etc.   2. Mothers—Handbooks, manuals, etc.
I. Schaffer, Lewis A., joint author.   II. Title.
HD6055.G73 1978   650'.1   78-3301
ISBN 0-690-01461-9

78 79 80 81 82 10 9 8 7 6 5 4 3 2 1

Contents

Acknowledgments

We are very grateful to the many people who helped us in the preparation of this book. In particular, we would like to thank Helene Kaplan, Rosalie Brody, and Cynthia Vartan, who encouraged us so warmly at the start, and Amy Bonoff, Diana Goldin, and Anne Tobias, who criticized us so constructively toward the end. We extend special thanks to Barbara La Mont, who made available to us the facilities of the Vassar College Library, and to Patricia Isom, who obtained much valuable information for us through the Northern Westchester Hospital Center Library. Our heartfelt thanks, too, to Mary Mercora and Patricia McClain, who typed the manuscript with endless good grace. And, though they know how we feel, a public thank you is in order for our families, who were unfailingly supportive of our efforts. Finally, we'd like to express our gratitude to all the working mothers who shared their concerns and coping techniques with us so that we might share them with you.

Introduction

During the three years I researched childhood in historical perspective for my book *Children Through the Ages,* I was repeatedly struck by the fact that few mothers have ever had the luxury of sitting around watching their children grow. In every era most mothers have been too busy tending crops, cooking, washing clothes, or working in factories. But though they did not devote themselves full time to child rearing, their children turned out to be, for the most part, well-adjusted members of their particular society. And though the women worked very hard, they did not seem to be under as great an emotional strain as the mothers who work in America today. As I thought about the contrast, it became obvious that working mothers fared so much better in earlier times and in other cultures because they got far more support from their family and society than their modern American counterparts. After further consideration, I also decided that Americans are experiencing an emotional time lag between the supposed ideal, mothers who devote their entire day to child nurture, and the real, mothers who need and want to work.

My musings led me to feel that the time was ripe for some no-nonsense advice for the working mother. I felt that she could use a book that would dispel the harmful and untrue myths surrounding motherhood and maternal employment, one that would enable her to cope more effectively with all the outside pressures in her life while strengthening her inner self and that would deal with the world as it is, not as she might like it to be—in short, a book that I myself as a working mother would want to read.

As the idea took shape in my mind, I discussed it with Dr. Lewis Schaffer, who had been a great help to me on *Children Through the Ages* and who had collaborated with me on various article ideas. Dr. Schaffer, a pediatrician with a private practice, deals directly with children and their mothers every day. Being one of those mothers, I know that the advice he dispenses is not only readily understandable but it works. After I finished outlining the project to him, he endorsed it enthusiastically and agreed to work on it with me. Eventually, he contributed to every aspect of the book.

Dr. Schaffer and I made our formal start by reading widely—everything from sociological, medical, and psychological tracts to popular treatments of the subject. Then we proceeded to send out more than 100 questionnaires to mothers from various socio-economic backgrounds who were either studying or were employed on a part-time or full-time basis. We also conducted numerous formal and informal interviews with working mothers and their husbands and children. The purpose of all this research was not to do a statistical analysis of working mothers, but to identify their major concerns and to find out how they cope with their many-faceted existence. Finally, we evaluated every piece of information against the single criterion: will it be helpful to a working mother? If not, then out it went.

Once we had decided what material we would use, we arranged the book so that it can be read either straight through in order or consulted at random. Should you choose to use it the second way, as a reference work, we urge you to start off by reading the first chapter even if you have been working for some time. Then look through the detailed Table of Contents to make sure you don't miss anything of interest, or check the Index for the location of specific information. Since one size does not fit all when it comes to advice, we also urge you to modify and personalize our suggestions as you go along. And now, since we know that you're strapped for time—off with the Introduction and on with Chapter 1.

HELP

A Handbook for
Working Mothers

1

15 Million Mothers
Can't Be Wrong

"Congratulations, mother, you got the job!" or "Congratulations, worker, you're going to have a baby!" Either way
you're in good company, because half the mothers in America
with children under the age of eighteen are now working. This
percentage is double what it was thirty years ago and seems
likely to escalate. In a recent magazine survey, three out of four
women under the age of thirty-five said they planned to combine
home and jobs, while fewer than one in ten in that age group
wanted to make homemaking her sole career.

Unfortunately, society is only slowly catching up with this
trend. On television mothers are still basically hausfraus ob-
sessed with getting the ring out of the collar and the shine onto
the floor. And magazines have only recently started to address
themselves to the problems of women who raise children and
work.

But even more serious than the media's reluctance to deal
with the mother as worker is the fact that many public schools
are still scheduling parent-teacher conferences in the middle of
the afternoon and many pediatricians are still giving child-rearing advice predicated on mom's being home twenty-four hours a
day. Moreover, despite the large number of mothers enrolled in
educational institutions today, many colleges and graduate
schools are still insisting on full-time attendance to obtain a
degree. Our legislators are even more obtuse than our educators.

A whopping 37 percent of all preschoolers have mothers who work—the overwhelming majority from economic necessity—yet politicians are resisting subsidized child care in any form. Indeed, America's governmental outlay for day-care centers is embarrassingly small when compared to that of other countries. But just let someone say the words "budget crunch," and even this pittance comes under attack.

It is left to businessmen to deliver the coup de grâce, however, for they seem the most insensitive of all to the special needs of working mothers. And who can blame them? Industry has so many applicants clamoring for five-day-a-week, 9–5 jobs that it has little incentive to experiment with job sharing, the four-day work week, and flexible scheduling—any one of which would be a boon to women with children at home.

After toting up all these factors, it is hard to escape the conclusion that as far as American society is concerned, the working mother is on her own. In fact she barely exists. Why? Why should a nation that has been so quick to accept the automobile, the TV set, and the computer be so reluctant to accept the working mother? Because old myths die hard, and one of this country's oldest and most strongly held beliefs is that the "real mother" is the one who stays home. Operating in splendid isolation, she alone is supposedly capable of doing a good job raising her children. And any mother who flouts this myth by taking a job is supposedly courting disaster. According to the conventional wisdom, her marriage will go on the rocks and her children will become emotionally deprived, depressed, delinquent, and every other terrible thing imaginable.

The "real mother" myth is so much a part of American culture that its veracity is accepted without question, not only by embattled housewives and male chauvinists, but also by many trained social scientists who ought to know better. It is accepted by husbands who are otherwise quite liberated, and—worst of all—it is probably accepted by you, the working mother. Indeed, the notion that maternal employment is detrimental to family life is the single greatest cause of guilt among working mothers. Since guilt is so harmful to you and to all you're trying to achieve with your children, you need to combat it with fact. And the fact is that children are not necessarily worse off—and may even be somewhat better off—when their mothers work.

Getting Rid of Guilt

Because a woman's place is supposedly in the home, her going out to work is often cited as one of the reasons for the disintegration of the family. Yet "when mothers are successfully and enthusiastically employed . . . the changes reported by their families, if any, tend to be in a positive direction. The myth dies hard." This is the considered opinion of Dr. Mary C. Howell, former professor of pediatrics and associate dean of the Harvard Medical School, who did a massive review of the subject for the journal of the American Academy of Pediatrics.

As Dr. Howell discovered, the divorce rate is no higher in families where the woman is employed than in families where she isn't. In fact, having that second income often improves a marriage because it relieves the husband of some financial pressure and allows him greater leeway in his own vocation. Furthermore, a survey discussed in the *American Journal of Sociology* showed that when wives are working by choice, both partners report significantly fewer marital tensions and significantly greater levels of marital satisfaction than those married couples where the women are full-time housewives.

Just as you are very much a "real" wife—despite the fact that you are working or because of it—so you are very much a "real" mother. Holding down a job in no way lessens the twenty-four-hour-a-day responsibility you feel for your children. You are still the one who makes sure Susie's white blouse goes into the wash on Wednesday so that she'll have it for assembly on Thursday; who senses when something's bothering Tommy although he's trying not to show it; and who makes the arrangements to get Lisa home from school when she's sick. For all these and a thousand other reasons you are as true a "psychological parent'' as any woman, even your neighbor who is devoting all of her energies to homemaking. Moreover, you probably spend almost as much time at parenting as she does. According to information gathered separately by the social scientists A. E. Siegal, A. C. Thorpe, and P. J. Stone, at-home mothers devote some 6^+ hours a day to child care, while employed mothers devote some 4^+ hours to it. The amount of attentive care, or what we usually refer to as "quality time," spent is estimated to be the same. And employed mothers report getting as much or more enjoyment from child care as do their nonworking counterparts.

These positive feelings must be transmitted to their children, because a study published in the *American Journal of Orthopsychiatry* shows that infant attachment to the mother is not altered by mother substitutes or by group care. Older children report feeling that they have received as much affection and emotional support from their working mothers as do the children of nonworking mothers. And they don't view maternal employment as threatening, either. To the contrary, most of the girls want to work when they grow up, while the boys evince a less stereotyped attitude toward male and female roles.

Many other studies have been done comparing the children of working and nonworking mothers in terms of school and social adjustment, peer relationships, intelligence, school grades and achievements, life aspirations, extracurricular activities, dependency-independency, and delinquency. After reviewing some 280 of these studies, Dr. Howell concluded: "There are almost no constant differences found between children of employed and unemployed mothers.''

Knowing that you are not doing irreparable harm to your children by working is the first step toward combating guilt. And combat it you must, because guilt is a counterproductive emotion that causes anxiety, chronic fatigue, and depression. Ironically, it is as potentially harmful to your ability to parent as any of the factors associated with maternal employment that you're feeling guilty about. It can make you so apologetic and overpermissive with your children that they in turn will become anxious and insecure. Moreover, they will quickly learn how to manipulate you through your guilt—a very unhealthy situation indeed.

You are likely to experience more guilt if you work out of personal desire rather than out of sheer economic necessity— and society will be more critical of you too. However, money and self-gratification are not mutually exclusive. According to a Department of Labor survey, most employed wives do work for the money, but a majority said they would work even if they didn't have to. No matter what your particular motivation, there is no reason for you to feel defensive about working. Instead, you should shed your guilt feelings by developing confidence in the rightness of your decision.

This will be easier when you realize that one of the best ways to make your child happy is to be happy yourself. A child's basic outlook on life is strongly influenced by that of his mother, so if you're usually in good spirits, chances are he or she will be too.* Conversely, if you're chronically depressed, he might very well be the same. It has been shown time and again that when a child has emotional problems, the condition relates not to his mother's employment status but to her own emotional troubles. Therefore, if working makes you happy, chances are you can credit it with making your child happy too.

Although we know almost nothing about the interdynamics of working and the ability to mother, we do know that job satisfaction correlates to a high degree with feelings of maternal satisfaction and competence. Perhaps working brings with it an increase in self-esteem that carries over to mothering. Perhaps, as one day-care worker observed, women who achieve can be more relaxed about their children's ability to achieve. Perhaps spending a certain number of hours in a rewarding environment

---

*This is the first and last time that cumbersome phrase "he or she" will appear in this book. From now on we will merely alternate the pronouns, which, in almost every instance, are meant to be interchangeable.

gives a woman a fresh perspective on mothering. Whatever the reason, you can rejoice over this phenomenon. It means that if you get satisfaction from your job for any reason—salary, social contacts, intellectual fulfillment, or increased status—you are probably a more secure and therefore more effective parent.

And positive thinking can help to make this happen. If you concentrate on the good features of your job, you will get more satisfaction from it. Likewise, if you focus on the positive effects of maternal employment, you will feel less guilty about leaving your child. As a starter, remind yourself that every member of the family benefits materially and emotionally from your salary. Then, instead of bemoaning the need for a surrogate parent or group care for a very young child, start to think of each arrangement as a good socializing experience. Finally, come to look upon your absence as a chance—one might even say a golden opportunity—for an older child to become more independent, to take on greater responsibility, to acquire new domestic skills, and to feel perhaps for the first time in his life that he is truly needed at home.

This is not to say that your child won't have problems. He will—but most of them will have nothing to do with your working. After all, kids have had a tough time growing up for centuries before mothers invaded the job market. So, while recognizing that it won't be all smooth sailing, we suggest that you expect your child to be okay. You should develop this attitude both because a child tends to live up to expectations of him and because, if he is like the vast majority of children, he *will* be okay.

Time is on your side in the battle against guilt. The longer you work and the longer your family survives it, the more justified you'll feel. Moreover, the older your children get, the less conflict you'll perceive in your dual role. If you're the mother of a preschooler, you should especially take heart. When your child turns six and starts to attend school all day, you will experience an enormous drop-off in guilt. Until that great day occurs, we suggest that you do your utmost to obtain the best help you can. The women who feel least guilty about working are usually those with the best or at least the most consistent child-care arrangements.

Banish guilt now before it becomes a habit by preparing your children for the new régime. If you know that they know what to do and where to go when you're out of the house, you will feel much better about leaving and so will they.

Setting the Stage, Rehearsing the Actors

Assuming that you've just landed a job, you'll have to convey the good news to your children. If they are above the age of three, they've probably known for some time that something is up. Still, you should make it a point to tell them directly. Not only is this common courtesy (which you hope they'll reciprocate some day), but it is a flattering indication that you consider them partners in your new life. Beyond that, a thorough discussion gives the children an opportunity to ask questions, express anxieties, and start to come to grips with the wider implications of your taking a job.

But don't feel that you have to broach the subject the very day you're hired. In fact, as a general rule the younger the child, the closer to the actual event he should be told. Until he is five or six, a child only knows that tomorrow and next month are not today. Since even older children often have trouble getting a fix on time, you could help them place your debut by speaking of it in relation to some familiar event, such as the start of school or the end of the Christmas vacation.

As with any other subject, your job should be explained to the children in a straightforward manner. Give them real facts, not just hints or euphemisms, but let the facts be appropriate to their ages. Also, only give them as much as they can absorb in one sitting, then plan to fill in the details later. We suggest that you start by describing the company you are going to work for, the job you will do there, and the daily routine as you foresee it. Then tell the children what arrangements have been made for them. It is absolutely crucial that you present all this information in the best possible light, lest you prejudice the children against your working before you even begin.

By the way, don't be surprised if your offspring are much less interested in your great new enterprise than in their own potential inconvenience. Children are self-centered by nature, and in their eyes they come first. One psychologically oriented woman we interviewed found this out to her chagrin. Having sat her son down and told him she was going to work, she awaited his reaction with trepidation. She had prepared herself to cope with deepseated fears and dark resentment. Instead, she got the single question, "But who's going to take me to basketball practice?"

After you've explained in general terms what is going to occur, you can get down to specifics. Children of school age find it reassuring to know what is planned for them day by day and, for the younger ones, even hour by hour. Drawing up a calendar will help you in this explanation. It will also enable your youngster to get a firmer grasp on his comings and goings than he possibly could by listening to a lot of confusing instructions. Of course, once he starts to put the new routine into practice, he will automatically go to Cub Scouts on Tuesday and to Mrs. Smith's on Wednesday. But until it becomes second nature, having a concrete schedule to follow will reduce his anxiety about being left alone or in the care of others.

In addition to making it clear to your children where they will be every hour of the day, you should spell out what will be expected of them under the new régime. While you're still home, have them cook, run the vacuum, and practice other new chores under your supervision. One woman who was about to return to hospital work on the 7-to-3 shift supervised her children just that way. Since there would be a two-hour period between the time she left for work and the time they left for school, she wanted to make sure they could get out of the house without her. For weeks she did less and less until, by the time she started to work, they were dressing, making breakfast, bagging lunch, and meeting the bus—all on their own.

It is valuable to prepare children for the unexpected as well as the expected. While you're still around, go over a number of contingency situations with them. Have them walk home from the bus stop while you, pretending to be a stranger, accost them. Have them start to unlock the door only to discover that they've lost their keys. Have them make believe they came home to a strange odor, a suspicious phone call, a power failure, a flooded basement, a flash fire. Drill young children on their names, addresses, and phone numbers and instruct them on how to go about calling the telephone operator and the police. The more they practice handling unusual situations, the more self-assured they'll feel and the less likely they'll be to panic when something out of the ordinary does occur. However, since you don't want to terrify the youngsters in the process, run through each situation calmly and, when appropriate, with humor.

It's best if you can start your child on her new routine before you start yours. Then you'll be able to stay with her while she grows accustomed to the day-care facility or the new sitter. If that's not feasible, she should at least be introduced to her caretakers before she's left with them. One final thing you can do ahead of time: take your child on a tour of the place where you'll be working. This will help her to visualize you when you're gone and allay her fears that you're vanishing off the face of the earth.

But even if you are not able to prepare your child for every eventuality (and you won't be), she will quickly adjust. Soon after you take a job, your working and her own new routine will seem totally normal to her.

Beginnings Are Always Hard

Beginnings are always hard because everything has to be consciously thought out. Tasks that you will zip through later on now seem to take forever. The start of a new job is particularly difficult because it involves learning so many tasks, meeting so many people, and enduring the unpleasant experience of being judged. Moreover, while you're striving to get acclimated on the job, you've still got to attend to all your duties at home.

How will you be able to get everything done? You won't, and rather than try, you'd do better to temporarily eliminate any extraneous activities from your life. Take a leave of absence from the ladies auxiliary, drop out of the weekly tennis game, and find a substitute to work with the Cub Scout pack. You can always go back to these activities later on. The remaining items will get done because they have to be done, but they'll produce less wear and tear on the nervous system if you plan for them in advance. They'll also be done better because, once you get things off your mind and onto a list, you can concentrate more fully on the task at hand.

Above all, don't try to be a perfectionist. You'll drive yourself crazy if you try to do everything at home as well as you did before. For the time being, anyway, aim for simply managing instead of trying to be magnificent. Like politics, the secret of successful working motherhood is knowing how to compromise. In your situation, just being able to cope can be considered a major achievement.

Of course, even if you're coping just fine, the rest of your family may choose this very moment to fall apart. Your eight-year-old may regress to the point where he needs you to tie his shoelaces and your husband may decide that he absolutely cannot face his annual sales convention without you by his side. While these tactics are annoying, they are also flattering because they show that your family is afraid of being neglected. And it's possible that you *are* neglecting them while so much of your energy is going into the new job. If you suspect that you are less attentive than usual, make it a point to administer extra T.L.C. Husbands find it difficult to be put on "hold" until their wives get themselves straightened out, and children find it impossible.

Like most women, you may experience a tremendous sense of exhilaration when you first start to work. But interspersed with those days when you are high as a kite will be days when you feel tired, frustrated, on edge, and out of step with your husband and children. Of course, you'd probably have such days even if you were still at home. Now, at least, when things go badly you can console yourself with the money you're making, the people you're meeting, and the satisfaction you're getting from doing "real work." Dwell on these rewards; they're good for your mental health. And don't overlook the salutary effects of a sense of humor, either. A few good laughs can go a long way toward dispelling the tensions of this period.

When you are feeling particularly overwhelmed, remind yourself that by definition beginnings don't last forever. Things do get easier as you go along. With experience—and the aid of this book—you can learn how to save time and energy through shortcuts, how to run your household more smoothly, and how to be more efficient on your job. You'll learn how to enlist the aid of "volunteers" and how to make the best use of professional services. You'll become adept at evaluating child-care arrangements, at diagnosing a sick child's condition over the telephone, and at heading off behavioral problems before they get serious. Above all, you'll become the best mother you can in the limited amount of time you have.

So, buck up! Fifteen million American women are holding down jobs and raising children at the same time. If they can do it, so can you.

2

Let's Get Organized

What really separates the working mother from the rest of the world is time. You probably have less of it in which to do more things for more people than most other men, women, and children on this earth. Since time is of the essence, organization is what you need. Organization allows you to get hold of and stretch time to its outermost limits. It helps you run your household more smoothly, become more accomplished at your job, see more of your family, do more of your errands, and have greater opportunities for leisure. At times it enables you to just plain survive. Fortunately, when you started to work, you acquired a basic structure to your life. Now all you have to do is get organized within that structure, a process that begins with scheduling.

The Fine Art of Scheduling

When something is about to start—such as a new job, a new semester, or a summer vacation—it's a good idea to physically block out a weekly family schedule. Setting things down on paper with pencil and ruler will not only make everyone's comings and goings more controllable, but will imprint the traffic flow more vividly on your brain. It will also enable you to see if one person is overscheduled or two people have a transportation conflict.

In addition to the family calendar, you will need a schedule for your own activities. On it block out time for routine chores, errands, and leisure. Keep these categories as general as possible since many of the specifics will change from week to week. Also leave plenty of room around the edges for last-minute emergencies and for running late. Time-management consultant Alan Lakein advises people to leave an hour a day unscheduled for the sake of spontaneity. We would go further and suggest that you also set aside one "catch-up" night each week for the sake of sanity. Of course, if you've been so efficient that you're all caught up, you can spend this time in bed with a box of caramels and a juicy novel. What an incentive to get your chores done!

To plan a realistic schedule, you will have to know in advance how long each activity takes. This means getting an exact fix on your daily routine. Since you probably have never paid attention to precisely where your time goes, we suggest that for the next week or two you jot down when you start and when you stop each chore. You will be fascinated to find out how long it takes you to empty the dishwasher, do a load of laundry, buy the week's groceries, and get up and out in the morning without rushing.

When you have this information in hand, you can proceed to the next step of scheduling: an appraisal of various times of the day. You will find that one hour is not as good as every other hour. There is something about 8:00 A.M., for example, that makes people frantic and something about 5:00 P.M. that makes them cranky. To avoid the morning frazzles, do some traditional A.M. chores the night before, such as laying out clothes, setting the breakfast table, and making the next day's lunches. To avoid the end-of-work, end-of-the-day "mean reds," don't do anything "meaningful" at all. Rather, when you come home plan to chat with your family as you start to prepare dinner. Give the starving ones something to tide them over and then gracefully withdraw to your bedroom—making sure to close the door. Take a cool shower or a warm bath, do a few sit-ups, lie down for a catnap, or just stare at a crack in the ceiling. Only when you feel the blood start to circulate again should you change into an at-home outfit and emerge. Many women find this private little interlude absolutely indispensable, because it enables them to unwind while making the psychological switch from office to home.

The wise scheduler also tries to take it easy when her energy level is low. If you drag through the early morning like a zombie, for example, there's no point scheduling anything more demanding then than a cup of coffee. And if you feel down and out after dinner, leave the dishes until you get a second wind. On the other hand, if you usually wake up full of vim and vigor, plan to do your exercises, scour the oven, and sear a pot roast while the family sleeps on. You will get more done with less resentment if you work *with* your energy cycle rather than against it.

Finally, take your total energy quotient into account as well as its ups and downs. Although Tillie Terrific down the block may be able to rush around for ten hours a day every day, you may not. If you haven't got the stamina for it, a perpetually hectic schedule will leave you feeling exhausted, tense, and irritable. Listen to your body. If it seems to be rebelling, cut down on the total number of activities you have planned and/or do them more slowly. There's no sense killing yourself for an hour so that you can rest for an hour if you're really more comfortable—and ultimately more productive—working at a leisurely pace for the entire period. Even a racehorse, whose whole *raison d'être* is speed, doesn't run his fastest for the entire race. He has learned how to pace himself, and so should you.

As all of this suggests, there is an art to scheduling. It takes soul-searching, observation, and practice. It also entails trial and error, because no one can really know how a schedule will work out until she has put it into gear. If you make up a weekly timetable and find that you're having trouble following it: (1) you may be attempting to do too much; (2) you may be trying to change too many things at once; (3) you may not have left enough room for the unexpected; (4) you may have trouble remembering what it is you're supposed to be doing; or (5) procrastination is your middle name. For stumbling blocks 1–3 we recommend simplifying your schedule. For hangups 4–5 we suggest trying that other key tool of organization, the list.

Lists and . . . "Look, Ma, No Lists"

Like making out a schedule, writing up a list helps you visualize what has to be done. A list turns the amorphous into the concrete, the possible into the official, the idea into the obligation that you are duty-bound to fulfill. A list can make you feel good, too, because crossing off something—anything—conveys a sense of accomplishment. Finally, a list helps you define your priorities. When you star or rank chores and goals A, B, or C in order of their importance, you are really determining the best use of your energy and your time.

Ideally, you should add something to a list when you think of it. However, at that very moment there is usually nothing handy except the corner of a magazine or a gum wrapper. After writing on one of these little pieces of paper, you tend to stash it away in your coat pocket and forget it, until one day—while searching for your keys—you come across it quite by chance. To improve upon this haphazard procedure, try carrying a small ring binder with you at all times. Not only will it provide you with a ready source of paper for your lists, but it will serve as a portable control center for all the fragments of your life. Physically, the notebook should consist of lined paper, dividers and, if possible, a pocket for tickets and receipts. In terms of information, it should contain a number of categories:

Dailies: The day's complement of appointments and errands—"Must Do's."

Chores: Less pressing duties, sometimes arranged by geographical location.

Work: Project reminders; long-range plans; people to contact.

Special Events: Party planning; volunteer obligations; vacation details.
Food: The running list; menu ideas.
Home: Repairs, including phone numbers of service people; items to
 buy.
Children: Clothes, including list of sizes; teacher's conference topics;
 etc.
Husband: His chores and errands; things to discuss.
You: Clothes; courses; shows; etc.
Calendar: Liaison between family calendar and office appointment
 book.
Mini address-book: Phone numbers of sitters, children's friends, and
 often-called stores, including your charge account numbers; ad-
 dresses of people to whom you frequently send gifts and cards.

Although your little black book is a great improvement over
the gum wrapper, even it won't be able to organize your life
unless you *read* the lists it contains. If you keep forgetting to do
so, prop your "Must Do" list behind the bathroom sink at
night. Then you will be sure to read it when you brush your
teeth in the morning. In addition, get in the habit of glancing
through your notebook before you leave work and rewriting the
"Dailies" section before you go to bed.

We think that the list is practically indispensable for the busy
woman. But we concede that its greatest asset can also be its
greatest liability, because getting chores onto paper gets them
off your conscience. Moreover, making out a list can delude
you into feeling that you've done something about a problem.
But of course you haven't. One working mother said that she
gave up making lists when she realized that the lists were
always very up to date while she was falling further and further
behind. Even worse, they constantly seemed to be accusing her
of things undone, which made her feel demoralized instead of
energized.

If you find that listmaking is not spurring you on to action either, drop it. Try doing last-minute chores as they come up and
making automatic commitments to the recurring items. Like

lists, automatic commitments build expectation and sustain energy until a task has been completed. They also save time and psychic effort, because you follow through by rote. Automatics actually function as both list and schedule. For example, you might reserve every Monday night for a shampoo and the laundry. Skipping Tuesday, which you could use to finish up the laundry if need be, you might set aside every Wednesday to water the plants, change the kitty litter, and clean the bathrooms. If your husband works late every Thursday, you might logically make that your night to market and take the kids out for a fast-food meal. Of course late meetings, last-minute dinner guests, and other unexpected occurrences will force you to switch things around somewhat from week to week. But as a result of having standard days on which to do standard tasks, you'll still get around to—or at least remember—what has to be done.

The first of every month makes a convenient target date for other recurring but less frequent chores, such as waxing floors, enriching your savings account, and checking your breasts for lumps. Tasks that only have to be done once a year are best linked to some holiday. Thus, you could make Thanksgiving the deadline for putting up the storm windows, getting snow tires on the car, and having the furnace cleaned. Designate Labor Day for going through everyone's winter clothes and Easter for checking out summer wardrobes. If you take these target dates seriously, they can be as effective as any written list. Indeed, they can weigh so heavily on your mind that you will find it less painful to do the tasks than to put them off. Once you've gotten to that point, you've accomplished the goal of all listmaking, manual or mental, and that is taking action.

Errands: The Spoilers

Most of your listmaking will revolve around errands—those unrewarding, never-ending, unbelievably time-consuming pains in the neck. Errands can wreck the best of schedules because they usually demand immediate attention, knocking your nice neat flow chart into a cocked hat. Yet even errands can be controlled through the techniques of organization.

First and foremost, since you could spend practically every nonworking moment running them, it is essential that you confine errands to specific time slots. Second, group them by location and do them in some logical sequence to avoid retracing your steps. Third, be sure to take your list with you, crossing off each task as it is completed. Crossing off forces you to keep looking at your list which, in turn, acts as a reminder of what still has to be done.

Another good device consists of leaving out in full view anything that has to be repaired, dropped off, matched up, or returned. This will mean unsightly heaps at your front door or some other conspicuous spot. It will also mean that your car often looks as though you are about to skip town with all your earthly possessions. But if you keep "must take care of" items discreetly out of sight, they will also fly discreetly out of mind. Moreover, having the goods on hand allows you to make the most efficient use of your time. If you've got your overdue books in the car, for example, you can drop them off at the library when you find yourself in that part of town. Or, you can swing by the repair shop with your broken toaster when you have an unexpected five minutes to kill.

Since most of your errands will involve purchases of one sort or another, your aim should be to get the greatest number of items in the fewest number of transactions. This means buying in quantity wherever possible. Look for a restaurant supply house that sells napkins, paper towels, toilet tissue, and cleaning supplies in bulk to retail customers. Stock up to avoid running out of—and out for—these household staples. Lay in as many canned goods and long-lasting boxed foods as you have room for, too. And if you have a freezer, investigate meat and food plans that could provide you with up to four months' worth of edibles.

Where it's not appropriate to buy in bulk, try to get the greatest number of items in the fewest number of stops. Patronize stores that carry a wide variety or full line of merchandise, and concentrate your efforts on these few places where you repeatedly find what you want. If possible, develop a personal relationship with salespeople. Knowing them can make it much easier for you to order by phone, take merchandise home on approval, or have things held until you can get down to the store to see them.

While usually more expensive than discount stores, department stores can offer all the advantages listed above. Moreover, these emporiums routinely accept checks, charges, exchanges, returns, and—what may be even more important to the working mother—they gift-wrap and deliver. Be sure to take advantage of this last service, even if it means that your gifts arrive three weeks early. That's far better in our opinion than having to ship them out yourself.

And, while we're on the subject of gift-buying, remember that it can be an enjoyable, guilt-free way to spend money—when you're in the mood. When you're under the gun, it's a drag. To avoid last-minute, nerve-frazzling searches, plan ahead. Keep a file of gift ideas so that you can come up with something suitable without dragging around from store to store for inspiration. Be on the lookout for presents when visiting craft shows, flea markets, museum shops, gourmet centers, and, above all, foreign climes. Everyone loves a native handicraft or at least something that wasn't made in Japan (unless you happen to be touring Japan). Since you can't keep too many hostess gifts or juvenile birthday presents on hand, try to acquire them whenever there's a sale. And, for goodness sakes, don't feel that each one has to be unique. In most cases the recipients won't know or care that you've given someone else the same thing.

When you take a present home, wrap it quickly before the children decide you've bought it for them. Identify the box with a small, removable label and place it on the highest shelf to keep it safe from junior explorers. Having a wrapped present in the closet is like having money in the bank, only better, because you don't have to make an extra stop to withdraw it.

Use the same approach for cards: when you see them, buy them. In fact, whenever you have a little extra time, drop into a drugstore and actively look for all kinds of greeting cards. Keep your cards in a file to be signed, addressed, and stamped as the spirit moves you. To make sure that you get them out in time, make up a master list of personal occasions and glance at it every two weeks. When you see that someone is about to have a birthday or anniversary, simply pluck the appropriate card from your file and drop it into a mailbox. One working mother keeps her master list in her bathroom above the toilet tissue. She claims she hasn't missed an occasion yet.

No matter what purchase your errand entails, you'll get it done faster when you can bring yourself to compromise. If the item is tremendously important or costly, then of course you cannot settle. But if it is of lesser magnitude—make do. You don't have time any more to hold out for the silkier blouse, the more original hostess gift, the cheaper towel rack. If you're unable to find something better than the one you see first, the original may be gone by the time you get back to it. And, taking into consideration the time and car fare needed for comparison shopping, the little bit you might save probably won't be worth the trouble. If you're the kind of person who finds it relaxing to browse around stores, enjoy. But if you're like the busy woman who told us, "I hate to shop but I love to buy," do your utmost to make every foray count.

In addition to the physical errands you run outside the house, there are always numerous mental "errands" that demand your attention inside. Most of these matters revolve around communications and many are initiated via the U.S. mail.

Mail, Ma Bell, and You

Like birth, death, taxes, and laundry, there's something predictable and inexorable about mail. The postmark changes but the mix is always the same: bills, advertisements, notices of meetings and, every so often, a personal letter or invitation. All of these missives demand attention or, even worse, action—and they demand it each and every day except Sunday. Although you might feel like shouting "Enough!" or hanging an "Out of Order" sign on your mailbox, you'll find it more effective to observe the following guidelines instead.

Time-management experts advise people to deal with each piece of information only twice: once to file it and once to take action on it. Of course, if you're super-efficient, you could take action on the spot, thus dealing with papers only once. And in many cases you don't have to deal with them at all. Like most people, you may be intimidated by unsolicited bids for your attention and your money, because it just doesn't seem polite to dismiss them without a hearing. However, we suggest that often you do just that. Keep telling yourself that questionnaires do not have to be answered, free samples do not have to be tried, cents-off coupons do not have to be redeemed, and charities do not have to be contributed to. If you don't open the envelopes, your sympathies cannot be played upon. So curb your curiosity and throw out junk mail unread. After a while you'll become a keen judge of what's worth your time and what isn't.

Often what comes in by mail requires that something from you goes out the same way. And, indeed, there's a lot to be said for putting things down on paper. Using the mails provides the receiver (and the sender, if you make a carbon) with a permanent record of the transaction. It is cheaper than phoning and affords greater flexibility too, because it doesn't restrict you to the hours people are at work or even awake. Finally, availing yourself of mail-order catalogues allows you to shop at home. This is such a great way to save time and energy that we cannot recommend it too highly for every working mother.

The major drawback to communicating in writing is that people tend not to do it. They put it off and put it off until they simply give up the whole idea. Lest that happen to you, make it a point to keep stamps, stationery, pen, and address book together in one place.* Then, when you're ready to write, make an official commitment to the letter by addressing the envelope first. We have found that this approach works particularly well with thank you's, condolences, and other short, obligatory notes. If you receive a letter that requires a reply, try penning your answer right at the bottom of it. Although not the most elegant, this procedure saves time and trees and induces you to take prompt action.

Since starting your job, you probably haven't written even one optional postcard, not to mention any long personal letters. Still, you might like to keep in touch with far-flung relatives and friends—without running up hundreds of dollars in phone bills. As a way out of your dilemma, we suggest the mass mailing, a favorite device of matriarch Rose Kennedy. Write out one newsy letter, photocopy it, append a personal line or two at the bottom, and send it out to everyone with whom you don't regularly converse. Although not as warm as a whole handwritten letter, the mass mailing gets out while the individual communiqué remains permanently in the "I really ought to write" stage.

Phoning has its place in your life, too. It is often more effective than writing because so many people simply do not answer their mail nowadays. It also brings immediate results. By calling up, you can quickly settle a disputed bill or find out if the store has your size. Everyone loves to receive an invitation by mail, but not everyone remembers to RSVP. When you invite people by phone, you know on the spot whether they can make it or not. Using the phone to locate goods and services is such a godsend that any working mother who doesn't "let her fingers do the walking" is missing out on the timesaver of all time.

In addition to all its other merits, the telephone is indispensable for making arrangements, keeping in touch with the children, and just plain socializing. The trick is to keep it under control. Unless you do, its imperious ring will take you away from everything, including the dinner table and important proj-

---

*See Appendix, Home Filing System, for guide to organizing your desk.

ects, to engage in often unimportant chatter. Learn to say, "May I call you back?" And when you have to contact someone who has trouble saying goodbye, try calling her at 8:00 A.M. You'll find that business gets concluded on the telephone far more rapidly at that hour than it does in the evening.

If you're the gabby one, don't get comfortable. You're far less likely to prolong a conversation when you're standing up than when you're sitting down. You could also try setting a timer to remind you of the fleeting moments. But if you're an incurable talkaholic, there's just a single, drastic remedy for your problem. Try restricting yourself to a pay phone—and one dime per call.

Whether or not you choose to talk your free time away is up to you. Outside of work you have it in your power to get as much or as little done as you wish, to sleep nine hours a day or five, to be organized or to drift. Sometimes you will want and need to let everything go, but as a working mother you don't have that luxury very often. You've got to keep track of too many things to be the perpetual flower child. Moreover, if you're not at least somewhat organized, a child of yours is going to find himself in a school play at some point without either his costume or his mom in the audience, because the event will have completely slipped your mind.

To prevent such mini-tragedies, embrace the tools of organization. They require a little time and effort, it's true, but we feel that they are well worth the trouble. The few minutes a day you spend making out schedules and lists or just thinking ahead will result in a calmer, more reliable, more productive, and happier you.

3

The Ins and Outs of
Child Care

Dependency on substitute child care is largely what separates working mothers from other working women. Household chores can always be done at 1:00 A.M. or delayed until the next day, but children are not so obliging. Until they reach a certain age they must be supervised, and supervised well, during the hours their parents are away from home. In this chapter we will cover a number of child-care options. You may immediately rule out some of them because of cost, availability, and your own preconceived notions of what is best for children. While there is little you can do about cost and availability, you can try to purge yourself of your preconceived notions. We strongly urge you to do so both because new studies are disproving old prejudices and because, things being what they are, you don't have the luxury of dismissing any child-care arrangement out of hand.

What Are the Options?

The most common arrangement for child care in the United States today is the individual sitter who cares for a single child (or siblings) in her own home or the child's. The group situation is another option being exercised with increasing frequency by working mothers. Group care comes in many sizes and shapes: cooperative ventures; family day-care homes; and three types of day-care centers—publicly funded, profitmaking, and private nonprofit. The last is usually sponsored by a church or community organization, but the provider may be a business, a hospital, or a college that runs the center as part of its early-childhood-education program.

You will probably narrow down your options quickly on the basis of availability alone. Your mother may spend her days at work, your mother-in-law may be loath to give up her steady card game, your closest aunt may hate children, and your other relatives may live out of town. If you reside in a sparsely populated area, you may not be able to find or provide transportation for live-out caretakers of any sort. The answer for you, then, would seem to be a live-in helper, but this much-sought-after human being is presently scarcer than hen's teeth. Indeed, some employment agencies are now reporting seventy applicants for every available live-in worker. Day-care centers are a boon—if you can get your child into one—but there are fewer than 20,000 licensed facilities in the whole United States of America and many of them have restrictions based on income. If you're really in a bind, you could start your own babysitting cooperative with a few other working mothers. But you should understand before going in that you will have to devote time to supervising the sitter(s) and that you might have to open your home to several rambunctious youngsters as well.

The other factor that quickly narrows the field is cost. Unless you can find a relative or neighbor who is willing to sit for nothing or practically nothing, you will have to shell out a considerable portion of your weekly salary for child care. Indeed, this will probably be the largest work-related expense you'll have. Many adult babysitters charge at least $1 an hour, whether they mind the child in their home or yours, on a one-to-one basis or in a group. If you locate the sitter through an agency or live in an affluent community, the fee may go much higher. The least expensive unsubsidized day-care centers charge a minimum of $35 a week, and housekeepers, whether living in or out, often charge at least $20 a day. Car fare, social security, unemployment, workmen's compensation, and disability benefits insurance can considerably increase the cost of having a regular employee—as can the food she consumes on your premises.

The only bright spot in this bleak financial picture is the recent amendment to the tax law giving working parents a $400-per-child reduction of their tax liability for child-care expenses (including housekeeping services). While this tax credit doesn't begin to approach what you actually spend for child care, it is better than nothing. Therefore, we urge you to find out if you are eligible for it, which you may be even if you are a student or a part-time employee.

Individual Care

Statistics indicate that the situation you finally settle on will probably be some sort of home-based care. Almost half the preschool children of working mothers are cared for in their own homes and just under a third are cared for in someone else's home. Home-based care tends to be cheaper and more available than any other kind. And since it takes place in a home rather than an institution and maintains the one-to-one ratio found in traditional mothering, it may also be the easiest for you to feel comfortable with. Sometimes the caretaker in this situation is a stranger, but often she is a relative. Indeed, 45 percent of all working mothers rely on relatives to watch their children.

The Relative as Sitter: Using a relative has several advantages. The first is cost. Indeed, without the volunteer services of a relative it might not be feasible for you to work at all. The second is that it is probably easier to feel good about leaving your child when you are leaving him with Grandma Rose or Aunt Susan, who is predisposed to love him or at least to feel a tremendous sense of responsibility toward him. Not only should the relative's feelings transcend that of a hired hand, but she should be more reliable too, because she has her reputation to uphold within the family.

Coming from the same general background, you and your relative-sitter are likely to have more or less the same attitude toward child rearing. This should minimize friction between the two of you and promote uniformity of care. But do expect things to come up as they would with any sitter. The drawback here is that you won't be able to handle them as freely as you would with just any sitter, both because this woman is doing you a favor and because she is related to you. How can you fire your mother, especially if she lives upstairs? Obviously, the situation calls for great tact. You have to voice your complaints, otherwise nothing will change except that you will grow more and more disgruntled. But try to state your objections as impersonally as possible. Appeal to the woman's desire to do the best possible thing for the child, even if it wasn't the way she did it in her day.

You may have trouble getting her to change her ways, though, not only because she's set in them, but because she may start to feel that the child is hers. As the all-day babysitter, she may feel that she knows best. Be sure that you're not unconsciously fostering this attitude by ceding her too much control. Burdened down with many other responsibilities, you might be giving in to the temptation to let her take over, especially if she is older and seems wiser regarding child care. Ultimately this state of affairs will be harmful to your ability to parent. Although you should back her up in the execution of her job, you must make it clear that you are the one who sets the child-rearing policy. You are the child's mother, after all, and you must have ultimate responsibility for him. Thank her profusely for her help, but let it be understood that you have to do things your own way. And if she feels entitled to intrude upon other areas of your life by dint of the fact that she cares for your child, thank her for her interest but tell her firmly, no thanks.

The nonrelative who watches a single child either in her own home or in the child's is also used by a large percentage of working mothers, but unless this type of sitter lives next door, you will have to do some investigative work to find her. Ask around among your friends and neighbors and the janitor in your apartment building. Place a newspaper ad, answer one, tack up a notice at work, and contact a local senior citizens group. If you can't find a sitter close by, look for someone near your job who would watch a child in her own home. When seeking a housekeeper, try going through a commercial agency or other people's housekeepers, who sometimes know of a likely candidate.

Although not related to you, many a paid sitter can develop such a warm relationship with your child that you will be able to go off to work with a minimum of guilt and anxiety. When you find someone who makes you feel that you're leaving your child in loving hands, do everything you can to keep her happy. However, just as with the relative, you will have to watch out for signs that the sitter is becoming too possessive of your child, possibly to fill a void in her own life. To some extent you can humor her in this, but when she begins to feel that she knows best because she's with the youngster all day, you will have to put your foot down. Make it clear that you are the mother and that she is your agent. If you don't get this straightened out, she may come to disregard your orders completely.

A more common problem is the sitter who interprets her title literally: that is, she sits. She sits in front of the TV, she sits next to the refrigerator, and she sits on the telephone. Her interaction with the child is limited to giving him the snacks that keep him quiet and to making room for him on the sofa so that he can watch TV too. Moreover, although there's always something one could be doing in the way of household chores, she doesn't seem to think of it.

This situation is discouraging, but it can be improved. You can prevent the sitter from turning your child into a cookie monster by giving her instructions about the time and exact content of every snack. You can promote exercise and fresh air by providing her with the kind of timetable that emphasizes outdoor play and limits the hours of TV. And you can stimulate her creativity by making available to her the materials for children's projects. As for the household chores, you could either make them a condition of employment or add them on for a small sum. Faced with the possibility of earning extra money, your sitter might be only too glad to do laundry, cook, or mend clothes. Not only would such an arrangement be very helpful to you, but it would probably benefit your child as well, because busy people are generally more effective people.

Live-in Helpers: You will have many of the same problems with live-in help that you have with a sitter—and then some. Living and working in the same place, and a home environment at that, she may forget that she has a job to do. In fact, it may be hard for both of you to know whether she's a friend or an employee, when she's on and when she's off. You also have to deal with her personality to a greater extent than you would if she lived elsewhere. And you will lose some privacy, although we think that the privacy factor is overrated in a household with children. Your husband, in particular, may suddenly become very proprietary about having someone else live in *his* house (which until this very moment was always *your* house).

Of course, live-in help also has some tremendous advantages over a regular sitter, the major one being that—once she shows up Monday morning—you know you're covered for the entire week. Even if she doesn't feel well or your child comes down with an illness, you can go off to work. Moreover, she spares you from coming home to all the dishes, all the laundry, all the cleaning—and often the mess the live-out sitter left behind. When you add up everything you're spending on sitters and services, you might find that live-in help will not cost much more while providing you with a flexibility no other arrangement can offer. If you work long or irregular hours, travel a great deal, live in an isolated area, have a very young child, or simply cannot seem to make satisfactory arrangements, this may be your best alternative. The question for you then is not *whether* to get someone to live in, but *how.*

Some imagination is definitely called for. After you've gone the commercial-agency/asking-around route, you might consider inviting a relative to move in with you. Or contact your church auxiliary, a social service agency, and local senior citizens groups to see if they know of a retired person who might like to move in with a family. You could also try the state employment bureau, or place an ad in a local paper or one that circulates through a rural community. If you live near a college or can offer a student transportation, you might be able to attract a young person who wants to swap light housework and babysitting for room and board. If her schedule meshes with yours, this arrangement could work out very well. By contacting your local high-school placement office, you might be able to find a young person who wants to work for a year in order to save money for college. Since teen-age boys can be very effective sitters/housekeepers too, don't overlook them in your search, especially if you have sons.

Of all the possibilities for live-in help, the least advisable would seem to be the import. Despite the dearth of Americans seeking jobs as domestics, the U.S. government is making it increasingly difficult, if not impossible, to sponsor a person from abroad who will work in your home. And someone who holds only a visitor's visa may not legally work here. For these reasons and because of the language barrier and training problems, we think you would do better to keep your sights fixed closer to home when looking for resident help.

When you do find someone—be she maid, sitter, or mother's helper—bear in mind that she is not a member of your family and it would be a tremendous strain on all of you, especially her, if you tried to make her into one. Keep some distance between you. Unless you distinguish her from a family member when she's off, you will not be able to treat her as an employee when she's on. Therefore, tell her right away that certain parts of the house "belong" to you and your husband at certain hours of the day. And since she needs her privacy, too, delineate certain places that are hers, no matter how small your home. Give her her own shelf in the bathroom, her own corner of the room she shares with your child, her own TV, and her own cache in the pantry or fridge.

These arrangements will also serve to minimize the inevitable friction that comes from living together. Familiarity breeds contempt, as the saying goes, and nothing could be closer to the truth when someone lives right in your home. An otherwise innocuous habit can become an abrasive irritant—whether it's cigarette smoking, loud radio playing, or a nightly shampoo that uses up all the hot water. You can talk some of these problems out, but others you'll have to learn to live with if you want to keep the woman on.

It's also a good idea to make her hours as regular as possible, so that what she does in the house will seem like a job. Set down what chores are to be done within those hours. You don't have to plan her day down to the last minute, but it helps people to know what has to be accomplished when, especially if they are somewhat inexperienced. But do be realistic in your expectations. No one works from 8:00 A.M to 8:00 P.M. straight, and a person who has to keep an eye on a toddler while cleaning is not going to be as efficient as one who doesn't have that extra burden. Professionalize the job further by requesting that appropriate clothes be worn, not an old wrapper and curlers. If you take her job seriously, she will too.

She may pack her bags on short notice, though, if your children start to give her a hard time. It is not unusual for youngsters to think of a live-in person as their own personal servant and to treat her accordingly. If you detect an arrogance creeping into your children's behavior, make it clear to them that she is there to help *you,* not them. You also have to make it clear that she deserves the same polite treatment they would accord anyone else. Since your children may subconsciously feel that if they can get rid of the live-in sitter, you will stay home with them, it is important that you let them know otherwise. Tell them that if she goes, they will have to do all her chores themselves. That should make them shape up—fast.

Since the live-in person is going to be doing at least some of the household chores, you will have to block out time to show her the ropes. You may have only a day or two to do this, so make your systems as clear and simple as possible. Label shelves and drawers throughout the house with masking tape to remind her where everything goes. Write everyone's name on the inside of clothes to make sorting easy, and give her a list of cleaning supplies to check off as she runs low. Help her keep track of the children, too, by jotting down their whereabouts: whom they are visiting, what the phone number is there, and when they are expected back. Also leave her a list of useful telephone numbers, such as those we suggest at the back of the book.

Some working mothers find it very difficult to ask someone else to wash out their toilet bowl or scrub down their kitchen floor. But these household tasks have to be done and if the domestic doesn't do them, you'll have to. Moreover, as one woman put it, "It's not a question of exploitation. She has her job to do and I have mine."

Group Care

Since there are an increasing number of working mothers with young children who need care and a decreasing number of people to give it to them, different kinds of group care are becoming more and more popular. Group care has several advantages. Because it is formalized, it is reliable—you can count on it's being there day in and day out. It is often cheaper than one-to-one care and it eliminates the worst abuses of the sitter syndrome: too much TV, too many cookies, and not enough meaningful activity. And though you're not on the scene to observe the group caretakers in action, at least you have other parents with whom to compare notes. The other great advantage of group care is that it provides your child with playmates. Children enjoy being with other children, but when you're gone all day this may be hard to arrange. Group care does it for you.

You may hesitate to use group care for fear that your youngster will catch an extraordinary number of diseases from the other children. And the probability is that he will get sick somewhat more frequently in a group situation than he would with his own private sitter, especially if he is under the age of two. But the illnesses he will get are essentially garden-variety colds and upset stomachs. Moreover, it has been our observation that the child who is an early mixer—and therefore acquires certain illnesses and immunities early—tends to miss school less often later on than the child who begins to socialize at an older age. (In other words, you only get the chicken pox once.) So, as far as we're concerned, the threat of sickness should not keep you from considering some form of group care for your child.

Parents' Cooperatives: If you work part time you might be able to participate in a parents' cooperative in which you would watch a few children in return for having your child watched while you are at work. Since all the labor under this arrangement is voluntary, the cost is nil. You can go off with a clear mind because you are extremely familiar with all the children and parents involved. And as one of the chief supervisors, you can do a great deal to influence the situation. As with any cooperative venture, though, round-robin babysitting requires a hardworking organizer and a firm commitment on everyone's part to do her share.

Group Sitter: If you and your friends work full time, you could expand on the cooperative idea to hire a sitter. She would watch the children in one of your homes and, depending on their ages and her training, she could initiate structured activities and even teach reading and writing as well as supervise free play. This kind of arrangement can be relatively inexpensive since there's no rental of property and all of you are pooling your child-care monies. It can also be highly satisfactory because day care often works best when parents are involved in the hiring and administration process. Here again, though, you will probably need at least one good parent-organizer in your group, all-around willingness to pitch in, and possibly extra insurance coverage and health and fire department approval if your cooperative is considered a bona fide "school." To find out if it is, contact the local office of your state's Department of Social Services. Then, if the cooperative expands to the point where an outside facility is rented, you will have to find out from this same office what the personnel and structural requirements are to obtain a license.

Family Day-Care Homes: If the cooperative venture is not for you, you might be able to find a woman who watches a few children in her home. She is often babysitting for her own child or grandchild and will take in your youngster and a few others to supplement her income. If the woman is kind and the other youngsters congenial, your child will probably adjust to this situation as easily as he would to having his own private sitter, and he might enjoy it much more. Indeed, for some children this is the best of all possible worlds. Family day care is winning more and more adherents because of its unique combination of personal, institutional, and social elements. Your city or county Department of Social Services will be able to advise you about any family day-care homes under their jurisdiction. Your friends and neighbors may be able to tell you about other ones.

Day-Care Centers: You can probably accept the idea of family day care as easily as your child because it takes place in a home, and Americans are accustomed to thinking that small children belong in a home. If you are considering leaving your youngster in a day-care center, on the other hand, you may feel your anxiety appreciably mount. And no wonder. It is a relatively new institution and one that has come under so much scrutiny and criticism that to say you're taking your child there may seem tantamount to saying that you are abandoning him altogether.

Yet the most recent White House Conference on Children stated in its report to the President that "the recognition of day care as a developmental service [has] tremendous potential for positively influencing the lives of children and families.'' And to some extent that potential is now being recognized. Studies of children in good day-care centers show that they are on a par with their peers in terms of physical and emotional development and, in some instances, are even slightly ahead of the home-grown in mental and social skills. Commenting on some recent studies, the psychologist Kuno Beller declared, ''Any statement now that day care is bad is as erroneous as the statement that parenting is good.''

At its best, day care can be very good. The facilities can be better equipped and the staff better trained or at least more closely supervised than they would be under any other arrangement. Many centers are open from 7:00 A.M. to 6:00 P.M. to give working mothers maximum coverage. Because they are geared for such a long day, day-care centers usually offer the most varied menu of learning, structured recreation, free play, and rest. And since they handle the largest number of children, they are the most likely to provide your youngster with playmates his own age. Therefore, though you might feel queasy at first about leaving your young child in an institutional setting, there are many reasons why the formalized day-care center might be the right choice for you.

You can find out what day-care centers exist in your area by looking them up in the Yellow Pages of your phone directory under ''Day Nurseries and Day Care Centers.'' Your pediatrician is another probable fount of knowledge, as is your local child-care information and referral center—if you are so fortunate as to live in an area that has one.

As you go about gathering information, you may find yourself becoming confused about sponsorship and funding. ''Sponsorship'' of a day-care center can mean almost anything from the donation of space to the total management of the program. Therefore, just because a center is located in a ''Y'' or carries the name of a reputable charity on its letterhead, you shouldn't automatically assume the center is an integral part of that organization. Nor should you assume that a government-sponsored center is necessarily better than a private center—or vice versa. Furthermore, "subsidized" can mean almost anything from a totally underwritten program to a small government allowance for food. Subsidies often mean lower fees, but not always. We were amazed to learn that one profitmaking Midwestern chain charges as little as many subsidized establishments. Since no two centers are alike, we strongly urge you to purge yourself of preconceived notions and judge each facility on its own merits.

The Screening Process

Having decided upon the kind of child-care situation that seems right for you, you will have to choose the individual person or place you will use. If the caretaker is a close relative, you don't have to do much investigating. You know her, you know her background, and you have doubtless already seen her in action with your child. When you go outside the family, however, it is a good idea to look into several options closely, because you learn as you go along. Moreover, your original choice may not work out and you will want to have others to fall back on. Only by doing some comparison shopping can you satisfy yourself that you're making the best choice possible.

When you start the screening process, try working solely over the telephone as this will save you time and considerable leg work. Describe the job thoroughly to potential sitters and housekeepers, because if they don't like your hours and wages, you might as well eliminate them immediately. If they accept the conditions of employment, chat with them a bit to find out how they got into this line of work, how long they've been doing it, and what they like about it. Ask for the name of two current or former clients. If you're interested in family day care, call the sponsoring agencies to obtain some information about the people in charge. And if you contact a day-care center, ask the director about the kind of program he runs. Then check out everyone's references. If they are encouraging, proceed to the next step of the screening process: the personal interview or on-site visit.

When you're interviewing a sitter or housekeeper, pay attention to her total demeanor. Is she neat or sloppy, relatively relaxed or tense, unusually hopped up or sluggish (either of which might indicate that she's taking drugs)? Does she seem to like children? Is she an American citizen? If not, insist upon seeing her social security number and the permit or "green card" that shows she is legally entitled to work in this country. If she is foreign-born, how good is her English? Unless she can make herself understood in an emergency and/or speak well enough to keep a preschool child company, it would be unwise to hire her. And if she's never held any job or this kind of job before, be very wary. Unlike the stay-at-home mother, you don't have the time to train a novice properly.

Listen carefully to what she is saying. Do you get the feeling that she has a chronic health problem that might cause her to cancel you out frequently or keep her from running after a toddler? Does she have an infirm mother who has first call on her time? Is she committed to making this a permanent job or do you sense that she is merely trying it out? And, when all is said and done, does this person give you the creeps or do you think you could be happy leaving your child with her? Although facts do count, your instinctive reaction is crucial too. You must feel good about the child's caretaker to feel good about going off to work.

If your child is going out to the sitter's, *see the premises for yourself*. Is the yard free of dangerous debris; is the interior of the house clean? Does the sitter have books and toys around that are suitable for your child? Does she seem to be warm, energetic, and sensible? Her personal characteristics are of paramount importance, because ultimately the quality of care will depend on the person in charge, not on her surroundings or equipment. When you're looking at family day care, investigate all the above. In addition, pay attention to the way the other children are interacting and count heads. Some experts feel that family day care works best when a woman has three to seven children under her roof at one time. Finally, find out if she offers any structured activities and if she takes the children on any excursions.

When you set out to observe a more formalized day-care center, it's a good idea to plan to spend the morning there. Notice whether the children are running wild or whether they're being kept under too-rigid control. How quickly is an unhappy child comforted, a dispute between children settled, a wandering youngster enticed into taking part in some activity? Do the personnel seem to interact warmly with the children or do they take a custodial approach to the job? Does the program seem varied, the equipment adequate? Again, count heads. Many commercial centers will accommodate as many as one hundred children with one teacher to every eight to twelve youngsters, but the younger the age group, the lower the child-teacher ratio should be.

Back in the director's office, ask about the staff. How many are trained teachers, teacher aides, and child-care workers? How long have most of them been at the center? High turnover, which is endemic to the day-care field, may prove upsetting to a young child. Find out whether the premises are inspected by both health and fire authorities, and make sure parents can visit at any time—that's a must.*

In evaluating group day care, don't set too much store by the fact that the home or center has been licensed by a social service agency or the state. The agency's supervision may be minimal, state requirements are usually low, and enforcement in either situation can range from spotty to practically nonexistent. As we suggested with hiring a sitter, rely a great deal on your own instinctive reactions.

As you get close to making your decision, take your child with you to the day-care center or have him sit in as you inter-

---

* For more detailed guidelines, send away for one of the pamphlets listed in the Resources section at the end of this book.

view the sitter or housekeeper. Watch how he interacts with the sitter, see how he feels about the group-care environment, and if other children are involved, observe the kind of overtures they make to him. The sight of your child in the actual situation may be all you need to help you make up your mind.

The probability of continuity could also tip the balance one way or the other. Continuity gives a child a feeling of security and enables you to develop that all-important trust in the caretaker. Although it is unrealistic to look for an instant "old family retainer," there's no sense going into a situation that doesn't hold out hope of lasting at least a year, especially when a young child is involved. There's also no sense waiting until something ideal comes along. Except for an increase in the number of commercial day-care centers, there probably won't be any discernible growth in the caretaking field in the near future. Besides, you need coverage right now. So make the best choice you can and then try to think positively about it. As one working mother said of the center where she sends her two preschoolers, "Oh, sure, it's not perfect. But then home isn't perfect either."

As you screen caretakers, remember that no matter what arrangement you make, there will be times when you'll need backup support. At the last minute the sitter will develop a raging toothache, the day-care center will be flooded, or your child will be quarantined with the chicken pox. Start looking for help in the likeliest quarters—mother, sister, best friend, next-door neighbor—and then go on from there. However, the time of crisis is not the time to begin finding out who sits. Keep gathering the names of freelance sitters, day workers, and group-care situations, and try to set up procedures with them in advance. Some day-care centers have provisions for drop-ins, for example, and if you give a home-based sitter a retainer to be applied toward her fee, she might take your child on short notice. Since substitute teachers are prepared to go to work at the last minute, look for one who would like to make extra money babysitting for a day. As always, try to introduce your child to the temporary caretaker in advance so that when she arrives on the scene, she won't be a total stranger.

Before-School, After-School, and Vacation Care

As soon as your child enters first grade, you can breathe a sigh of relief—the worst is over so far as his supervision is concerned. Now you only have to make arrangements for the few hours when he's home and you're not. If you leave the house before he does in the morning, you may have a particularly difficult time getting coverage, both because you're asking someone to come in so early and because you're asking her to stay such a short time. The best solution might be to drop your child at a neighbor's house. If you can't do that, find out whether a nearby day-care center or home-based facility takes children for breakfast. If these are not viable alternatives, you might succeed in hiring a woman who will cover for you at home if you expand the job to make it worth her while. One teacher we know who did this lengthened the hours and added laundry and cleaning to the job description. She had to pay a little more but she got someone—and she came home to a clean house every day too.

If your child's day ends before yours, you should look for supervised after-school activities right on the school grounds. And if his school does not offer such a program, we urge you to lobby for it. Like other good institutionalized care, it is reliable, sociable, and enriching. What youngster could resist the marvelous smorgasbord of classes offered by Amy Carter's public school in Washington, D.C.? According to an article in *The New York Times:* "The [Stevens School] offers an extended day that keeps the children of working parents busy until 6 p.m. when they can be picked up. After school, children as young as three study ballet, gymnastics, sewing, carpentry, photography, music, or dramatics taught by high school and college students who are paid with funds from Federal and local youth programs."

If you can't get a program like this going on your school premises, you should investigate the offerings at a nearby "Y" or community center. You could also try banding together with a few other working mothers to hire a companion to take your children back and forth to various activities. And you might even consider enrolling your child in a private school that offers an extended day. Although this is an expensive alternative, it might not amount to much more than the combined costs of private lessons, transportation, and adult sitters—when you can get them—and it would offer greater continuity besides.

Another common solution to the after-school problem is the teenager. Teenagers can be marvelous, hardworking companions and they are universally preferred by children to adult sitters. Unfortunately, teenagers often have so many other claims on their time between homework, extracurricular activities, and the orthodontist that they find it difficult to handle all of them and a permanent job too. To get around this problem and to stave off employee boredom, some working mothers have hired different teens for different days. This can work out well, especially if the girls or boys will cover for one another in a pinch. But these part-timers must feel as committed to your job as they would to a five-day-a-week obligation, which is often the stumbling block with part-timers of any age. When you're hiring a teenager, we also suggest that you check first with his or her parents. Unless they approve of the arrangement, you could find yourself involved in a constant tug of war with them over their child's time.

If you have a teenager of your own, it's a fine idea to have her baby-sit from time to time or even one or two days every week. But since you can't in good conscience obligate her to spend every afternoon child-watching, her employment will probably be a sometime thing. However, if she wants to sit regularly in order to earn money, it might work out beautifully for all of you if you took her on. You'll have to make sure that she understands that this is a real job, though—she can't leave you in the lurch just because she's your daughter.

Teenagers can fill in for you during school holidays and summer vacation as well as after school. Though they're almost always short-term employees, the children take to them so easily and they pick up the household routine so quickly that it could be worth your while to hire one on a temporary basis. If they can swim and drive, they could be the answer to your prayers. You can locate a young helper by contacting high-school and college placement bureaus. But whether she lives in or lives out, don't be surprised if she charges well for her services.

Another solution for summer vacation is camp. Among all the day camps and "sleep-away" camps, church-sponsored camps, Girl Scout and Boy Scout camps, sailing, tennis, weight-loss, hiking, biking, travel, music, and gymnastics camps in America—there is bound to be one that fits both your pocketbook and your youngster's interests. Ask around for recommendations and send away for the camping guides and brochures listed at the end of the book. When you've narrowed down the field, have the directors come to your house with their slide shows and photo albums. Ask them for the names of campers you can call, because you'll want to consider their evaluations and those of their parents, as well.

You'll learn what to look for as you go along, especially if you ask a lot of questions, such as: How many campers to each counselor? How old are the counselors, what is their training, how many return each year? Is the camp program highly structured or is each child more or less on his own? Is the atmosphere competitive, is the individual sport or the team game stressed? Is there a religious component you should know about? What precautions have been taken for the children's safety, especially at the waterfront? Is there a doctor or a nurse on the premises at all times? Although you can't guarantee your child a good summer, the more thorough your investigation and the more positive your feelings about the camp, the better his chances for success.

As Time Goes By

Alas, your job is not over once you have chosen a care-taker—be it sitter, day-care center, after-school program, or teenager. You must constantly monitor the situation to see how it is going. Your continuing evaluation will not only help you influence events, but will further your education as an employer or child-care consumer.

The day-care center is the easiest to evaluate because, if the program is a good one, your youngster will soon begin to show an improvement in motor skills and language ability and to demonstrate knowledge beyond what he is learning at home. Moreover, most centers welcome visitors throughout the week and hold parent-staff conferences at various times throughout the year. Speak up during these conferences. Your comments will alert the day-care worker to your child's particular habits, reactions, and interests. She will work harder for your youngster and do more to fulfill his individual needs if you show you care. Indeed, you "train" her during these informational exchanges.

And she trains you. If you pay attention to what the day-care worker is saying, you can gain valuable insights into your child's behavior. She sees him in relationship to other young-sters his age, which gives her a perspective that you as the mother of one or two children cannot possibly have. On the other hand, you have an insider's view that she doesn't have. So when her opinions are at odds with yours, don't automatically conclude that she has to be right, even if she is older and more experienced.

When you take your child to a sitter or she comes to you, evaluation is more difficult. All we can suggest is that you ar-range some overlapping time at the beginning or end of the day to observe the two of them together. How do they seem to in-teract? How does she say it's going? When other children are involved, a pause at the door may be enough to tell you a great deal, but do verify your impressions with the other parents.

With any employee, you must bring your concerns out into the open, but try to state them as impersonally and constructively as possible. Because your sitter may be very touchy about her ability to parent, you should employ great tact. Suggest that her way of doing something undoubtedly works very well with her own or other children, but that you feel another way would work better with your particular youngster. The right kind of criticism can actually be a morale booster, because it shows that you care about the woman's work. It is also the only way you can hope to bring about an improvement. Some working mothers are so afraid of a confrontation or of hurting their sitter's feelings that they keep their objections to themselves. But they're not doing the sitter any favor because inevitably the situation deteriorates to the point where she must be fired.

Since you have a large stake in keeping the competent sitter happy, be ready to pay her on the appointed day with her exact salary in whatever form she wants—usually cash. Make every effort to take over for her on time at night. And if you are unavoidably detained, at least give her the courtesy of a call so that she can make contingency plans for her own household. In other words, be as considerate of your employee as you would like your own boss to be of you.

If you notice that tension is developing between the two of you as time goes by, ask yourself if you have unconsciously been changing the conditions of employment. Are you now expecting the sitter to come earlier and stay later? Are you giving her more to do? Are you switching her days off at whim? Are you asking her to take a bus home whereas you always used to drive her or give her extra money for a taxi? Once you've established a pattern of employment, you're committed to maintaining it. Unilateral modification of any sort usually leads to trouble.

When it comes to camp and after-school activities, you should try to visit once or twice when the program is in full swing. Introduce yourself to the staff and try to get a line on how your child is doing. If the program is a residential one, you will have to depend on your child's letters and calls until visiting weekend. But if his reports indicate that something is seriously wrong, put in a call to the counselor or director right away. They might be able to make some change that would immediately set things to rights.

In evaluating any caretaking situation, not only the residential one, you must take your child's reactions into account. How does he look and how does he act? Is he unusually droopy or cranky at the end of the day or is he so hopped up that it takes hours to calm him down? Are there any troubling changes in his patterns of sleeping and eating, is he misbehaving at home or not performing up to his usual standards at school? Anything out of the ordinary that lasts more than a month or two into the new situation should be brought to the attention of your child's physician, teacher, or school psychologist.

When it is a baby that you are leaving, you will have to observe him with particular care because he cannot tell you how he feels. Remember to expect a very young child to demonstrate separation anxiety, especially between the ages of nine and eighteen months, even if he has been left with the same caretaker every day of his life. Since the unhappiness he displays at separation shows that he has made the proper attachment to you, you shouldn't consider it an unnatural or even undesirable occurrence. However, the more familiar he is with the caretaker, the sooner he should stop fussing once you're gone. Try to find out just how soon he does settle down and be alert to any real aversion he may show toward her.

If your child is in the midst of the Terrible Two's, he may not want to go anywhere or be with anyone, no matter how wonderful the place or how loving the caretaker. So don't leap to the conclusion that there's anything wrong with the sitter—he may just be going through a negative stage. As your child enters the nursery-school years, you can still expect some clinging and some signs of anxiety when you say goodbye in the morning, but they should be relatively mild and short-lived. Then, if everything is going well, he should greet you at night with an eagerness to show you what he made, sing you the songs he learned, and tell you about something exciting that happened. When your child is able to express himself well, encourage him to tell you how he feels about his caretaker. Chalk up about 50 percent of what he says to a vivid imagination and a bid for your sympathy. But if something in the other 50 percent is disturbing, check it out.

In order to see your child's reactions in the proper light, you will have to be honest about your own. If you feel anxious about leaving him, he will feel anxious about being left. If you feel sorry for him, he will feel sorry for himself. And if you feel antagonistic toward the caretaker—whether out of guilt, jealousy, or personality differences—your child probably won't like her either. Therefore, we urge you to look for the pluses in the situation instead of the minuses. And the pluses for your child could be very much in evidence: greater independence, a more outgoing nature with strangers, and an increased degree of comfort in new situations.

It is also worthwhile to concentrate on your caretaker's strong points, because you want to retain her if at all possible. Continuity is very important in any child-care situation. It makes your child feel secure and it enables you to develop trust in the surrogate. In light of that, and because the pickings are so slim, we urge you to stick with whatever arrangement you've made as long as it meets the basic requirements of health, safety, emotional nurture, and reliability. You can't get hung up on how well a sitter cleans if she has to keep her eyes glued to a two-year-old at the same time. And it's hardly productive to get annoyed about the fact that the day-care center doesn't serve a hot lunch if it provides a loving atmosphere at a price you can afford. Work with the caretaker, overlook her idiosyncrasies, try to improve her performance, but don't seek perfection or a child-rearing style that's exactly the same as yours. Neither one exists.

Sometimes, of course, the basic requirements will not be met, no matter how carefully you investigated the situation beforehand. We would advise you to get someone else lined up before you let the ax fall, however. If you fire your present sitter in a huff, not only will you be stuck for coverage the next day, but you're likely to make another unsatisfactory arrangement because you have to make it so quickly. There is one exception to this: if the sitter represents a clear and present danger to your child, you'll have to fire her on the spot.

The Child Who Stays Home Alone

"Latchkey child" is as negative and emotionally charged a term as "day-care center." Yet the millions of preteens and early teenagers who are largely unsupervised after school lead lives that are almost indistinguishable from those who are supervised. Kids in both categories often dash into the house, wolf down some milk and cookies, grab their bikes or mitts, and are gone until supper. Or they visit with friends, participate in extracurricular activities, and do their homework. Indeed, most unsupervised children bear little resemblance to the melancholy stereotype of the "latchkey child" who sits around forlornly in a darkened house. Most real-life youngsters are doing very nicely, thank you, and many of them have come to prize their independence.

Who can stay alone? A child who is at least ten or eleven years old; a child whose home and neighborhood are relatively safe; a child who has been brought up to accept responsibility and to use his own judgment in everyday matters; and a child whose mother has confidence in the arrangement. An interesting study of urban fifth graders found that the unsupervised youngsters in the sample population were not more frequently delinquent, late, or absent from school, nor were they less conforming in behavior than their supervised classmates. The study also indicated that they were higher in intelligence and—when they had more responsibilities at home—that they were also higher in cognitive achievements and intellectual maturity. Of course, one could argue that it was just those more intelligent, mature, and responsible youngsters who were chosen by their parents to stay alone after school, but it is also possible that circumstances helped them develop their potential.

If you think your youngster is a candidate for self-supervision, work out a few basic procedures for him. Map out the way he is to come home from school and give him an alternative route, too. Make up a set of keys for him to carry, and hide an extra set outside the house or, if you live in an apartment, leave one with the superintendent. Have your youngster call you when he gets home from school or when he goes anywhere except to a prearranged destination. Teach him how to answer the door or phone without divulging much information, especially the fact that he is home alone.

Make sure your home environment is free of hazards that could injure the child. Have faulty wiring fixed, cement loose steps, throw out oily rags, and recycle old newspapers. Keep a flashlight handy and prominently display emergency numbers near each phone. Buy small fire extinguishers, put in smoke alarms, and hold fire drills. Talk about the best ways to handle any number of situations that might come up when the youngster is home alone.* Go over basic first aid with him, using the material found in our Appendix, the Girl Scout and Boy Scout manuals, or Martin I. Green's book, *A Sigh of Relief*. Once a month review your first aid and safety equipment to make sure it's in place and in working order. From time to time do some role playing to reassure both you and your child that he knows what to do.

Once you have taken the basic safety precautions, establish a few social rules regarding your child's time alone. While these do's and don't's will reflect your own particular situation, they will probably encompass: who may and may not visit; what ac-

*Refer him to the list of useful phone numbers found at the back of the book.

tivities your child and his friends may pursue; what rooms they may go into; what equipment they may use; and what food they may eat. You will also want to set certain geographical limits and give him a standard time to come home. To help him meet that deadline, you might want to make him a present of a rugged watch.

Since you can't cover all contingencies in advance and your child can't remember a thousand and one directions, only create rules for the most important matters. But make sure your child takes those few rules seriously because—while you don't want to make him unduly nervous—staying alone is serious business. If your child seems to be chafing under your directions, assure him that these rules don't mean that you consider him a baby— if you did, you wouldn't be leaving him alone in the first place. But for his safety and your peace of mind, you've both got to know what is permissible and what isn't.

As time goes on, go over the basic rules again, updating them to keep pace with your youngster's increasing maturity. And every so often play a fast game of "What would you do if. . . ?": if you saw a stranger prowling around the house; if you got a frightening phone call; if you smelled smoke; if you couldn't get into the house?

With all his after-school activities, religious instruction, organized activities, pickup games, and visits to friends' houses, your child may rarely come straight home from school. But for the times he does, we suggest that you help him develop a routine to stave off loneliness and make the hours pass more quickly. His routine might include picking up the mail on the way in, giving you a call, making himself a snack, and perhaps watching a half hour of TV. Some children like to use this quiet time to get their homework out of the way, while others like to use it to do their chores. If your child is old enough to stay home alone, he is old enough to give you a hand running the household. Of course, he will have to be thoroughly familiar with all the appliances he has to use, since you won't be on hand to give him directions. But with a little advance preparation he should quickly become competent enough to do the work on his own.*

Often there is more than one young member of the family at home after school. You may find this comforting because there is supposedly safety in numbers; however, when they start to fight, you may begin to wonder if each one wouldn't be better off alone. Many working mothers complain that their older child tends to throw his weight around and the younger one responds by hassling him. Since you won't be on hand to act as referee, we suggest that you try to keep the peace in advance. Make it clear to them that while the older child has overall responsibility, the orders he gives are really yours, and they are neither to be given arrogantly nor disobeyed flagrantly. Moreover, when the two children are home alone together, they had better get along—or else.

Despite the temporary immaturity brought on by the presence of a sibling, self-supervision generally helps make a child more resourceful, self-confident, and grown up. When your youngster sees that you trust him, he has to feel better about himself. And when he knows that he's expected to take on more responsibility, he tends to rise to that expectation. Of course, your motives for encouraging him to become more self-sufficient are not entirely altruistic, but that doesn't make the net effect any the less beneficial. In our opinion, you are giving your child a great deal by allowing him to stay alone. You are grooming him for the true state of adulthood—independence.

*See Chapter 9, "Pitch In!"

4

Your Husband: Booster or Spoiler?

Like good child care, a supportive husband can make the difference between happy and unhappy maternal employment. Fortunately, more and more men seem to be taking a greater hand in the household chores. Indeed, in some homes husbands and wives now go fifty-fifty on everything from window washing to child rearing. Moreover, these men wholeheartedly endorse their wives' professional aspirations. If you have such a supportive spouse, consider yourself blessed. But if you don't, consider yourself in the majority, because in most American families today the wife still bears the major burden at home whether she works or not. And if she does work, her husband is likely to have serious reservations about her employment.

His Possible Objections

A marriage is like a seesaw in which rights, privileges, duties, territories, and IOU's weight the ends of the board. When a wife starts to work or go back to school, she upsets the seesaw's delicate balance and the board may begin to swing wildly. The length of time and number of tradeoffs it takes to restabilize the marriage will depend in large measure on the husband's attitude. If his mother worked, if he was born liberated, or if he has recently seen the light, his wife's new venture may barely give their seesaw a quiver. But if the husband feels that her employment will send his end of the board crashing down, it will take a lot of hard work to get their relationship back into alignment.

If your husband has a negative attitude toward your working, it could start with your salary. Since most men have been brought up to feel that they alone should provide for their families, a second income may seem to imply (whether it is true or not) that they cannot make an adequate living—and therefore that they are not adequate men. Largely for this reason, the working mother is neither a status symbol nor a source of pride in many circles. She's an embarrassment. If you are contributing substantially to a joint treasury, earning more than your husband, or, especially, if you are the sole support of the family, your husband may be particularly sensitive on this point.

Assuming that you want to keep the marriage going, be as tactful as you would like him to be under similar circumstances. Don't wield your income as a club or decide unilaterally on its use. If yours is the lesser salary, you might suggest putting it aside for major purchases or long-term savings. That way your husband's income will pay for the family's day-to-day maintenance, which should enable him to go on thinking of himself as the principal breadwinner. Later on, when he is more secure, you can throw everyone's money into the same pot if you so desire.

In addition to your economic independence, your new physical independence may be making your husband uneasy. First, it flies in the face of the age-old idea that a woman's place is in the home. And second, it doesn't square with his own fond memories of being greeted by his mother with hugs and kisses when he returned from school. While you can understand your husband's affinity for the cozy idea of having a wife at home, you can't sacrifice your life to indulge him in it. In most instances you will not be able to work at home, so he will just have to accept your leaving. But you could defer to his wishes to the extent of forgoing jobs that entail a great deal of travel or nighttime and weekend work.

To many husbands a wife's leaving the house signifies her meeting other men and this thought, too, makes them anxious. While such concern is not the end of the world for a marriage—to the contrary, it could make it come alive—you don't want to push a jealous husband too far. Don't dress up for work and neglect your appearance at home, for example. And do bring him up to the office to meet "the guys" or have them and their wives over to the house. Once he sees the competition in the flesh it won't seem as formidable.

Actually, what your husband may really be worried about is not your becoming less dependent on him economically or physically, but your becoming less involved with him psychologically. Despite his contempt for "keep 'em barefoot and pregnant" machismo, he may suddenly find himself very jealous of your new interests. Being human, you may not be able to resist flaunting your enthusiasm for work. And, being human, your husband may grow resentful of it. The situation could worsen if you're successful, for then the underlying competition that is present in every marriage might start to surface. But it might not surface in an identifiable way, either because your husband truly doesn't know what's bothering him or because—to quote Nena and George O'Neill, authors of *Open Marriage*—"Men are not accustomed to expressing their feelings, least of all about job jealousy." As a result, the two of you might find yourselves bickering over a host of trivial subjects while the real issue of job envy is never discussed.

Choose to find your husband's attitude flattering rather than annoying. Of course, you can't falsely pretend to live for him alone, but you should evince a lively interest in his life and you might also want to try to soft-pedal your own for a while. Then, when you sense that he's feeling less threatened, you can hold forth on your experiences at work.

Either to cover his own self-interest or because he's genuinely concerned, a husband will often object to his wife's working on the grounds that it takes her away from the children. This objection is the hardest of all to deal with both because good child care is so difficult to come by and because you too are worried about your youngsters' welfare. All you can do is look for the best possible caretaker, monitor the children's reactions, and reread—with your husband this time—our first chapter disproving the old maxim that maternal employment is harmful to children. As with your husband's other objections, this one should fade in time.

The attitudes we've been discussing can be found in homes of every socioeconomic stripe. But the middle-class woman who does not have to work may encounter opposition of another sort. Her husband may feel that taking a job voluntarily is crazy and, while he wouldn't go so far as to stop her, his every remark belittles her efforts. If your husband cannot identify with your aspirations, try to convince him that woman does not live by bridge games alone. If that doesn't work, try to involve him in your new undertaking. One woman whose husband had been totally opposed to her applying to law school swung him over to her side by sharing the devastation of a rejection notice with him. A dance teacher overcame her husband's indifference by asking him to work the stage lights for her recitals. And an elementary schoolteacher always brought her husband along for moral support on back-to-school nights. After such exposure, no husband—including yours—could long remain aloof from his wife's enterprise.

At some point the indifferent or hostile husband may magnanimously "allow" his wife to work. Yes, he will go along with it as long as his favorite meals are still served piping hot and on the minute; as long as his underwear is always freshly laundered and tucked away neatly in his drawers; as long as the children can keep up their round-the-clock schedule of extracurricular activities; and above all, as long as he does not have to lift a finger to help. This husband is a throwback to earlier times. If he belongs to you, we suggest that you try to bring him into the twentieth century with some of the following techniques.

Be Fair but Firm

A husband's emotional support may not be easy to get, as we have just noted, but his physical help may be even harder to obtain. Tradition-bound husbands flatly refuse to do "women's work," and even men who are ideologically in favor of working wives tend to balk when their own want to hand over some of their responsibilities to them. Try to hand them over anyway. Although your husband may earn a larger salary than you, your time is valuable too. Although you may be working out of choice, you're as tired as he is at the end of the day. And although you probably took care of everything by yourself before, you simply cannot go it alone any more. Convince yourself of these key points and then set to work convincing your husband.

Do it without getting upset—your voice will get high and quavery. Do it without screaming, hurling epithets, or assassinating his character—you'll only stiffen his resistance. And do it without crying—it's hard to be taken seriously when mascara is running down your face. Instead, adopt the businesslike approach we call "Fair but Firm." Write down all your chores and responsibilities in one column (you'll need a very long piece of paper) and then do the same with your husband's. When he sees the disparity in the two lists, he may be impressed enough to move some items from your column to his. For extra clout you might want to tell him that a recent study in Michigan concluded that married working women do four times as much housework and child care as married men.

Once you've made the point that you're overburdened, don't get bogged down in philosophical discussions of what men and women were put on this earth to do. Rather, get right into the specifics of what needs to be done and how best to do it. Ideally each of you should have an equal say in this matter, but realistically either your husband won't know where to begin or else he may demand to run the whole show. If the latter is the price of his cooperation, we suggest that you pay it (assuming that his division of labor is fair). Like your children, he's more apt to carry out plans he's made himself and often his ideas are good ones.

While your husband is growing accustomed to the new routine, help him out as much as possible. Tactfully suggest some of the systems and time-management techniques we discuss later on in this book, give him written lists to jog his memory, or make up standard schedules for him to follow. Since your husband has probably never paid much attention to housework before, you will have to keep your instructions as simple and specific as possible. You will also want to work alongside him for a while to demonstrate what has to be done. Some couples find that they like the companionship and speed of this collaborative effort so much that they keep it up even after the husband has become as good a housekeeper as his wife.

If your husband has definite ideas of what constitutes women's work and men's work, you might want to start him out in jobs he feels comfortable with, such as washing windows, and gradually ease him into more "feminine" chores, such as doing laundry. If he is having a hard time switching over, try incentives, tradeoffs, cajolery, humor, and appeals to his sense of fair play. Point out what a good idea it is for him to do the mending while you manage the household accounts, since the buttons you sew on always fall off again and the totals he arrives at never match the bank's. Of course, after you've huffed and you've puffed, your husband still may refuse to pitch in—at all. At that point you have three choices: you can do everything yourself; pay a substitute; or let the household go to pieces.

Even with a husband who is cooperative about doing household chores, you have to keep your "Fair but Firm" doctrine at the ready. Otherwise errands will end up where they always have, right in your lap. Few husbands realize how time-consuming and energy-sapping the minutiae of life are, because they've always had a mother, wife, or secretary to take care of things for them. Do not allow the "secretary syndrome" to pervade your marriage any more. If the family car is going to be sold, for example, don't let your husband automatically assume that you'll be the one to advertise and show it. Likewise, if the two of you are taking a trip, decide up front who will make the reservations, who will arrange to have the paper delivery stopped, and who will pick up the sun tan lotion. (The answers to the above should not all be you.)

If your husband is not doing his share, it might be because he senses that you will do it for him. Is he right? Though you feel he should call the theater, are you on your way to the phone the moment the two of you decide to take in a movie? Do you just go ahead and clean the house, buy the presents, do the marketing, balance the checkbook, invite the guests, and chauffeur the children without even giving him a crack at it? If so, you've only yourself to blame when he doesn't volunteer—you're preempting his every move.

You're also issuing a tacit warning to him to stay off your turf. By doing all these things yourself, you're saying that you don't think he can do them or do them as well as you. This is a mistake. If you want your husband's help, cede control along with the responsibility. Moreover, make up your mind that no matter what the results of his attempts, you're going to love them. Give your husband tremendous support and encouragement and never, ever deride his efforts.

To the contrary, go overboard in showing your appreciation. Sometimes a woman will become so overwhelmed by the logistics of managing a home and job that she will take her husband's help for granted. Treating him as some kind of hired hand, she even neglects to say thank you. Make sure that woman isn't you. The next time you find yourself ordering your husband to take the swim team carpool because you've had such a beastly hard day—stop. Did you ask him what kind of a day he had? "Fair but Firm" does not give you license to become unloving, uncaring, and inconsiderate. It should be used instead to forge a true partnership in marriage.

Money Matters

Next to a husband's pitching in at home, money is the most ticklish problem a working couple faces. Depending on how it's used, money can undermine or strengthen any relationship. Generally speaking, though, a second income should improve a marriage, because the simple fact of having extra money means fewer tensions and greater opportunities for a better life. In addition, where the wife's salary makes a substantial contribution to the family's income, she becomes a fuller partner in the marital enterprise. To make a second income enhance your marriage, choose the financial plan that suits you best: full pooling, partial pooling, or no pooling at all.

With full pooling all the family money is thrown into one pot and every expense from barbers to boilers is considered a joint outlay. If you and your husband have essentially the same spending habits and budgetary priorities, full pooling is the way to go. It prevents the proprietary attitude that often crops up when only one spouse's salary is used for purchases. It eliminates the need for a family council every time an unexpected bill appears. And it reinforces the idea that you and your husband are playing on the same team.

Despite these advantages, working couples often feel more comfortable with partial pooling. Under one version of this system you would use your salary for your personal and job-related expenses: lunch, commutation, babysitters, cleaning services, and perhaps your clothes. What is left over would then be combined with your husband's salary to pay the rest of the bills. Partial pooling is of particular benefit at certain stages of life, because it clearly delineates what it costs you to work and forces the family to live largely on your husband's income. If you were to retire temporarily, for example, your family would not have to lower its standard of living as much as it would under a full pooling arrangement.

Under the following no-pooling arrangement your family

might not have to lower its standard of living at all if you were to stop working. According to this plan, the wife's total income is considered found money and is put into a savings account for retirement, the children's college education, or other long-range goals. This is nice if you can afford it. If you can't but still like the idea of not pooling your salaries, you could draw up two different budgets to be administered and paid for separately. Thus, you might be responsible for everyone's personal expenses while your husband takes care of the home, insurance, and taxes. Obviously this version of no pooling will work best if both you and your husband are competent money managers.

Where one spouse is clearly more adept at finances, we feel that person should be put in charge of them. However, since the one who minds the treasury gets stuck with a lot of extra work and tends to feel more involved (i.e., worried), a certain amount of job sharing should always take place. If you draw up the budget and pay the bills, for example, there's no reason why your husband couldn't take the money to the bank and balance the checkbook. Then, once a month you should both look over the family's financial status, and once a year you should jointly redefine your financial goals.

No matter how good a system you and your husband work out, there are still bound to be some differences between you as to how to spend the money. For that reason we strongly recommend individual "squander funds." This private money corrects the worst feature of any joint financial venture: the need to get permission for every purchase. It also allows each of you to keep up that expensive hobby or go on a shopping spree without guilt, criticism, or damage to the family budget. Squander funds can be endowed through weekly salaries or sudden windfalls such as overtime pay.

When differences over money go deeper than squander fund expenditures, some basic changes in approach may be needed. If you're a disciplined shopper while your husband is an impulse buyer, for example, he may have to put himself on an allowance. And if he needs a year's salary in the bank to feel secure while you need none, you should hand over the savings book to him. But in discussing your differences, don't assume that the more conservative partner is always right or that the larger wage earner always has the final say. Rather, try to decide each case on its own merits. And above all, retain that measure of interest in financial matters that separates the women from the girls.

Money can be a constant source of friction in a marriage or it can be one of the ties that bind. Make sure it's the latter. After all, when funds are running dangerously low, who else is going to eat spaghetti with you nine nights in a row—and laugh about it with you afterwards?

And who else is going to worry with you over your son's reading problem or share your relief when he overcomes it? Just as you and your husband do better by working on your finances together, so the whole family will come out ahead if you both look upon child rearing as a cooperative venture.

Shared Parenting

Your husband's moral support is crucial in bringing up the children but, as with housework, his physical help is also necessary. Be "Fair but Firm" in seeing to it that he does his share. How can he help? Let us count the ways: he can sit up all night or stay home all day with a sick child; he can hunt down a pair of pink tights size 4–6x during lunch hour; he can ferry a son back and forth to the dentist; he can have conferences with teachers; he can correct posture and oversee homework; and he can talk to, discipline, and worry about the children as well as love them. In short, everything you do, he can do.

Since all of this takes time, a father may not be able to do it without some change in his accustomed pattern of living. He can no longer leave the house before the kids get up, return after they have gone to bed, and spend all his weekends on the golf course. Nor will he be able to bury his head in a newspaper when he's on duty, if that has been his wont. Moreover, under a true cooperative parenting arrangement, your husband will not only have to give of his time, he'll have to become *responsible* for many unrewarding but necessary child-related chores that he merely used to *help out with* before when asked. And when he starts to correct table manners and enforce language codes, he'll have to take the flak such reminders evoke. But as a result of his increased exposure to the children, he will get to participate in those wonderful shared moments that make it all worthwhile.

Despite these rewards, it is the rare husband who volunteers for nannyhood. Therefore, you may have to actively encourage his participation. It would be best if he decided on his new responsibilities himself, but since he's probably new to the game, you may have to give him some rather broad hints. "I'd like to take a breadmaking class Saturday mornings at ten," you might say. "Could you take care of the children then and put off your jogging until one?"

Cooperative parenting does not necessarily mean splitting time and responsibilities right down the middle. It does mean arriving at some sort of equitable arrangement. If your husband travels all week, for example, you cannot expect him to make up for it by babysitting all day Saturday and Sunday—or he may never come home. Still, since you are working *and* parenting while he's away, he should do a little extra when he returns.

Your husband may be apprehensive about spending time alone with the children if they are very young or he's never done it before. To ease him into it, suggest organized activities to make the time pass more quickly and/or find chores they can do together. Not only will the latter get things accomplished, but it will give the children an opportunity to see Dad running errands and doing housework. This sight will do more to combat rigid ideas of sex roles than a thousand lectures from you.

In addition to the "quantity" time described above, your husband should spend some quality time with the children. This would give him a real chance to get close to them while at the same time taking them off your hands. Help your husband to be more than a caretaker by suggesting some of the ideas we put forward in Chapter 10, ''Closing the Communications Gap.'' Show him how he could enjoy a hobby with them or how he could arrange time to talk. Since it is hard to orchestrate quality time with more than one child, you could occasionally divide up the brood. Just be sure that you don't always follow the same equation when doing so: mother-daughter, father-son, or mother–younger child and father–older child.

Some men relish the prospect of spending time alone with their children. Others view it with resentment, if not horror. Yet once they get into it, almost all of them find it a rewarding experience. Indeed, every man we interviewed for this book cited a closer relationship with his children as one of the real advantages of having a working wife. These men claim that they have gotten to know their children better than they did in the days when their wives were always running interference for them.

Although cooperative parenting strengthens the father-child relationship, relieves the working mother of many chores, and endows her with that rarest of treasures—time to herself—many women do not encourage it. In fact, each time they call upon their husbands for help with the children, they interfere and criticize so much that the men give up in disgust. If you, too, are loath to leave your husband and children alone, you may be the victim of guilt, jealousy, or an image of motherhood that's so all-encompassing it leaves no room for fatherhood.

On the other hand, you may be reluctant to bring your husband and children together because you disapprove of his parenting style. You may feel that a father should be a pal while your spouse prefers to be an authority figure. Or you may want him to behave in a dignified manner, while he likes to get down on the floor and roughhouse with the kids. But just because his way is not your way (even if you've read all the child-rearing books and he hasn't), that does not mean he's wrong and you're right. If he cares enough about the children to spend time with them, what he's doing can't be all bad. In fact, just by being on the scene to provide a role model, he's doing a lot of good.

Still, you and your husband have to be careful not to work at cross purposes. Once the children see that they can play one of you off against the other, you're sunk. Therefore, even if you're strict and he's permissive, get together on basic policies regarding allowance, bedtime, acceptable dress, permissible language, homework, and discipline. But hammer out these decisions where the children can't hear you and do so in the spirit of compromise. Decisions are rarely so monumental that by themselves they'll change the course of your children's lives, so why go to the mat on each and every one of them?

This need to arrive at mutually agreeable solutions can be a pain in the neck. From time to time you'll yearn to make just one major decision without discussing it with your husband first. But in the long run you'll all be better off for having raised the children cooperatively. They'll enjoy a richer home life and you'll enjoy a more rewarding marriage. Moreover, you need your husband's help with the children right now. And you can't very well ask him to do the work without letting him have his say on how the children should be raised. Even though you might like to.

Your Marriage

One reason why you may resent consulting your husband about child rearing is that, since you started working, relations between the two of you have become strained. No matter what's bothering him, he may seem to blame all his problems and tensions on that new factor in his life—your employment. Do not let him get away with this. Empathize with his unhappiness but point out where the real cause of it lies. If you don't, your job may become the whipping boy for everything that goes wrong in your husband's life from now on.

You also have to be careful not to duplicate this syndrome yourself. Just because he's *there,* your husband may seem to be at the root of all your problems when in fact he has nothing to do with them. The stage of self-motivation you're going through could be contributing to this irrational conviction. You may have worked up a rage against the status quo in order to gather the courage to go out into the world. And once you've decided that the whole of American society is conspiring to keep mothers down, what else could your husband be—no matter how supportive he is—but a male chauvinist pig?

Now that you're already seething, your resentment may boil over when you have to thank him for doing the least little thing around the house. Nor do you love it when the other women sing his praises for taking the kids out on Halloween or picking up some groceries at the store. Despite the fact that you're holding down a job too, everybody just expects you to attend to the house and children, and nobody sings your praises for it either. This is patently unfair and you have a right to be angry about it. Fortunately, our society is moving toward greater equality on the home front; unfortunately, we're not there yet. But rather than let the gap between real and ideal tear your marriage asunder, try to focus not on what anyone is saying but on how much more your husband is doing than (a) his father, (b) his friends, or (c) he used to.

A raised consciousness is not the only change being wrought in you as a result of work. The way you look, handle situations, deal with people, regard your future, and think of yourself may be undergoing major metamorphoses as well. Yet your husband may be oblivious to most of it. It's not that he's necessarily obtuse or resistant to the changes; in fact he may like many of them. It's just that he's grown accustomed to thinking of you as "my-wife-the-housewife," and it's hard for him to conceptualize you any other way. Creating a new image for oneself is never easy, as secretaries find out to their chagrin when they try to climb the managerial ladder: they often have to move to another company in order to be taken seriously. Unless you want to move to another family, all you can do is patiently chip away at your husband's (mis)conceptions of you.

But be aware that your husband's attitude is colored by the way you behave at home, and you may be sending out mixed signals there. Although you clamor to make decisions befitting a mature woman of the world, you may shrink from taking responsibility when they turn out wrong. Although you demand that your husband respect you, you may become flighty, unmechanical, or even unable to count if it will get you out of doing some tedious chore. And although you complain that he's a tyrant, you may tacitly encourage your husband to be "masterful" either because you find it sexy, you need a father in residence, or you feel deep down that's how a man should behave. Everyone likes to be babied from time to time and no one should have to be competent in every area from diapers to carburetors. But if your old, manipulative dependency act is casting doubt on your new working woman competence, drop it. Otherwise, how will your husband know it's the New You?

And it *is* a New You. Since a paycheck carries clout in our society, you are probably thinking more highly of yourself since you started receiving one. And since working is a kind of assertiveness training course, you're probably feeling more self-assured, speaking up more at home, and trying to become a more equal partner in your marriage. Unfortunately, many men don't take kindly to equality. They tend to think of relationships in terms of dominant-subordinate roles. "If I'm no longer the boss," your husband may be worrying, "will you be?" But if you don't let your new assertiveness become aggressiveness and your husband is not an unredeemable reactionary, your marriage should emerge stronger than ever after a period of adjustment.

Some women never find that out. They don't bring their new assertiveness home, because they are afraid that it will turn off their husbands sexually. Instead, they continue to play a passive role that bears no resemblance to the real them. If you, too, are pretending to be a shrinking violet in order to hold on to your husband, you may be underestimating him. Like many men he may just find an independent wife even more exciting than a passive, dependent one—especially as he learns that when she feels better about herself, she feels sexier. Indeed, the satisfaction that accompanies taking a job can add dimension and sparkle to a sexual relationship.

But taking a job may bring with it a new set of problems too. According to psychiatry professor Dr. Carroll M. Brodsky, "You carry your job experience and the way it affects you . . . into the bedroom." This is another way of saying that a good job experience is good for your sex life and a bad one is not. Moreover, even if your job experience is very good, the fact that you're working at all could affect your physical relationship. Because the two greatest enemies of sexual pleasure— anxiety and fatigue—are your constant companions, the possibility of sexual dysfunction is increased.

While you want to be alert to this possibility, you don't want to be too quick to assign blame. Firstly, there are no statistics linking female employment and sexual problems, so no one knows for sure if there is a direct relationship between them. Secondly, a number of factors such as health, age, and mental attitude are so closely intertwined here that it is almost impossible to extricate female employment from the matrix. And finally, sexual dysfunction is such a widespread phenomenon—Masters and Johnson report that 50 percent of all married couples have sexual problems—that a wife's employment could not be the single or even the greatest cause of it. Take heed! If you are using work as an excuse to avoid your husband in bed, not only will he become hostile toward your job, but you are overlooking the real cause of your sexual dissatisfaction.

The way you and your husband relate sexually has tremendous bearing on your total marital relationship, and vice versa. Therefore, you'll want to make each as strong as possible. This means setting aside time, storing up energy, and generating real interest in your sex life. It also means paying attention to what's going on between you, because familiarity has a bad habit of breeding not so much contempt in marriage as ennui. You can't drop all the romantic amenities in the interests of efficient living and still expect to remain "in love."

A key factor in keeping your romance alive is spending time together away from the children. It is hard to perceive one another as sex objects when you're always playing Mom and

Pop. Therefore, set aside time each day for adult talk and get out together once a week, even if it's just for a pizza. In addition, try to arrange an occasional weekend without the children. You may be reluctant to leave them after working all week, but rest assured that they won't be harmed by your absence while they will benefit from your strengthened marital bond. The kind of weekend we have in mind does not have to be elaborate or costly. In fact, if the kids are boarding at a neighbor's, you don't even have to leave the house. Without them around, holding hands in the living room will seem like a trip to Paris.

As you've gathered by now, making a go of the two-career, two-parent marriage is not easy. But you can do it if you keep your goals realistic. Don't expect your husband to immediately empathize with your desire to work if he truly believes you should stay at home. And don't expect him to suddenly embrace sweeping the floors, giving the kids their baths, and cooking dinner every other night if he's never done these things before. It is crucial that you give your husband time to adjust to the two-career marriage. But keep nudging him toward greater acceptance and participation while you wait. By handling the situation this way, you could help to create the perfect counterpart to the New You—a New Him.

5

The "Real World"

How you feel about your job—enthusiastically positive, bleakly negative, or somewhere in between—may depend upon how the rewards you reap and the demands you face balance out. Everyone feels better about working when the job delivers satisfaction and a decent salary. But a mother has a further requirement: the obligations of a job must not seriously impair her ability to carry out her duties at home.

For the fact of the matter is that when you step into an office or classroom, you will be treated just like every other employee or student. There will be no exceptions made and no special dispensations granted just because you're a mother. It's not that people in the "real world" don't understand that you have a family—it's just that they don't want to be inconvenienced by it. Therefore, before you commit yourself to any situation, you have to be sure that it will be compatible with family life and at the same time meet your vocational or educational objectives.

Some General Considerations

Whether you're entering the job market for the first time, switching to another company, or embarking upon a course of studies, you should be realistic. Is the field you're considering crowded, the work low-paying, the opportunities for advancement limited, and the chances of transferring skills slim? If so, it's probably not a good choice even if the work itself seems interesting or the hours amenable to child rearing. There's little point getting a master's degree in education, for example, if there are 300 applicants for every teaching position in your city and student enrollment is falling. There's also no point looking for work that would seriously undermine your role as wife and mother. Why try out for a play that is going on the road for six months or apply to a firm that demands frequent relocation? Situations like these could have a disastrous effect on your family.

Another key consideration is how the job will advance your career. Too many women are stuck in unsatisfactory positions because they didn't do any advance planning. Unfortunately, it isn't always possible to know what you'd like to be doing five or ten years from now, or to get started on that goal even if you did. Very often you have to do what's right for you at the moment. But paying attention to the present and near future can work out well too. A good case in point is Lucy Wilson Benson, Under Secretary of State for Security Affairs, Science, and Technology, the highest position ever held by a woman in the State Department. "I never really thought of public administration as a career," said Mrs. Benson. "When I was a high-school student, my only thought was to get to college. When I went to Smith, my goal was economic independence."

If your present goal is an economic one too, make sure it's being met. It costs so much to work, especially if you have to pay for child care, that you might very well find you'd come out ahead if you stayed home. Payroll deductions, commutation, lunches, new clothes, and extra convenience foods could use up all that wonderful money you had been counting on. You may still decide to work for psychological reasons or to get a toehold in your profession. But if the figures are not there, don't fool yourself into thinking that your job is an economic bonanza.

Another factor you should bear in mind is the commute. Many mothers find that traveling more than half an hour each way takes too big a bite out of their day, and for some women even that half hour is too much. But many others welcome a trip at either end of their day because it enables them to unwind and to switch gears from home to office. Indeed, they say they wouldn't know what to do without this peaceful lull in their otherwise frantic lives.

Finally, you have to know yourself. When contemplating that wonderful smorgasbord that is the "real world," many women get very big eyes. They heap their plates with responsibilities, opportunities, and plain hard work. Then, when they start to dig in, they find that their appetites have shrunk considerably but by then it's too late—they're committed. Lest you, too, find yourself in over your head, estimate ahead of time how much physical stamina you have and how much pressure you can cope with. Calculate how much inconvenience your husband will put up with and how much responsibility your child's caretaker will take. Then, when you have a good fix on what all of you can handle, go on to evaluate the specific arrangements you might make.

Conditions of Work and Study

Things are so competitive in every area of life today that in order to get your foot in the door—and accommodate your family at the same time—you may have to accept something that's less than ideal in terms of wages, hours, and conditions. Still, not all compromises are equal. To obtain the arrangement that suits you best, we suggest that you weigh the following pros and cons.

The 9 to 5 Job: Most working mothers work full time and they do so for good reason. Full-time jobs usually offer the most money, job security, opportunities for advancement, and fringe benefits. They are the most plentiful too, which means that among them you're most likely to find the kind of work you want to do. And you can't beat them for status and responsibility, either. The "real world" operates on a forty-hour week and the only way to truly become a part of it is to be on the scene for the full forty hours.

The great disadvantage to full-time work is that it leaves you very little time for yourself and your family. It could put you under a great deal of pressure, too, because as a full member of the team you have people counting on you. You also have a large personal stake in doing well. Therefore, you may start to carry your work around with you both mentally and physically, which could put an additional strain on you at home. Although this can happen with any work arrangement, it's most likely to occur when the commitment is 9 to 5.

Part-time Work: Many mothers look upon part-time work as the ideal arrangement, and in many ways it is. Part-time work is especially good for getting back into the world again. It gets everyone in the family accustomed to the idea of My-Mother-the-Worker, especially Mother, and it gives her a chance gradually to build up her confidence, working wardrobe, and home systems. When a woman has small children, part-time work enables her to get out of the house and earn some money while still spending a great deal of time with the youngsters. It can also benefit the woman with older children, because it brings her self-satisfaction, sociability, and financial reward, yet leaves her enough time for housework and family without feeling overwhelmed.

Unfortunately, there's not much of it around. Although there has been a great deal of talk about job sharing and other part-time arrangements, employers would rather not work around someone else's schedule if they can help it. Nor do they want to be bothered with anyone who doesn't seem to be committed either to the company or to her own professional advancement—especially when the world is full of people knocking down their doors to work full time. Employers usually get interested in part-time work as a way to save money, temporarily fill an odd slot, or accommodate a valuable employee they would otherwise lose. But no matter what their reasons, the work they assign to a part-timer is not usually considered crucial to the company's existence.

As time goes on, even the part-timer herself may grow disillusioned with the arrangement. She may find that she is spending a great deal of time at home on the telephone trying to coordinate her work with that of the employees who are always on the premises. Moreover, she may have to lay out as much for clothes, carfare, and lunches as a full-timer without receiving the same pay, promotions, on-the-job training, or fringe benefits (including paid holidays and sick leave) as they. As one part-time speech therapist said, "I used to think that I had the best of all possible worlds. Now I think that the agency has the best of all possible me."

Odd Hours: Many jobs—full time and part time—entail nighttime and weekend work. Don't dismiss a job with odd hours out of hand, because it might work out to your advantage. It could provide you with free babysitting if your husband or your mother who lives with you works the day shift. Since one of you would always be around, your children would be assured of constant supervision in their own home by a close relative. One beautician told us that Saturday was actually her favorite day to work, because it was the one time she didn't have to worry whether the teen-age sitter was going to show up: her husband was on duty. Working at night could make it more convenient for you to shop and do errands, and being gone while your children are asleep could mean that you're around more when they're awake.

If you are a student you might be able to get your education at night, on weekends, or through intensive short-term courses. Again, you might find it easier to get babysitters at these times than if you attended regular daytime sessions. The major disadvantage of working or going to school at odd hours is that you might see your husband only when he's coming and you're going, or vice versa. It might also prevent your family from regularly interacting as a total unit. However, if you can surmount these obstacles, you might find that odd hours are for you.

Working at Home: For many reasons working at home can be a godsend. It enables a mother to earn money without giving any of it back in the form of carfare, lunch money, extra clothing, or babysitting fees. By working at home she can actually earn less and wind up with more. And by not commuting, she can save time and energy. In addition, when her children are at school she has at her disposal a free, quiet environment for six or seven hours a day, and when they're home, she's available to them. If a child gets sick, the mother doesn't have to scramble around at the last minute to find a sitter so that she can go to work. But while this is all true, there's a darker side to the picture as well.

Despite all the articles in women's magazines, there just isn't that much one can do at home to bring in real money. Moreover, working at home day in and day out can be lonely and depressing. Not too many people are cut out for this solitary life, nor do they have the enormous—some say superhuman—discipline to produce without the structure of an office routine. Because she is also responsible for the house, a mother may find it even harder to get the work out if she is constantly surrounded by so many legitimate reasons to procrastinate: a load of laundry that has to be popped into the dryer, a roast that should be basted, a parsley plant that cries out for repotting. And for some reason these chores always seem to need doing during prime time.

Moreover, since other people usually don't take the work-at-home seriously, she finds it hard to take herself seriously. Friends think nothing of calling up for lengthy chats and inviting her to play tennis or check out a sale, offers perhaps too tempting to refuse. And when she tries to combine work with babysitting—the most highly touted advantage of all—she is likely to find it a losing battle. "Don't disturb me unless it's an emergency!" she roars, only to be disturbed a few minutes later by a serious little person who swears, "Mom, it's an emergency. I can't find Huggy Bear's shoe." If she has small children, she usually resigns herself to working at night.

But if you're stouthearted and would like to give it a try, here are some suggestions from other women who have worked at home. Get dressed and put on your make-up in the morning—every morning—or you'll soon grow depressed. Make lunch dates and take (short) telephone breaks to combat the isolation. Decide how many hours a week you are going to work—and what you're going to drop to make room for them—then draw up a time sheet to make the commitment real. Even better, establish regular business or study hours and notify one and all that you're incommunicado during that period. Then don't make even one bed or dust one table until you've fulfilled all your business obligations.

You'll find this easier to do if you have a room to yourself or, at a minimum, a corner where you can set up your equipment permanently. Try to inculcate in your children a tremendous and well-founded fear of touching that equipment. Also try to teach them to answer the phone in a professional manner, to depart the scene when you're transacting business, and to leave you alone when you're working. However, little ones can't be expected to entertain themselves for long and big ones can't be expected to tiptoe around the house every day after school. Therefore, you may very well find that the amount of work you are turning out is small while the emotional wear and tear on you is great. If this is so, consider taking some space outside your home.

Your Own "Office": Having a work space outside the house does away with many of the disadvantages of working at home: you feel that you're really going to work, you aren't tempted to clean and cook, you don't have the problem of children underfoot, and, if there are other people in the building, you aren't so lonely. You also have fewer outside interruptions because people take you more seriously when you have an office. Indeed, if you don't bring your mending from home, the whole environment can be much more conducive to work. Though you may initially feel sheepish about renting an office when you've theoretically got a whole house at your disposal, your increased productivity may soon justify it.

How do you find a space you can afford? Start with the library, which is free. You could either carve out a niche for yourself in a quiet corner, set up business in the typing room, or ask the librarian to open up a little-used conference room to you. For a more permanent arrangement, look for an odd piece of space in someone's office to accommodate a desk and phone. Or try to find a small suite with a separate entrance in someone's home and get a few women to go in on it with you. Obviously, if you don't have much money, you'll have to use your imagination. An artist we know got the management of her apartment building to clear out a basement storeroom for her, and three law students of our acquaintance took a hotel room together to cram for exams. But if you can afford it, there's a new setup custom-made for you: the individual, furnished office in a commercial building that's available on a short-term lease.

Freelance: Like working at home and sometimes in conjunction with it, a freelance job appeals to many mothers. They like the idea of being able to phase in and out of the job market at will, set their own hours and/or meet many new people, and work in many different environments. Indeed, for women with limited vocational goals, freelance work offers a number of advantages.

But for women who are serious about working, freelancing is not all it's cracked up to be. According to the mystique that has grown up around it, a freelance can pick and choose among her assignments. In reality, unless she's a superstar, she's grateful for whatever work comes her way. Indeed, a freelance often lives in a state of anxiety, not knowing for sure whether her phone will ever ring again. She is aware of the fact that when an employer has a job to be done, he thinks first of the person he used last or the person most likely to say yes. Therefore, unless a freelance has another job, she always says yes. And once she's accepted, she *has* to show up, whether her child has a temperature of 102°, the sitter has canceled, or she has ten people coming for dinner. She must be there, both because she is irreplaceable for that day and because she doesn't dare risk being thought unreliable.

As for the financial rewards, they too are often overestimated. The work is rarely steady, the pay often insufficient to live on, and the fringe benefits nil. Unlike the staff worker, the freelance does not get paid when she is sick. Those women who do make their living at freelance work are constantly hustling and/or they have an understanding with a company that guarantees them a certain amount of work each year. But a woman generally gets this plum only if she's already been on the staff of that particular company or in the field for many years. Depending on the profession, a person can advance herself through freelance work if she builds up a good portfolio, a fine reputation, and a host of contacts. However, in order to branch out she may have to take a staff job, because an employer will only call a freelance to do something she's expert at. He's not going to spend time training her if she's just coming in for the day.

Finally, rather than being conducive to a smoothly running household, freelance work can be at odds with it. It's hard to arrange for irregular child care, hard to honor your commitment to the carpool, and hard to plan a regular schedule of housework when you don't know what days you'll be home and what days you won't. Therefore, if you want to work less than a forty-hour week, perhaps you should consider taking a regular part-time job rather than seeking freelance assignments.

Starting Your Own Business: Again, because of the flexibility it can afford, going into business for themselves holds strong appeal for many mothers. Those who are already on their own also cite the advantages of not having to please a boss, not having to contend with an institutional structure, and not having to turn over the profits to anyone as particular delights of this situation. Holding their destinies in their own hands, they experience a unique sense of control. Being able to put their ideas directly into practice, they feel a new surge of energy. And after building up a business from scratch, they have the satisfaction of knowing "I did it myself."

Alas, few of their ventures turn out to be truly successful. Not many people have the capital or marketing skills to withstand the competition of big business and often the things they pursue, such as one-of-a-kind crafts, are inherently unprofitable. From the individual's point of view, too, the situation may soon lose its charm. If the business is so small that it puts the owner under no pressure, it usually isn't bringing in enough money to warrant the effort she's making. And if, on the other hand, it does grow large enough to actually support her, she may suddenly find herself staying up all hours of the night wrestling with paperwork and problems. Moreover, when they try to turn their hobbies into profitmaking ventures, many women report that they no longer enjoy them, at least not on an eight- or even four-hour-a-day basis. Therefore, if you're considering starting your own business, ask yourself whether you have the fortitude and special skills required to be an entrepreneur, or whether you're willing to settle for pin money.

Going to School: There are many advantages to going to school while your children are still at home. Taking classes provides an exhilarating change from parenting and cleaning, yet it can be compatible with them. If you followed a standard academic schedule, you would be available to your children during the summer and most holidays. By going to school you would be enhancing your self-esteem and stretching your mind. And, whether working toward your first degree, accruing additional professional credentials, or switching to a new field, you would be laying a solid foundation for your future.

But take it slowly at first. If you haven't been a student for a number of years, it may take some time to get adjusted to it again. Every returnee feels insecure, and if your classmates are much younger than you, you may feel especially self-conscious and intimidated. Moreover, between exams, term papers, field work, and the need to acquit yourself well in class, you may feel much more pressured than you would in a routine job. The time requirements alone are tension-producing. Indeed, if you're taking a full course load, you might find yourself putting in sixty hours a week or more. If you don't think you can cope with all that and motherhood too, perhaps you should take on only a partial academic load.

Not only do you have to consider the stress factor when weighing a full-time versus a part-time program, but you must take into account the financial ramifications as well. As a full-time student you might be eligible for scholarships and aid, but as a part-time student you might be able to find a job that covers the cost of tuition. A prestigious school might cost more and have a less flexible program, but it might guarantee you a better job when you graduate—an important consideration if the field you're preparing for is highly competitive. Whatever choice you make, you will need a quiet place and a block of time daily in which to study. Make sure you have both before plunking down your money for tuition.

Since the work or study situation you ultimately choose may depend largely on how ambitious you are, now is the time to evaluate how high your aspirations go.

Indian or Chief?

Today women are being told not only that they *can* make it to the top, but that they *should*. They're supposed to want to climb the ladder of success because, like Mount Everest, it's there. But merely holding their own is a struggle for many working mothers, and the additional pressure of trying to get ahead could do them in altogether. If you can't give any more to your job than you're already giving, don't feel like a failure. Putting limits on how far you'll extend yourself is a perfectly acceptable practice. And if you are content with whatever professional status or financial rewards you already enjoy—more power to you.

On the other hand, if you're naturally ambitious, this is a good time for you to be alive. In the past you would probably have had to sublimate your ambitions or realize them through your husband and children. Today society permits you to have direct outlets for your drive. And because there are more opportunities now than ever before for a capable woman, you are more likely than ever before to find a position that will give you the kind of responsibility, satisfaction, and—dare we say it?—power that you seek. Let us mention here, too, that though ambition has recently been maligned as compulsive workaholism, we see it as a positive life force. Moreover, we think that it can occur just as naturally in a woman as in a man.

But even if you were born ambitious or have become so over the years, you should be realistic about your chances of making it to the top. Look around you—how many people do you see who are fantastic successes? Moreover, when you find out what it takes to make it to the top, you may not even want to enter the fray. With increased responsibilities come increased headaches; with greater opportunities, greater pressure; and with more risk, more likelihood of failure.

It's hard enough for a man to make it to the top, but it's close to impossible for a woman. The business world is still largely a man's world. Indeed, only 2.3 percent of American executives earning $25,000 a year or more are women, and even breaking into middle management is considered quite an accomplishment for a female. Despite recent legislation mandating equality of opportunity, a woman usually has to push harder and be better than a man to obtain the same position, and once she has attained it, she will usually be paid much less than he. If yours is a second income, an employer may be even more reluctant to bring your salary up to par—if he'll hire you at all. According to testimony given at government hearings and the findings of research studies, women with young children are often discriminated against in the marketplace because employers think they are less responsible than men, abundant evidence to the contrary notwithstanding.

You may also find it difficult to fight your way to the top because your upbringing may not have prepared you for it. Girls in America have traditionally been raised to be unadventurous, sweet, loving followers. In return for their passivity, they were awarded security and approval. So you should not be surprised if the assertiveness needed to get ahead produces a conflict within you. The realization that a co-worker may not like you because you are a threat to his job may in turn be threatening to you. You may also be afraid of seeming less feminine by becoming successful, especially if your mother always told you to let the boys win.

Then, too, you've got to be realistic about the fact that careers and child rearing do sometimes collide. First of all, there's the matter of logistics. To get ahead you may have to stay late, travel, and relocate on command. To be a good mother you may have to be home at a regular hour, be available on weekends, and not pull up stakes every few years. It's not only that you feel guilty when you're away—it's also that you miss the children very much.

Then there are the physical burdens of keeping a house clean versus the physical drain of working and commuting. You can't underestimate this, because in most cases, unlike a man, you're not just exchanging home for office; you're *adding* office to home. And there is the danger of mental clash between being the psychological parent/housekeeper and the effective worker who is always sharp of eye and clear of mind. If you have to remember to buy the snowsuits, arrange the piano lessons, put toilet paper on the list, and cancel the appointment with the pediatrician, you're less likely to be thinking of twelve new ways to improve your company's filing system.

Finally, there can sometimes be a conflict in emotional commitments. If your heart is breaking because your youngster is overweight, failing in school, or hanging around with an un-savory bunch of kids, you'll have trouble caring passionately about whether the deodorant you're advertising expands its share of market or not. And when your husband comes home one day and says: "I'm being transferred," what will you reply? "I'm not going. My future with the company lies here"?

As an ambitious employee, loving mother, and devoted wife, you are trapped between two sets of expectations: always being available to your family and always giving your all to your job. Yet no one can do both, and the attempt may tear you apart. As Margaret Hennig and Anne Jardim, authors of *The Managerial Woman,* said of working mothers: "You find some who want to be the perfect wife, the perfect mother and the perfect vice president at the same time. . . . It's a losing battle." The trouble is that there are no limits to any of your roles. How good is a good mother, how top a top executive?

The competition in academia, the professions, and the business world is so stiff and the pace so killing today that in order to get to the top, one has to practically devote one's life to the task. Many women choose not to make that commitment. In interviews with medical doctors and college professors who are also mothers, the familiar theme is sounded over and over: they often won't travel to attend conferences, they don't publish as much as they should, and they tend not to seek the chairmanships of departments. Any of these things would take too much time away from their families.* The women who have backed off this way say they don't resent making professional sacrifices nor do they regret having had a family (although some would have limited the size of it), but they do acknowledge that they have scaled down their ambitions, at least for the time being. It is their bargain with life—and almost all of them think it is a very good one.

---

*Domestic duties are a consideration, too. A recent survey of female physicians in the Cleveland area revealed that a whopping 75 percent of them do their own housework!

Onward and Upward

If, after taking all these factors into consideration, you're still excited by the prospect of getting ahead, discuss the ramifications of this decision with your husband. You need his support and, yes, his approval, if you are going to make a successful run for it. He might prefer to have you wait until the children are older, but both of you have got to be realistic about the fact that the longer you wait, the less employable you'll be and the slimmer your chances will be for becoming a real success. In many fields forty is considered over the hill and women starting out at the age of thirty-five are often looked at askance. So if you eventually want to attain a high position, now is probably the time to start shooting for it.

Once that decision is made, life becomes a matter of working hard, harder, hardest. There's always a lot of competition for the better jobs and, when you're up against men and women without children, you start out a few lengths behind. To be taken seriously, you'll have to be especially reliable, conscientious—and good.

For the most part, we think that the idea of getting ahead through gamesmanship is just plain silly. As Under Secretary of State Lucy Benson said, "The important thing is to find what you like to do, and then do it as well as you possibly can." Still, you can't be totally naïve about office politics. You'll go further if you become professionally friendly with everyone in the office and can find one experienced employee to act as your mentor.

Because men apparently find it easier to confide in a woman than in another man, you may discover yourself in the role of office confessor. However, don't make the mistake of confiding back—at least not about your children. Whether out of guilt or pride, many women have a compulsion to talk about the kiddies, and in most cases it bores the listener silly. It also gives others the impression that you consider yourself a mother first and an employee second. While your boss might approve of your priorities, he won't promote you on the strength of them. In fact, if he's like the overwhelming majority of Americans, he's apt to disapprove of your working altogether if you have young children. Therefore, if you want to get ahead, don't keep reminding people at work that you're a mother.

Just as you can't be naïve about office politics, so you shouldn't underestimate the importance of appearances. In the outside world you get marked up or down on the basis of looks. Because you're a mother as well as a worker, you'll have to strike a compromise between beauty and practicality. Thus, you should find a hairstyle that's flattering but easy to keep up— something in between Farrah Fawcett-Majors and Carol Burnett. Make sure that your clothes go to work when you do. If you have to worry about hitching up your slip or tripping over your spike heels, you'll find it hard to concentrate on what you're doing. And if you wear clothes that are too tight, short, low-cut, flashy, bright, or extreme in styling, associates will find it hard to concentrate on what you're saying. Every expert states emphatically that calling attention to yourself this way will not help you get ahead.

What will help you get ahead is a quiet, understated elegance. Fortunately, you can achieve this look with a minimum of clothing if you stick to simple styles, neutral colors, and coordinated separates. Look for seasonless fabrics that work well in overheated or over-air-conditioned offices. And if you travel a lot for business, count on darkish, wrinkle-resistant, layered ensembles to see you through.

In addition to covering your body and enhancing your appearance, clothes can be a form of advertising. Indeed, if you want to get ahead, they should correspond not to the job you have but to the job you would like to have. That means that if you are a secretary hoping to be a supervisor, you should probably wear long-sleeved blouses and pants suits when all the other secretaries are wearing T-shirts and jeans. And if it's the corporate ladder you would ascend, you might want to consider buying a

"Dress for Success" business suit. Except for the fact that it comes with a skirt, this suit looks exactly like the one worn by men—down to the four-in-hand tie! Some people feel that it is insulting for a woman to have to dress like a man to get ahead,* but corporate women say this kind of uniform works. As a marketing associate for the Continental Can Company put it: "There are enough obstacles in a woman's way. Why go against conceived dress codes? If you want to be an individual and differentiate, do it in other ways."

What a Job Can Do for You and What It Can't

Just as the ease of making it to the top has been overestimated, so the benefits of working have been oversold. Women have been falsely led to believe that a job is the panacea for all ills. They have been told that once they land it, they will "find" themselves, tap creative inner resources, and be off to a flying start on the road to fame and fortune. When you've been mopping floors and changing diapers all day, that's heady stuff.

It's also largely fictitious. After all, how many first jobs—or even second and third jobs—are exciting, creative, or a direct conduit to the "big break"? Most jobs are ordinary and consist of routine tasks. Women still benefit from them, but if they go in expecting the moon, they are likely to feel that the job—and they themselves—are abysmal failures. They grow ashamed and angry because they are unable to find the self-fulfillment they were assured is out there. Everyone experiences a letdown when the excitement of starting a new job wears off. But if a woman's expectations have been raised to unrealistic heights, the letdown will be that much greater. She might even go into a real slump.

If you feel that you're in such a slump, try to pull yourself out of it by focusing on the positive aspects of your work. And the fact is that although your job is not giving you everything, it

*Fashion designer Kasper is of this opinion. When asked what he thought a woman should wear to an interview at IBM, he replied with tongue in cheek: "That's easy. She should wear a machine."

is probably giving you a great deal. For one thing, it is providing you with money, social contacts, and participation in the working world. For another thing, if it is satisfying, it is increasing your sense of competence, achievement, and self-worth. Surely you would find it hard to develop that kind of self-esteem—and have the world stamp it "Valid"—if you were still sitting at home. Nor might you be as effective a mother or have as happy a marriage, at least not if you wanted to be out and were stuck in.

Therefore, try to find work that you like and that pays you a decent wage. Then be realistic about how much satisfaction you're going to derive from it. Once you stop demanding more from a job than it can deliver, you'll probably find that you like it a lot better. And once you rid yourself of the notion that only through work can you "develop as a person," you're likely to find that you're much more relaxed. With some perspective you can see that the "real world" is not the be-all and end-all. Still, if you put a lot into it, you can get a lot out.

6

"Mommy, I Don't Feel Good"

Working mothers worry about their children getting sick out of proportion to reality. They worry because (a) they are mothers; (b) it is an acceptable way for them to vent their guilt; and (c) illness sometimes necessitates extraordinary arrangements, such as staying home from work. If it is any consolation, nonworking mothers seem to worry even more. How often have you heard them say, "Oh, I couldn't work. What would happen if one of the children got sick?" What would happen is that they would cope. And you will cope, too.

You must adopt this positive attitude, because your child *is* going to get sick. Even if you dose him with megavitamins, put him to bed each night at seven, and never let him near a draft—if "it's going around," he's going to catch it. According to pediatric studies, your child will develop eight to ten illnesses a year for at least the first three years that he is regularly exposed to other children. After that he will get two or three a year on the average.

Physicians can and should immunize children against polio, diphtheria, whooping cough, tetanus, measles, mumps, and German measles. But that still leaves well over 100 viral and bacterial agents that a child can acquire in his susceptible years—and during some winter sieges it seems as though he's out to get them all. But it is not necessarily bad for children to get sick. It is natural, inevitable, and in some instances even good for them. By getting and overcoming minor illnesses, children become immune to them. Moreover, a childhood case of most contagious diseases is usually far milder than an adult one.

"Where Does It Hurt?"

As a working mother you may find it hard to accept this benign view, because children do tend to get sick at the most inconvenient times. Just as you are about to leave for work, a pasty-faced, watery-eyed little creature may appear before you to declare woefully, "Mommy, I don't feel good." Since you've got to decide on the spot just how significant his complaints are, we provide you with the following thumbnail guide to common symptoms and what to do about them.

Fever: Fever is not a disease. It is usually an indication that a child is coming down with something. Its significance varies tremendously from child to child and from disease to disease, so a 103° reading on a thermometer does not always have the same or a dire meaning in every case. Since both running around and climate can elevate temperature, be careful of a high reading on hot days or after exercise. Anything on the thermometer registering 100° or below is not really fever. Anything above it may require some aspirin or the like, but in most cases is not by itself cause for alarm. It is, however, cause to keep a child home until you see what develops.

Temperature becomes significant when it lasts more than a day or two with or without symptoms, if the child looks and acts sick, or if other symptoms and signs develop. The exception to this is the child under six months of age, when reactions to illness are vague; then fever in and of itself becomes a reason to call the doctor promptly. Very hot children who are irritable, shaky, or delirious may need to be sponged down with tepid water or even put into a tepid tub, but ice water enemas, which are both unnecessary and extremely dangerous, should never be given.

Coughs: Coughs come in all sizes and descriptions: loose, wet, tight, nighttime, constant, and so on. Coughing is simply a sign of irritation of the respiratory tract and may be totally benign, as with a chronic winter cough from an overly dry house. It may be symptomatic of more serious problems, though, such as pneumonia or bronchitis. Simple coughs with colds unaccompanied by fever or any other breathing problem can be ignored for several days or treated with simple nonprescription cough medicines. Coughs that persist or are accompanied by any difficulty in breathing, shortness of breath, or fever lasting more than twenty-four hours can be considered significant and should be reported to the doctor.

Runny Noses: Runny noses abound, especially in the winter months and with children under the age of eight. By themselves runny noses simply mean "cold" or, as the doctors say, "upper respiratory infection" (U.R.I.), but if they're chronic, they could mean allergies. When the runny nose is not accompanied by other complaints, employ tissues and patience. Spring has to come sometime. When it's chronic, whether seasonal or not, contact the doctor at a convenient time.

Sore Throats: Sore throats are significant because they may indicate a strep throat and therefore need to be examined. Notify the doctor if your child complains of a sore throat even if the throat doesn't look sore and no other symptoms of illness are present. The exception to this is the sore throat that occurs only in the morning—which usually indicates nasal drip, mouth breathing, or over-dry air, and usually disappears an hour or two after rising.

Swollen Glands: The cervical glands in the front of the neck under the jaw often swell slightly in children, as do the glands up and down the back of their necks. Occurring without other symptoms, this usually means that a child has had or is having some sort of infection, usually viral, and is successfully fighting it off. Glands that are simply visible under the chin when the child picks up his head or can be felt by you along the back of his neck when you comb his hair should be ignored. If, however, the glands are markedly enlarged, tender to the touch, have any redness of the overlying skin, or are accompanied by a persistent fever, they need to be examined by the doctor.

Earaches: Earaches are generally significant, especially if accompanied by a runny or stuffy nose. Even in the absence of fever they are to be considered middle-ear infections until proven otherwise and should be checked out by a doctor. Sometimes the earache may stem from a mouth or jaw problem or from constant exposure to water, resulting in "swimmer's ear"—but let the doctor make that diagnosis. Also be alert to any hearing loss, either gradual or sudden. Even if unaccompanied by pain, the hearing loss should be brought to the doctor's attention, although it does not have to be treated as an emergency.

Headaches: Headaches in children can be caused by many things, the most common of which are tension, viral infections, and fever. If there are no accompanying symptoms, headaches can be treated initially with aspirin and a little sympathy. If they persist for more than a day, or recur, bring them to the doctor's attention.

Stomachaches: Vomiting, diarrhea, abdominal pain, and loss of appetite alone or in combination may be very significant—indeed, a true emergency—or quite insignificant. They are caused by many factors, the most common of which is viral gastroenteritis and the most worrisome of which is appendicitis. Two key factors to take note of are the frequency and amount of the vomiting and diarrhea. Small, infrequent amounts of either may not be cause for great concern, especially with school-age children. But infants and small children get dehydrated easily, so massive amounts of fluid loss, whether in frequent, small eliminations or in infrequent, large losses, can be very significant. If a child is having frequent, loose bowel movements or is vomiting in a pattern such as one of those described, the doctor should be called quickly. Loss of appetite may and usually does accompany these symptoms or it may be the only manifestation of an upset stomach. Loss of appetite can be ignored for several days if unaccompanied by more serious signs of abdominal trouble.

As a general rule periodic abdominal pains, especially when the child seems perfectly well between episodes, do not constitute an emergency. But when abdominal pains are localized in any area, persistent, intense, and present in a child who looks or acts sick—they need to be treated as significant. Remember, appendicitis does not occur in five minutes or even an hour: it is the persistence of symptoms that usually dictates that the child be seen.

Constipation: Constipation is a symptom, not a disease. It involves infrequent bowel movements that are hard or dry and sometimes difficult to pass. Infrequency alone is of no consequence. Children and infants, including those on breast milk, may have only two or three bowel movements a week. This should be considered a normal pattern as long as the stool is of reasonably pasty consistency. Don't let your baby's antics mislead you into thinking that he is constipated. He may screw up his face, grunt mightily, turn red, and draw up his legs even with a normal stool. Since this routine is probably just a manifestation of his immature nervous system, no treatment is necessary as long as he manages to get out a softish BM with reasonable frequency.

Some infants will develop harder stools when they change from breast feeding or formula to cow's milk. And some children who lose fluid through the skin because of hot weather or fever might develop real constipation. If your child's stool has become quite hard, increasing his fluid intake, feeding him some fruit, or adding a small amount of bran to his diet may be enough to remedy the situation. If it isn't, call your physician. Do not give the child an enema or laxative on your own.

Musculoskeletal Complaints: The majority of these complaints are minor sprains, strains, and similar traumas that need only heat, some rest, and maybe some aspirin. Limps that persist for more than a day need to be seen. Limb pains with temperature but with *no* symptoms of flu or grippe-type illness need to be checked out. If a child has acute pain after a fall or some other accident that does not disappear rapidly and that is accompanied by any serious limitation of motion of the affected part, he should be seen by a doctor. But a child who complains repeatedly of arm and leg pains yet does not limp and has no fever can be sent off to school, perhaps to be seen at a more convenient time for both of you.

Rashes: Rashes of an acute nature that appear rather suddenly are generally caused by one of the following: allergy and/or contact with something such as poison ivy; viral or bacterial illness; localized problems such as impetigo, bug bites, or frostbite. Rashes associated with viral and bacterial illness are usually the easiest to identify because the child has some other symptom such as fever or sore throat, although viral rashes can occur without other noticeable symptoms.

In the vast majority of cases, rashes do not mean a sick child. They mean a well child who happens to have a bunch of funny red marks on his skin. But sitters, camp counselors, and school or camp nurses usually don't like rashes at all, because they tend to feel that all rashes are a sign of some horrendous contagious disease. They often demand that the affected child be excluded immediately from all contact with other human beings until the doctor sees the rash, pronounces it something less than leprosy, and signs a note to that effect. If the rash pops up before work, try to get it seen as early as possible. At the least, speak to the doctor on the phone and get the right treatment started if treatment is called for. Unless you are absolutely sure that the rash is benign and are willing to fight those in power on your own authority, this is probably the least time-consuming approach.

Urinary Tract Complaints: These are common and may well be acute in onset. Painful urination, any changes in the color of the urine, and any change in urinary habits—such as frequency or wetting at night in a previously dry child—are significant either alone or in combination. They require a trip to the doctor or, at the very least, a trip to a laboratory with a fresh specimen of the child's urine.

Eye Complaints: These often consist of red eyes with discharge. With or without an accompanying cold, this condition probably indicates either conjunctivitis or a foreign body in the eye and requires a doctor's attention. Puffy, itchy eyes are probably the result of allergy and can be relieved at least temporarily with cold compresses. Vision complaints usually can wait—unless the complaint is double vision, particularly if accompanied by fever and/or headache. In those instances the doctor should be called right away.

Teething: Teething is neither a symptom nor a disease, but we include it here because there are undoubtedly more misconceptions about this normal occurrence than any other event in a child's life. Here and there a baby may develop a cyst over an erupting tooth and have a day of honest discomfort, but he is the rare exception. Indeed, the cutting of most teeth is as imperceptible an occurrence as the growing of fingernails. Yet almost every symptom we've mentioned in this section—plus pain, fussiness, crankiness, sleep disturbances, and increased susceptibility to infectious diseases—is blamed on teething when it occurs in the young child. While this thinking in and of itself is harmless, the danger of it lies in overlooking the real cause of the child's discomfort, which then goes undiagnosed and untreated.

We recognize that all these diagnostic guidelines are extremely general. How you apply them depends on such factors as your child's age, his particular makeup, and what's happening in school that day. Is he the sort who overreacts to illness, especially on test days, or does he usually minimize his discomfort in order to attend—especially if there's basketball practice that afternoon? Does he complain of a stomachache every Monday morning, but has he now vomited in addition? Paying attention to your youngster's physical reactions over time will enable you to evaluate them more accurately at eight o'clock one morning.

We also recognize that these guidelines leave a wide margin for error. No matter how experienced you are, there will come a day when you will stay home from work to be with a "sick" child who miraculously recovers as soon as the school bus pulls away. Or you will leave a "well" child at the sitter's, only to pick him up half an hour later because he has started to vomit. Everyone has those days. But to keep them to a minimum, trust in your "mother's radar."

Often this "radar" will detect something significant in the vaguest of symptoms. When this sixth sense tells you that something is up—even if you can't pinpoint it exactly—call the doctor before leaving for work. He will set your mind at ease and may ask to see the child for himself. For your sake, don't feel you have to bring long-term complaints to the doctor's attention before you leave for work, and for his sake, try not to do so at 5:30 P.M. Like you, he's put in a long, hard day by then and the last thing he wants to hear at that moment is that little Johnny has had a funny rash for the past two weeks. Of course, you must call him at 8:00 P.M. if that's when ears start to hurt, or even at 3:00 A.M. if that's when croup develops. Doctors understand that. But if you want to establish a good rapport with yours, make nonemergency calls at a more convenient hour.

Finally, bear in mind these two axioms of pediatric care: Sick children look and act sick beyond such chronic conditions as circles under the eyes, tiredness, and vague malaise. And, *anything persistent must be brought to the doctor's attention.*

Be Prepared

As bad as early morning diagnoses are, at least you are on hand to make them personally. Later on in the day you will have to depend on others or the child himself to describe his condition over the phone. Minor ailments are hard enough for some people to deal with, but bleeding foreheads, vomiting, and temperatures of 104° make them absolutely frantic. To be sure that you, the caretaker, and the child carry on as calmly and efficiently as possible, we suggest that you begin preparing for medical problems well in advance.

We recommend that you start by contacting your child's physician. Tell him that you are working now and that if Susie gets sick he may be hearing from Mrs. Jones, the sitter. Ask him who covers for him when he's away, what hospital he's affiliated with, and what other information you should have to pass on to your child's caretaker. Then contact the school nurse, alert your neighbors, and discuss emergency transportation with a local taxi company. Finally, instruct your co-workers to *find* you when a call comes in from the caretaker or school. Since you know the child best, we think you should be the one to evaluate his condition. Instruct the caretaker that unless a super-trauma occurs, she should discuss the situation with you first; then, if you feel it is warranted, contact the doctor yourself.*

On the home front, post a list of emergency numbers near the phone and give the sitter an identical one to carry with her. Obtain a good first aid chart from your fire department or the Red

---

*See the Appendix for a check list of symptoms to help both you and the sitter zero in on what is bothering the child.

Cross and go over it with your sitter and the child who stays home alone. Make them aware of the information contained in the Appendix of this book, too. Remind them that the first principle of first aid is to remain calm. The second is to know what steps to take, and the third is to take them quickly and effectively.

No matter what your job, you cannot be next to the telephone every minute of the day. Therefore, help your caretakers by writing out each step to be taken in a medical emergency. Include a map or explicit directions for getting to the nearest hospital and explain how to be put right through to the doctor, fire department, and police. You should also leave telephone change, taxi money, and a notarized letter containing:

The child's name, address, age, height, and weight; a listing of all inoculations and allergies; and other pertinent medical information.

Names, addresses, and phone numbers of those doctors other than the pediatrician who might have medical information concerning the child (ophthalmologist, orthopedist, dentist, etc.).

A short statement to the effect that the person bearing this letter is authorized to obtain emergency medical attention for the child by virtue of the parents' signatures.

Whoever accompanies the child to the hospital emergency room or doctor's office should ask the physician to write out (clearly) the instructions for home care. Since more than one person will be following them, there should be no doubt as to what they are. The doctor should state explicitly how long the prescribed medication should be given and what it is supposed to do—suppress the cough or cure it? He should also spell out the procedures he wants followed for other treatments such as vapor inhalation and hot soaks. If you are present, ask the doctor to describe the usual course of the ailment. Although he may have to be vague about timing, he should be specific enough about the sequence of events so that you will know whether recovery is taking place or complications are setting in. He should give you some guidelines for the child's return to his normal activities. If you are not present (and it is often not necessary), phone the doctor for this information later on in the day.

Whether your child's condition is serious or mild, the sitter will be able to manage it better if you have seen to it that the necessary medical supplies are on hand. It is remarkable how often a vial turns out to be devoid of pills after a mother has left for work or the pharmacy has shut down for the night. Don't let this happen in your house. Make out a list of the medications your family uses, tape it to the inside of the medicine cabinet door, and check your stock against it regularly. While you're at it, make sure the medication is up to date and clearly labeled with name, proper dosage, and time lapse in between doses. You should do this for nonprescription drugs, but you'll have to ask your physician to instruct the pharmacy to do it for prescription drugs. In addition, affix a label to each bottle indicating its use, such as "for coughs" and "for cramps."

The actual contents of the medicine cabinet are up to you and your children's doctor, but we have some suggestions to get you started:

Aspirin: Aspirin or aspirin substitute should be kept on hand for fevers and minor pain. Make sure the dosage for your children is marked on the bottle by adding your own label to the manufacturer's. Since this dosage will change over time, be sure to keep it up to date. Thus, it might read for baby aspirin:

Caroline: 6 tablets, every 4 hours
Catherine: 3 tablets, every 4 hours

Cold and Cough Medicines: Nonprescription and prescription decongestants, cough medicines, and nose drops are available alone and in combination. Their variety is as great as the range of opinion as to whether they work or not. The type of cough or cold medication appropriate for your child and the dosage to be used should be discussed with your child's doctor.

Antihistamines: These are medications specifically designed to be used for allergic symptoms. Again, multiple medications are available, but if your child tends to suffer from minor allergic symptoms, seasonal or nonseasonal allergies, hives, and so on, his doctor may want you to have antihistamines on hand.

Skin Medicines: If you have a baby, a good diaper rash cream should be left with the sitter. You might also have handy a nonprescription antibiotic ointment to combat the infections that occur after burns or scrapes. If your youngster tends to suffer from poison ivy or eczema, a steroid cream might also be prescribed by the physician for your medicine cabinet. By the way, ordinary cuts and scrapes need only soap and water.

Gastrointestinal Medications: These come in three major categories: one for upper G.I. pains, one for lower bowel problems (cramps and diarrhea), and one for controlling vomiting. Again, there is much controversy as to the general efficacy of such medications, so check with your pediatrician for his recommendations.

Special Medications: In addition to the generalized preparations just mentioned, you will want to have on hand the specific medications for certain problems to which your child is prone. Make sure the supply of these drugs is adequate and the instructions for their use clear enough to be understood by those responsible for administering them in your absence. Since you may forget from one episode to the next how and why to use some important drug, write down the instructions as soon as you get them and tape them to the bottle itself.

In addition to these drugs, we suggest that you keep the following first aid supplies on hand. And woe to the child who raids them to play doctor on a rainy day!

Basic Supplies:

Band-Aids, at least three sizes including the very large
Adhesive tape, ¼-in. roll
Gauze pads, individually wrapped, several sizes
Telfa or other nonstick pads
Cling bandage or roll of other gauze bandage
Sharp scissors
Ace bandage, 2- or 3-in. size
Ice bag
Heating pad or hot water bottle
Ipecac syrup, 1-oz. bottle (to induce vomiting after ingestion of certain toxic substances)

Just having the medical supplies on hand is not enough, of course. When prescribed, they have to be dispensed properly. Since it is usually necessary to space medication out over the day, this means that someone else besides you will be responsible for at least one dose. The giver should know the name of the drug, its location (some medications must be kept in the refrigerator), the time it should be given, and the amount. In many school systems, the nurse will dispense medication only if she has a note from a doctor with the above information on it—so don't forget to get such a note from him at the same time that you get the prescription order. When the medication must be sent to a school or day-care center with your child, you might want the pharmacist to bottle or package the medicine in two containers (one for school, one for home) with proper directions on each.

Sometimes there is a question in your mind as to whether the sitter is giving the child his medicine. To be sure, put the day's dosage in a small bottle before you leave for work. The emptiness of this bottle when you return should indicate that the medication has been given—and taken. Sometimes you might have the opposite problem: with more than one caretaker involved, there is a possibility of the child's being double-dosed. To avoid this, tape a check-off chart to the medicine cabinet door and have each person initial it after administering the required teaspoonful.

The last—but certainly not least—thing you can do in the way of preparation is to talk with your youngster about illness from time to time and again when he seems to be coming down with something. Make a point of telling him what arrangements have been made for his welfare. He'll find them reassuring. A child often becomes upset when he gets sick, especially if he is away from home or separated from his parents, and he will cope much better if he is confident that he will be taken care of. But *do not* lead him to believe that you will come flying to his side. It is amazing what kids will manufacture to bring this about.

With young children, role playing is a good way to dispel anxieties related to illness and trauma. Initiate a psychodrama in which your daughter pretends to throw up, break a leg, or get a headache. You take the part of the doctor or sitter who treats her condition. Or you could change places: you pretend to be the child who gets sick and let her be the adult who nurses you back to health. If you handle incapacity with humor when your child is well, she will be able to handle it with aplomb when she gets sick.

Sick in the Space Age

Now we come down to the real nitty-gritty. Let's assume that your child *is* sick or broken or spotted, but you cannot sit home holding her hand while she mends. All your guilt about working overwhelms you, all your backup troops fade into oblivion, all your child's resolve to be a good soldier crumbles. She clings, you capitulate, the impossibility of being a working mother is writ large on the sickroom wall. But wait. . . . The scenario can, and should, read entirely differently. Sitter discovers child is sick; child sees doctor; doctor prescribes medication; child convalesces quickly; child returns to school with note; life goes on.

Your attitude toward your own ailments will set the tone. If all your not-so-latent hypochondriacal fears leap to the surface and you respond to every sniffle by taking to your bed with the heating pad, pills, and a vaporizer—guess who is going to follow suit? But if you view illness as nothing more than a nuisance, your child will take it in stride too.

You are not being cruel and selfish to encourage your child to carry on in the face of physical adversity. To the contrary, your attitude is medically sound. Today, with antibiotics and other effective medications against many childhood diseases, bed rest and home confinement are about as relevant as bloodletting. Yet many people who eagerly embrace the new medicines just can't seem to let the old ways go. Bed rest is a hangover from the days when doctors had few other specific treatments and felt they had to prescribe something. But the fact is that a child will not worsen his condition by getting out of bed or leaving the house.

There is no medical evidence, for example, that a child with upper respiratory illness will increase his chances of complications such as pneumonia, bronchitis, or infected ears by being active or being outside. Feeling chilled, fatigued, or "funny" a day or two before the U.R.I. becomes evident is part of the incubation phase and therefore the *result* of oncoming infection, not its cause. Studies of major illnesses show that even something as serious as rheumatic fever responds little or not at all to bed rest, while infectious mononucleosis, pneumonia, and influenza require rest only during the acute phase.

Nor is the sick child an excessive danger to his schoolmates. He is actually contagious *before* symptoms appear, during what is called the "prodomal phase." According to the American Academy of Pediatrics' Committee on School Health: "Generally, school-propagated communicable disease is widely spread by the time it is recognized and runs its course until most susceptibles are infected.'' In other words, anyone who has been in contact with the child for two or three days before his illness has already been exposed to that illness and will probably get it if susceptible. The committee concluded that ''it is impossible to isolate all young children with respiratory tract infections and still have sufficient days of school attendance to educate them.''

If bed rest doesn't help, there is some evidence that it can harm. Psychologically, it can make a child overanxious about his health; persistently demanding, as a result of the temporary moratorium on discipline; and expert in using real or imagined illness to focus attention on himself. Physically, too, bed rest can have an adverse effect. It can worsen a phenomenon doctors refer to as P.I.P., ''Post Infectious Poop,'' by allowing muscles to lose tone and encouraging fatigue. Sleep also comes harder to the bedridden child. A youngster who really needs extra rest will always get it simply by falling asleep early or taking extra naps.

If your child has been out of the action for a while, when is it time to let him get back in? Generally speaking, when he has had no fever, vomiting, or serious diarrhea for twenty-four hours; when his cough is manageable; and when he has attained his normal activity level. Let him be your guide and you will probably not overestimate the state of his health.

With some diseases such as ringworm, impetigo, infected ears, and conjunctivitis, a child can return to school as soon as treatment starts. With other diseases such as strep throat, only a day's wait is necessary after treatment begins. Chicken pox must be isolated for only three to four days after the last sore has appeared, and mumps only until the swelling has started to regress. As far as the other infectious diseases are concerned, only hepatitis still requires some period of isolation. Children who have suffered sprains, fractures, or lacerations should be encouraged to move around as soon as possible too, even if their activities have to be curtailed or they have to rely on crutches and slings. Don't forget the doctor's note if the child has to be excused from gym or camp activities.

Keep telling yourself that a child recovers faster in an environment that takes his mind off himself than one in which he dwells on his ailment—i.e., his home. Most children want to be well. Moreover, your child has to learn how to cope routinely with illness just as he has to learn how to cope routinely with other adverse situations.

When is a child old enough to recuperate alone? There is no general rule about this, but a child who is old enough to stay alone for long periods when he is well, who can walk, and who has someone he can reach by phone (or who will look in on him during the day) can stay home alone when he is sick. To say that a fourteen- or fifteen-year-old cannot take the responsibility of staying alone while recuperating from an illness or injury is to deny that child a maturing experience. Of course, a child of five or six confined to bed with a broken leg cannot possibly be left by himself. Between those two extremes is that large gray area in which you will have to use your own discretion.

As we have pointed out, most of the illnesses that children get today last a relatively short time. Yet there are some conditions that go on for so long (sometimes forever) that they affect not only the child's health but also his behavior, his schooling, his relationships with people—indeed, his whole life. If your youngster has a chronic disabling condition, you will want to learn all about it. What are the treatments, the limitations on activity, the special dietetic requirements? How will it affect his growth and development? Only when you understand exactly what's entailed will you be able to come to grips with the fact that no amount of feeling sorry for the child (and yourself) and no amount of personal attention will change his basic condition.

To the contrary, reorganizing your life around the child or overcompensating in other ways will probably add psychological problems to the physical ones he already has. A child wants to be treated as normally as possible. Although he may sometimes try to manipulate you through his condition, at heart he wants to live like every other kid.

Your attitude will be of paramount importance in providing

that normal childhood. Although it makes you feel better to keep doing for the child, you ought to insist on his trying to do for himself. And though it is in a sense easier to cater to his whims and to forgo reasonable discipline, you will only be increasing the child's sense of differentness and vulnerability if you do. Pity is as counterproductive as guilt—and in your particular situation you're all too familiar with both. But rather than quit your job, hover over the child, or commiserate with him ad infinitum, you should help him to participate in life to whatever degree he can. You won't be doing either one of you a favor by making him into a "case."

Whether he is afflicted with a chronic condition or a short-term illness, there will be times when your child will feel rotten. If your husband or other suitable caretaker cannot stay with him, you may want to go into work late on those occasions, leave early, or take the day off. You may lose some pay by doing so, but under normal circumstances you won't be fired and you won't be passed over for a promotion for doing so. Most bosses understand that emergencies do arise. But as we have stressed throughout this chapter, "emergencies" usually lie in the eye of the beholder. When everyone involved is well prepared and well rehearsed, most would-be emergencies can be taken in stride.

Of Prevention, Precautions, and Peace of Mind

Despite everything we've said up to this point, you may still be clinging to the belief that you can prevent your children from getting sick. To this end you may be dousing them with disinfectant mouthwashes, loading them down with clothing, or mixing blackstrap molasses into their pancakes. But these actions mainly serve to make you feel as though you are doing something constructive. Under close scientific scrutiny, none of them has yet proven to be of any value in preventing childhood illnesses. Exposure to others is the problem. But since children need that exposure in order to develop emotionally, you can neither isolate them nor protect them from ever getting sick.

That is not to say that all preventive measures are hogwash. Indeed, some are very beneficial and have ramifications far beyond childhood. To start with the most important, inoculations are now available that can protect your youngsters against a number of childhood diseases. We recommend that your children be immunized at the following times:

2 months	DPT*-TOPV†
4 months	DPT -TOPV
6 months	DPT -TOPV
1 year	test for TB
15 months	measles, mumps, rubella (German measles); given together or separately by age two
18 months	DPT -TOPV
4–5 years	DPT -TOPV
14–15 years and every 10 years thereafter	diphtheria and tetanus

This schedule seems simple enough, yet it is estimated that as many as one out of every four American children is deficient in all or part of it, sometimes with serious consequences.

Regular checkups provide the doctor with an opportunity to administer these shots, to collect data for school and camp forms, and to get to know your child—and vice versa. They also allow him to check on the youngster's growth and development and, occasionally, to discover some unknown medical condition. The commonly recommended timetable for these visits is six to eight checkups during the child's first year of life, four checkups the second year, and roughly one per year after that.

If you can possibly manage it, we strongly urge you to be present. You will feel better about going off to work if you have established a rapport with your child's doctor, something you

* DPT—diphtheria, pertussis (whooping cough), and tetanus
† TOPV—trivalent oral polio vaccine (Sabin)

can't do either with a sick youngster in tow or via rushed telephone calls. Being there enables you to size up the doctor and to get a line on his opinion of working mothers. It also allows the doctor to observe the relationship between you and your child, and to see whether you tend to be ultra casual, quickly concerned, or somewhere in between when it comes to your offspring's health. These observations will stand him in good stead later on, when he has to assess the youngster's condition over the phone.

How much you learn during a regular checkup is largely up to you. While some practitioners have a set speech regarding the Terrible Two's or a pat list of do's and don't's for the parents of teenagers, your doctor may prefer to take his cue from you. Don't be shy, don't be intimidated by a full waiting room, and don't let your mind go blank. Keep a running list of the things you want to discuss and make sure to refer to it during the visit. Consider any topic legitimate from nail biting and rapid weight gain to school failure and fear of fossils. Indeed, if it relates to the child and is bothering either him or you, bring it up. If you absolutely cannot make the appointment, send the questions along with your substitute and discuss them with the doctor during his telephone hours.

In addition to her regular medical checkups, any child over the age of three should have regular semi-annual visits to the dentist. You should also see to it that she takes fluoride daily either in the water or via a special supplement and that she brushes regularly with a good fluoridated toothpaste. Such measures are of great preventive value, as is limiting the consumption of refined sugars. Above all, do not use the bottle as a pacifier or bedtime companion, because prolonged contact with the sticky milk will probably guarantee your child a mouthful of cavities by the time she is five.* And since you're gone so much of the day, be strict with your sitter on this score too.

---

*In November 1977 the American Academy of Pediatrics and the American Academy of Pedodontics issued a joint policy statement that said, "Prolonged bottle feeding of infants over 12 months of age can lead to 'nursing bottle caries,' a severe form of dental decay."

Over and above these sound procedures, there is little you can do to prevent your child from getting sick. But there is a great deal you can do to prevent her from getting hurt. You can buy toys, children's equipment, and household items with an eye toward safety. You can put all medications under lock and key. And you can childproof your home, doing it several times more thoroughly than you would if you were going to be there all day. Tape the sharp edges of tables, remove tippy lamps, plug up electrical outlets, and place breakable treasures out of reach (as much for your sake as the child's). Although your home may not look too glamorous this way, its peculiar appearance is a small price to pay for your child's safety and your peace of mind.

A good pamphlet on accident prevention will aid you in your safety efforts.* Study it closely and then give it to your sitter to read. Impress upon her the need to take precautions, especially where hot liquids are concerned. Tell her to keep bubbling pots on the back of the stove with their handles turned in and to place cups of hot coffee beyond your child's reach. Also caution her against referring to medicine as "candy" in order to get the children to take it. If you're entrusting her with a baby, by the way, make sure she knows he's never to be out of her sight. "I just took my eyes off him for a minute!" is one of the saddest laments in the hospital emergency room.

Once your child is out of the infant stage, there is much you can do to train her for safety. Insist that she use a car seat or seat belt and set an example by wearing a seat belt yourself. Instill in her a healthy respect for hot ovens, boiling liquids, moving cars, deep water, and other potentially dangerous factors in her environment. You don't want to turn your daughter into a Nervous Nellie, but you shouldn't ignore the realities of life in order to keep her anxiety-free, either. She'll find something to be anxious about no matter what you do, so you might as well make her fears work for her.

---

*See the Resources section at the back of the book for some suggestions.

Once you've taken all the precautions you can, try to stop worrying. Ask yourself honestly if accidents can't happen when a mother is on the scene as well as when she is at work. See if your neurotic fears are turning your child into an insecure if not neurotic person herself. And evaluate whether your preoccupation with safety is preventing you from concentrating on your job. From the answers to this little quiz, you can see how worrying without concomitant action is strictly a counterproductive activity.

Far better to spend your time thinking up ways to give your children good eating and exercise habits. These habits won't prevent the youngsters from getting sick, but they will make them feel better now and throughout their lives. The first step is to cease and desist in using food as a pacifier. If you stuff your child's face every time he cries, you're setting up a lifelong correspondence between succor and ingestion. You're also encouraging overeating, which leads to overweight, which leads to a number of physical and psychological problems. Moreover, baby fat has an unpleasant habit of sticking around to become adult fat. So, since children can be overweight at any age, you should try to regulate how much yours eat from the cradle on.

You should also try to monitor *what* they eat. Although you can't control what goes into their mouths when they're out of the house, you can eschew junk foods and prepare nutritious meals (very quickly, too) when they're home. You can talk to them about the relative merits of various foods and teach them to read the ingredient lists on labels. Moreover, since eating habits are established early in life, you can get your children off on the right foot by removing the salt shaker from the table, reducing their intake of high-calorie, fatty foods, and increasing their consumption of fruits, vegetables, and whole grain products. Learning to eat this way now may help prevent cardiovascular diseases in the future.

You should also encourage your children to keep moving. Get the younger ones out to the park and the older ones up on their bikes. Don't be so quick to drive them everywhere on weekends and find rides for them during the week. Try to inter- est them in lifetime sports, too, by building family outings around such activities as hiking, jogging, tennis, and swim- ming. Encouraging your children to take part in active pursuits will do more for their health in the long run than all the vitamin C ever produced. Admittedly, it is much harder to put these plans into operation if you have to work through a sitter, but it can be done. For suggestions, see the "Individual Care" section of Chapter 3, "The Ins and Outs of Child Care."

All the suggestions we've made in this chapter should con- tribute to that rare commodity, peace of mind. When you are aware of what various symptoms indicate; when you have the medicine cabinet properly stocked; when you're confident that everyone knows what to do in emergencies; when you've taken precautions to keep those emergencies to a minimum; and when you've packed a nutritious school lunch—you can stop thinking about your family and start concentrating on your job. Now *that's* peace of mind.

7

Action House

Now that you've got the psychological and medical preparations for work out of the way, we suggest that you turn your attention to a physical task: organizing your home. When you know where things are, you can spend your time doing instead of looking. And when each item has its own place, by some miraculous law of gravity it tends to stay there. Like successful time management, good household management not only saves you time but makes you feel you are in control of your life.

Environmental disorganization has exactly the opposite effect, yet many people resist shaping up their homes. The roots of their behavior may go back to childhood experiences. According to Stephanie Winston, who operates a service called The Organizing Principle: "When a person is continually disorganized, there is a strong parent in his past saying, 'Clean your room.' And the person is saying, 'You can't make me.' "

Whether or not Ms. Winston's analysis applies to you, you may find it hard to get your household under control or you may be reluctant to try. After all, the job has so little sex appeal. As the successful clothes designer Calvin Klein remarked: "I can't be bothered. . . . Quite frankly, I don't have the time any more to worry what's in the house if six people are coming over for drinks." At another point he said, "My socks just don't interest me that much." They probably don't interest you that much either, but you don't enjoy the services of a secretary, business assistant, and housekeeper as does Mr. Klein. You don't even have a wife to take care of the time-consuming details of life. So there you are, left holding the bag—which in your case probably contains a lot of dirty laundry.

Although it can be unpleasant to be *it* when it comes to household organization, it need not be the end of the world. If you employ a few of the time-management techniques we discussed in Chapter 2, "Let's Get Organized," and incorporate some of the simple systems we are going to suggest here, you should be able to run your home as well as or even better than you did before you took a job. And you'll do it in less time. You can then apply the hours you save to more meaningful activity, such as lying in a hammock, which is why you wanted to be organized in the first place.

Form Follows Function

Make a tour of your home, measuring it against the primary tenet of modern industrial design, "Form follows function." If your furnishings actively fight this principle or only half-heartedly conform to it, you may want to gradually redecorate. Eliminate the eight little pillows that have to be artfully arranged on your bed each morning, and replace the sofa's soft cushions with firm ones that need no plumping. Choose floor tiles that don't show dirt, put away all but your most beloved bric-à-brac, and pick up scatter rugs that easily get scattered. There, your home is beginning to look like an Action House already.

But the changes will have to go deeper to make a real difference. Since your time at home is so limited, you want to spend it doing rather than setting up and taking down. Therefore, you will need a safe place to leave a painting-in-progress or an unfinished dress until you can get back to it. Ideally, this should be a room of your own, but realistically it will be a converted closet, a screened-off corner, or a roll-away table—if you're lucky. For the less enjoyable, more businesslike activities attendant upon householding, you will need a home office.

This spot should include a real desk, a filing cabinet, and all the supplies necessary to balance a checkbook, straighten out a bill, or write a thank you note.*

Another must for the Action House is a good system of communications. Every telephone should be equipped with a pad and pencil, and woe betide the youngster who swipes them for ticktacktoe. Then the kitchen or some other central location should be outfitted with a cork board for the prominent display of messages. Next to the cork board should be hung the calendar of family activities, and next to that, if you wish, receptacles for keys and laundry tickets. These receptacles are particularly handy if two or more family members share the car and the errands.

In the true Action House all storage follows the same principle: possessions are kept as close to the site of usage as possible. Thus extra towels, toilet paper, and soap should be stored in the bathroom, not in the linen closet down the hall. Sheets should be kept in a bedroom dresser and the vacuum cleaner should reside in the closet nearest the carpeting even if you have to nudge aside your best coat to make room for it. Taken to its logical conclusion, the Action House storage principle would result in doubles of everything for the second floor: mop, pail, ammonia, vacuum, and so on. Not only is this plan a great time- and step-saver, but it is a prod to cleaning at odd intervals, because all the supplies are always right at hand.

Actually, *all* the often-used accoutrements of living—be they for cooking, cleaning, or dressing—should always be right at hand. To get at them quickly, mentally rank your storage space A, B, or C in order of convenience, then stock it accordingly. This means that panties and stockings, items you wear every day, would be moved to an A spot, usually the top drawer of your dresser, while the leotards you wear just once a week would be demoted to a C position in a lower drawer. Some

---

*For more detailed instruction on setting up a home office and filing system, see the Appendix.

items are not even of C caliber and should be eliminated from the line of fire altogether. If you haven't worn girdles since 1972, for example, they have no place in your lingerie drawer just because they're underthings. Store them in your attic or, preferably, give them away.

As you become more proficient at organization, you can start to rank items within a drawer as well as drawers within a room. At this point determine your arrangements by use, not by size. Some experts warn against nesting more than two objects in a third, and others would like to see you forgo even that much stacking when it comes to everyday items. They would rather have you put your most-used possessions in the front of a drawer and the less-used items behind them. If you rarely serve pizza, your pizza cutter should not rest on top of several other gadgets even if it is the smallest of the lot. Rather, it should be moved behind the can opener, the slotted spoon, and the soup ladle (providing you serve a lot of soup). In addition, certain items lend themselves to storage by affinity: sifters and rolling pins can logically reside next to baking pans, while stockings can be stuffed into the same compartment as the shoes with which they are worn.

When it comes to your personal closet, think in terms of categories. Group your shirts, sweaters, pants, and skirts together, blending them from light to dark if many items are involved. Put the dressiest clothes (or least used) in the least accessible spot and your work outfits (or most used) in the most accessible spot. For a fast getaway in the morning, hang whole outfits together, including pins and necklaces, and keep coordinating shoes and bags nearby.

Unfortunately, sorting alone is often not enough to keep closets and bureaus in order. Indeed, no matter how conscientiously you shift around your belongings, they may become jumbled as quickly as ever. If that's been your frustrating experience, then you may simply have too many possessions. If you really want to do something about it, you'll probably have to give some of them away.

Learn to Love Giving Away

Most people have too much for their storage space, too much that they will never use or even look at, too much to enable them to zero in on what they do use. Whether this indiscriminate saving results from a fear of loss, as some psychologists have suggested, is part of our Puritan heritage of thrift, or is a throwback to the days of copious attics, garages, basements, and outbuildings, the fact is that many people are practically drowning in possessions.

If you're one of them, try to practice the golden rule of household organization: *Get rid of 20 percent of everything.* Not even the most fanatical neatnik would suggest that you make a clean sweep of all your earthly possessions, because familiar objects lend continuity and comfort to life. However, possessions that are not used, loved, or even looked at contribute nothing but clutter. In the true Action House objects have to *do* something for you to merit retention (although a thing of beauty needs no further recommendation). Once you can look at things in terms of how useful they are, not how much they cost, you will find it easier to free yourself of the role of custodian, especially for things that you don't like or use.

Nor do you have to be a custodian for things your children probably won't like or use either. The chances are that your offspring will lead a more nomadic life in more crowded quarters than you and that their tastes will differ widely from yours also. A box of mementos for each child, some good jewelry, a few nice objets d'art, and a photo album are lovely to hand down; beyond that it's probably a waste of space to save anything for your children that you yourself are not enjoying.

When you've convinced yourself that you'll be a happier and more organized person once you are rid of unnecessary possessions, it's time to take the plunge. To get started, you may want to make a tangible commitment to the project—such as buying a storage box—but don't make elaborate plans beyond that. Just get started! And for best results take it one drawer at a time. If you try to tackle the whole house at once, you could become so overwhelmed that you might be tempted just to crawl back under the clutter and never try your hand at organization again.

When you are faced with a heap of your own possessions, it is not always easy to determine what should stay and what should go. To help you make up your mind, ask yourself if you will ever "need" that last issue of *Life;* if the fuchsia sweater that has never matched anything in the past is likely to do so in the future; and how upset your daughter would be if she noticed that the ceramic ashtray she made you five years ago is gone. If some of your questions are less clear-cut, you might try working with a third party who can be more objective about your possessions. A friend or your husband are both likely recruits or, if the job is a large one, you might even consider hiring a professional organizer. A few hours of expert, dispassionate advice could save you days or even weeks of anguished decisionmaking.

A professional organizer can suggest novel storage arrangements for the possessions you are retaining. In addition, she will probably tell you to set out four receptacles for the possessions you are discarding. The first of these is a trash barrel. The second is a give-away box for friends, service people, and sitters. The third is earmarked for charity (and carries with it a tax deduction on all donated items). The fourth is for a garage or tag sale. If you haven't got enough merchandise to hold a sale of your own, team up with a few neighbors and hold one together. Not only will it bring you in some money but, perhaps more importantly, it will force you to review all your possessions by a certain date.

Unfortunately, the job of sorting through papers does not lend itself to the deadline of a tag sale, and this deadly chore seems to consume even more time. In recent years there has been an information explosion, with a huge fallout of mail, reports, books, and magazines, much of which is saved but not reread. Indeed, in the course of his research for the Action Office, the industrial designer Robert Propst discovered that 80 percent of all papers put into office filing cabinets are not retrieved even once. You should try not to duplicate that situation in your home. Unless you are going to need a piece of information in the next six months, or it is irreplaceable—*throw it out!*

Since most information reaches you via the U.S. mail, you'll have to be particularly careful not to let it accumulate. For some reason, unless it is taken care of right away, mail has a tendency to scatter or grow into an ominous pile that can require several days and/or several Scotches to plow through. One good way to prevent accumulation is to create an interior mailbox—a large basket will do—to contain the inflow. Then, each evening after everyone has had a chance to sift through it, sort and place the mail in the appropriate places: wastebasket, magazine rack, bills folder, son's desk, and so on. A two-drawer filing cabinet or even a divided box will expedite the sorting procedure. But whatever system or aids you use, use them nightly or you'll fall further and further behind in the battle against print.

Indeed, most of the trappings of life could result in clutter if you aren't on your guard. Loose photographs, for example, have a tendency to scatter and get lost; therefore, it is important not to leave them around. When you get a roll of film back from the processor, try picking out the best shots, putting them in your album that night, and discarding the rest. Or carry them straight to the photo box, where they'll repose until the rainy evening you designate as album night. Try a similar approach with the magazines that cross your threshold. Once every two weeks or so (on a shampoo night!), thumb through them purposefully, clip out items you want to read and/or save, then throw the periodicals away. It's also a good idea to equip your kitchen with a large file for recipes and a plastic envelope for cents-off coupons. And you might want to try hanging a shopping bag on the back of your closet door for the empty hangers to be returned to the cleaners. Only through such perpetual collection and divestment will you be able to contain household clutter. The secret is anticipation. If you don't let clutter take you by surprise, you're halfway there.

As you get into the swing of giving away, a strange psychological phenomenon may occur: you grow to like it. In fact, you may eventually get as big a lift from giving away as from buying, because in each instance you feel you are doing something for yourself. Moreover, in the process of divestment you become better able to focus clearly on what remains. And more often than not, freed from their matrix of clutter, old possessions suddenly look fresh and interesting. So, to treat yourself to something new—without the psychic pain of spending money or the hassle of shopping—merely give something else away.

Create-a-Space Storage

Even after divesting themselves of 20 percent of everything, many people find that their cabinets are still overflowing. If that happens to you, obviously you'll have to either give away more or create more space. Assuming you choose the latter course, you have a number of options to choose from. Indeed, many magazines feature ingenious ideas for holding and hiding things, as do the numerous do-it-yourself books on the market. Moreover, you don't have to be an engineer to solve your storage problems. Some of the most effective solutions require only a hammer and nail or a plastic bag.

If a lack of hanging space is your problem, you could easily convert a linen closet into a clothes closet by taking out the shelves and replacing them with a tension rod that needs no special installation. You could also double the capacity of an existing closet, provided that it's deep, by adding another rod and hanging the clothes two deep. Or, if you plan to stay in your home or don't mind leaving something behind, you could have a closet constructed in a dead corner, often behind a door.

If shelf space is what you need, search your home for unused nooks and crannies. Shelves can be sneaked into empty spaces under stairs, on the inside of closet doors, on walls, and above toilets; wire shelves can be suspended from other shelves; and drawers can be easily installed under counter tops and hanging cabinets, even by the novice.

Storage does not always have to be horizontal. Shoe bags, tie racks, toothbrush caddies, belt hoops, and a thousand other specialized holders can help you organize and store your belongings vertically. One manufacturer has even come out with a molded plastic liquor caddy to attach to a living room or kitchen door. All you need is a surface on which to mix the drinks and you're ready to give a party. Less exotic but probably far more useful in your home are the pegboards and the metal clips that can hold anything from a shovel to a spool of thread. And when you are storing a tote in the blackest recesses of your closet, a penny nail will do just fine. No matter what they consist of, hanging units turn every wall into a potential storage area, keeping objects orderly and accessible and freeing scarce horizontal surfaces for other uses.

Although most people think of adding space to create storage, dividing it up is often just as good. You can organize a multitude of items in a single drawer when you crisscross it with dividers, for example, and the objects in it will stay neater too. Extendible slats and open shoe boxes are good for this purpose, as are the plastic bags that are especially handy for keeping clothes in order without constant refolding. You can acquire almost twice as much space in your closet by dividing it horizontally: hang shirts and sweaters overhead, skirts and folded pants below. Or, if you don't want to get into construction, buy multiple hangers and you'll achieve almost the same end.

Specialized containers make the most of your shelf space through division also, and there is hardly an object they can't accommodate. Indeed, manufacturers have outfitted boxes to store everything from blankets to packets of dehydrated soup. The fanciest ones come in quilted print fabrics with see-through plastic windows. Though lovely to look at, these units are usually expensive. If you don't care to pay the price, paste wallpaper on some shoe boxes and grocery cartons and you've got yourself a custom-made look. But whether you go fancy or plain, be sure your storage containers have rigid sides. Shopping bags are simply too hard to stack and too easily ripped to do the job properly.

Finally, when you think create-a-space, think of free-standing units. Nowadays a great deal of furniture is made with storage in mind. There are headboards that hold blankets, end tables that double as filing cabinets, piano benches that can store sheet music, and room dividers that provide space for dishes. With some free-standing units it's hard to distinguish between storage and display, especially when china, wooden bowls, and other good-looking but utilitarian objects are brought out of hiding. Not only do these possessions lend interest to a home, but they tend to get used more when they're kept out in the open—and use is what the Action House is all about.

A Woman's Work Can Get Done

Now that you've geared your house for action, you have to face the problem of keeping it clean. We suggest that you start off by trying to keep it neat. As you well know, you can't clean a messy room until you have first straightened it up. But if you can keep it looking tidy, you'll be able to get away with cleaning it less often because everyone will equate the orderliness with cleanliness. Since you have so many other things to do with your spare time besides dust, we think you ought to trade on this optical illusion as much as possible. Then, when you've got your house reasonably neat, you can proceed at your own pace to get it clean.

Somewhere along the line before you took a job or before you had a family, you may have developed very high standards for your home—and lived up to them. But if you're still trying to keep things as spic and span as they were before you became a working mother, chances are that your life is a study in frustration. It's a problem that even the new household conveniences can't seem to solve. In fact, these appliances may be exacerbating the situation, not appreciably reducing the hours of housework. *Scientific American* reported that women today put in three hours more per week on household chores than their grandmothers did fifty years ago.

The most practical solution is probably to revise your standards downward. Take a tip from the workwife who said: "I no longer live by the credo, 'Anything worth doing is worth doing well.' My motto now is, 'It's good enough.' " If you simply must shine something, pick out one conspicuous object a week and scrub and polish it to your heart's content. Then, by practicing selective vision, you may be able to obtain almost as much satisfaction from that single gleaming object as you used to get from an entire clean house.

If, on the other hand, you're strictly from the "I hate to housekeep" school of cleaners, you may have to raise your level of involvement even to get through the basics. Buy a housekeeping book, try out new products, and make it a point to read magazine articles on spots and stains (how many sex surveys can you pore over, anyway?). You could also try to raise some interest in cleaning your home by decorating it with plants or fresh flowers. Then, if all else fails, you could fall back on the old entertaining ploy. The idea here is that entertaining will force you either to give your house at least a cursory going-over before the guests arrive or to stand exposed as the rotten housekeeper that you are. Faced with the latter alternative, even the most adamant anti-cleaners usually pick up a dust rag and set to work.

No matter what your attitude toward housekeeping, as a working mother you want to do it as efficiently as possible. According to the experts, that would ideally mean doing the same tasks in the same way at the same time each day or week. Decisionmaking uses up time and energy, so routine execution puts you ahead on both counts. Moreover, programming yourself to act generates energy and helps keep it high until you've completed the designated task. Fortunately, since most household chores are repetitive, they can be done by rote. One working mother we interviewed makes her bed as she rolls out of it (a task that she almost does in her sleep!); another always runs a vacuum over the upstairs hall before descending for breakfast; and a third always departs for work with a briefcase in one hand and trash for the incinerator in the other. Although it might become a standard family joke to say, "If it's eight P.M., Mom must be doing laundry," routine works.

The philosophy behind the working mother's routine is simple. In fact, it can be boiled down to one word—prevention—because it is so much easier to *keep* a room clean than to get it clean. Some women promote showers so rings won't form around their tubs, and others instruct their children in the fine art of toothpaste dissolution so that their sinks remain spotless. Those women who sweep the kitchen floor each night have to wash it less frequently, while those who vacuum the bookcase each week can stave off the need for wiping down the volumes by hand. Even a superficial cleaning, done on a regular basis, can keep things looking shipshape without your having to resort to that procedure guaranteed to bring out all your hostilities—the thorough cleaning.

In the course of such preventive housekeeping, you'll want to cut corners wherever you can. You can speed up bedmaking by eliminating the top sheet and using a comforter or quilt instead of a spread, for example, and by making up one side of the bed completely before turning your attention to the other side. When it comes to laundry, it pays to think ahead by turning all your garments right side out as you take them off; putting separate hampers in each bathroom for bleach and nonbleach items; and pinning socks together to avoid the inevitable search for missing partners. Coordinating tasks saves time too, as you will find out if you put clothes in the washing machine while you simmer food on the stove, or allow pots to soak at the same time that you vacuum the rugs.

Finally, be on the lookout for new devices that could make your housekeeping operation a more efficient one. Did you know that a manufacturer recently introduced innovative bedding called "The Dreamer" in which the pillowcase, top sheet, and bottom sheet are all of a piece for instant bedmaking? Did you know that you can now buy an in-the-wall central vacuum system in a do-it-yourself installation kit? And have you kept up with the latest improvements in self-cleaning ovens, self-defrosting refrigerators, and no-wax flooring? If you haven't, you may just be missing some good bets for simplifying your housekeeping chores.

As you look into new housekeeping aids and experiment with routine systems, you should be able to lop considerable time off the daily and weekly grind. But major household tasks that come up less frequently require a different approach to make them more efficient—or even to get them done. It is to these major tasks that we now turn our attention.

Whatever Happened to Spring Cleaning?

Years ago, large-scale house cleaning took its cue from the weather, and certain chores, such as washing storm windows and painting porch furniture, are still guided by it. By and large, though, air conditioning and all-weather fabrics have done away with the seasonal imperative. Moreover, since the family is not likely to complain about a messy garage the way it does about not having clean socks in the drawer or not having dinner on the table, we tend to let optional chores go—and go. What if I don't get around to the attic this April, you rationalize, what difference will it make? The difference could lie in the sense of control you feel over your home environment and the pride you take in the way it looks. When you do something for your home, you're actually doing something for your mental health.

But how to start doing and stop procrastinating? If you're like most people, you need some pressure in order to produce. Create this pressure by giving yourself a deadline, preferably one with a certain logic behind it. You're more likely to clean out the spare room when your mother-in-law is about to come for a visit than when no overnight guest is expected, for example. And you'll get more cooperation in weeding out the toy box before Christmas and birthdays than at other times of the year. In fact, your children may even volunteer to throw out some of their old possessions if they know that new ones are on the way.

Sometimes your self-imposed deadlines could be in the nature of long-range goals. Setting up such goals conditions you to the idea of action. Thus, if you make a pact with yourself in June to get closets cleaned out by Labor Day, sleepless nights and rained-out beach days would find you reorganizing shelves. To make a long-range project seem both less formidable and more immediate, break it down into a series of mini-projects, each with its own deadline. Write out all the intermediate steps involved and post them in a conspicuous spot. They'll serve as a constant reminder that you should get moving on the project—now.

Once you've set down your goals, buy an organizing or cleaning aid to help you get started. A little reward initially soothes possible resentment at "wasting" your time on the house. It also gets you to begin, if only to try out your new toy. In addition to some tangible enticement, declaring that you'll spend five minutes on a task and no more could also con you into action. Poking holes in a big job this way is called the "Swiss cheese" approach by the time-management consultant Alan Lakein. He contends that it is an effective weapon against inertia, procrastination, and downright hostility to a task. It is also remarkably efficient. Although the hope is that you will become involved and stay with a job longer, even five minutes a day could make a big dent in it. If you decided to rearrange your kitchen, for example, you could start out by organizing one drawer, one group of pots, or one shelf in the refrigerator, any of which could be completed quickly. Eventually—and rather painlessly—your entire kitchen would get done.

But such an approach is not for everyone. If you're the sort of person who finds stopping and starting very frustrating, then you'd do better to jump in with both feet. Set aside a whole Sunday for your project, import playmates for your children or ship them out for the afternoon, then plunge right in.

Once you've made a start, you've got to find ways to stick with your project. Wear comfortable clothes, put on your favorite record, sing, sip a cup of coffee—whatever you can think of to make the situation more pleasant. It also helps to give yourself intermediate rewards such as a rest break or a phone break. A "work break" can be surprisingly refreshing, too, and quite productive. If you enjoy polishing shoes, for example, do that as a respite from a more onerous chore such as shampooing rugs. All along, keep reminding yourself how good it will feel to finish. Promise yourself a shower, a quiet time with the paper, dinner out, or whatever else spells "reward" for a job well done.

But when should you collect that reward? Only you can decide when a job is finished or at least finished for the day. If you have a problem calling it quits (and many people do), setting a physical limit may help. Say to yourself that tonight you will gather all the loose photographs in the house and that tomorrow night you will paste them in an album. Or decide to polish all your silver knives, forks, and spoons on Saturday, but let the tea service go until the following week. Since housework expands to fill the time allotted to it, setting a time limit also helps. But you must be sure not to attempt more than you can finish in any one period.

As a working mother, you will enjoy living in an Action House. You've got so many things going on in your life that to spend precious time hunting for objects, doing chores the hard way, or painfully putting them off is worse than a waste—it's a sin. Yes, you agree, but what if a person was born disorganized? Even that person (could it be you?) can run a more efficient household if she will (1) use concrete systems, including lists, written deadlines, and organized equipment; (2) add innovations slowly; and (3) concentrate on one task at a time rather than attempt to overhaul the entire house at a stroke.

Just think, with your home functioning smoothly, you'll be able to concentrate on living in it instead of caring for it. And you'll have increased time and energy too, which you can then devote to more vital areas of your life, such as your family and your job.

8

All About Food

The problem with food is that the need for it recurs daily—in fact, twice or thrice daily. Whereas other areas of your life lend themselves nicely to procrastination, food is not so accommodating. It must appear on the table or in the lunchbox at the appointed hour, and pity the poor working mother who regularly serves late, is always short of a key ingredient, or relies on the Kentucky Colonel and other "caterers" several nights a week. If you can identify with this description, you might do well to apply some basic principles of organization to food.

Laying the Groundwork

The marketing process actually starts at your desk. Try to schedule a quiet half hour there alone with your cookbooks and your weekly menu—a sheet of paper divided vertically into seven days and horizontally into three meals. As you decide what your family will be eating, enter it on the weekly menu and check your larder to make sure you have all the necessary ingredients on hand.

It is usually easy to figure out what you'll be making for breakfast, because most people eat the same thing every morning. It wouldn't hurt to provide a little variety, though, especially on weekends. If you're looking for nutritious ideas, dieticians recommend that you choose among juice, fruit, a good cereal, whole wheat bread, cheese, an egg, some meat, and a glass of milk. These high-protein foods are particularly valuable at breakfast because they are digested slowly and release energy as the morning wears on. If your children tend to quickly rush out without eating, you can get some nutrition into them via a homemade milk shake.

In comparison to breakfast, lunch is a little more complicated to plan. At noon kids are hungrier, demand more variety, and unless they come home to eat, need a meal that is portable. Consult your children to determine which days they'll be buying lunch and what food they want to bring the rest of the week. Then, since minds do get changed at the last minute, make sure you've got all the standard fixings on hand. If your kids seem bored with their usual fare, remember that a bagged lunch does not have to mean a sandwich. It can consist of cheese and crackers, pieces of cooked chicken, or leftovers stuffed into Mediterranean bread. Nor does it have to mean something cold. With all the insulated containers on the market, you can send your children to school with soup, meatballs and spaghetti, tuna-noodle casserole, or any other hot dish you've had for dinner in the last few days.

Evening meals demand the most planning of all, because they are the most elaborate. Now that you have a job, you can't take a chance on inspiration at 6:00 P.M. If it doesn't strike or you can't come up with the necessary ingredients when it does, you may have to fall back on an expensive steak or an equally expensive and not very satisfying fast-food-chain meal. Far better to decide what to cook when you're not under the gun. Eventually you will build up a set repertoire of meals that you can simply rotate over time. To do this, save and date your weekly menus and, if you want to score even more points, give a copy of the current list to your husband or post it in the kitchen. Then, as you bring out the filet of sole you won't be greeted with his familiar, disappointed cry: "Oh, I had that for lunch today."

Although the weekly menu serves as the basis for your marketing list, it does not take into account the office meeting that runs late or the dinner guest who drops in unexpectedly. Prepare for these contingencies in advance by stocking your larder with the following items: "kid" foods, such as peanut butter and jelly, crackers, soups, hamburger patties, hot dog rolls, cooked chicken parts, spaghetti and spaghetti sauce; one company-caliber main dish; a dessert; and a crock of cheese guaranteed to last until the year 2000.

You'll also find yourself ahead in the planning game if you maintain a running list all week. If you've never kept such a list, you can make one up by placing a blackboard or a large pad in some central spot in the kitchen. And, if you're smart, you'll make everyone responsible for contributing to it. Thus, the child who eats a certain cereal for breakfast each morning must note that it's running low *before* marketing day or do without it the following week. If that child can't spell yet, encourage her to participate in the listmaking anyway by telling you, getting an older sibling to write it down, or sounding it out phonetically. In the last instance some mental gymnastics may be required on your part, but gradually you'll be able to crack her code.

Theoretically, everyone should reorder before the last Chewette has been chewed and the last drop of window spray sprayed, but somehow they don't. Therefore, you will have to make a fast sweep through your kitchen before setting off for the supermarket. Shake containers and peer inside them, because someone may have returned an empty box to the shelf or opened a new box while the old one was still half full. When you've finished your review, transfer everything from the running list to the marketing list, grouping items by category and aisle. Some working mothers have facilitated this procedure by buying or making up and photocopying a standard check list, which serves as a memory jog as well as a timesaver.

List in hand, you are ready to make your purchases. Your time is so precious that we recommend your sticking with one convenient supermarket. By getting to know it well, you will be able to zip down its aisles, plucking goods from their expected places. And by shopping the specials there, you will be able to save as much money in the long run as you would by searching about for bargains. Even if your market is out of an item, we feel that it is preferable to revise your weekly menu on the spot rather than seek the item elsewhere. But do ask your manager to order whatever is missing, so you'll have it for the following week. Then, when checking out, have the packer put all your frozen foods in one bag and all your meats in another to expedite unpacking later.

When you get your supplies home, place them on their designated shelves. Push the older products forward and place the newer ones behind them. Have your husband, your children, and your sitters participate in this system of rotation too, teaching them to observe the dating guide on perishables: older date forward, more recent date to the rear. You should use the same method in stocking your freezer, but add a label to meats identifying their cut and date of purchase.

Since you should be bringing in a week's worth of food, your kitchen will be full to overflowing for a day or two. One way to relieve the crush is by putting fruits and vegetables into bowls and placing them around the house. Not only is this practical and decorative, but it has the further advantage of encouraging your children to reach for an apple instead of a cookie. You will have to monitor the ripening process, though, to make sure none of the fresh produce spoils.

As you stock your shelves, try to do so in some logical fashion. For example, you could put soups on one shelf, cereals on another, crackers on a third, and baking supplies on a fourth. Some working mothers arrange spices and soups alphabetically and group canned fruits and vegetables by color, but this degree of specialization may not be necessary unless you keep a large supply of food on hand. You can organize your refrigerator along the same lines, too: one shelf for dairy, one for drinks, one for breads, and another for leftovers. The idea behind these systems is that they save you from frustrating searches—usually when your hands are full of flour. But once you've done the initial arranging, it's up to everyone in the household to adhere to the system or you'll be right back where you started. Explain to them where things go and then affix identification labels to the shelves if you feel they'll need some reminding.

Cook Ahead—Sometimes

After the planning and the marketing comes the cooking, and at some point you've simply got to take a deep breath and do it, although now that you're working, that point may not be 6:00 P.M. Take advantage of your energy cycle. If you feel terribly fatigued right after work but get a second wind at ten, you could start the next night's dinner before going to bed. If you are chipper first thing in the morning, start it then. But if you don't feel up to cooking at any time during the week, devote a Saturday or Sunday to it. Then weekday nights really become a time of quick assembly rather than nitty-gritty food preparation.

As a working mother, you'll want to experiment not only with new times to cook but also with new ways. Your old gourmet extravaganzas may have tasted divine, but you simply haven't got the leisure to make them any more. Become flexible about what constitutes a "meal." One mother we interviewed said she had come to rely more and more on the salad as a main dish, for example, both because it was fast and offered great variety and because it provided so much valuable fiber for her family's diet. There is no rule of thumb for determining how long dinner should take, but one experienced mother has gotten meal preparation down to twenty-five minutes during the week. In that time she gets frozen vegetables into a pot, heats up a prepared casserole or starts to broil some chops, cuts up a grapefruit, assembles a salad, and puts out dessert.

To find meals that lend themselves to such a speedy routine, we suggest that you thumb through cookbooks for children. The meals described usually look good, consist of a few nonexotic ingredients, are easy to prepare and, perhaps most important of all, are sure to get eaten. Nor are they all on the level of ginger-bread men and scrambled eggs. One woman confided to us that she had gotten her best company recipe for chicken divan from a book for junior chefs. Cookbooks for teens and brides also offer the kind of stripped-down recipes you feel you can cope with at six at night. Like the children's cookbooks, they get you off to a fast start with ready-mades and other shortcuts, but then they go on to incorporate a few gourmet touches that make the finished product a more sophisticated one. Finally, keep a constant lookout for paperback books and magazine articles featuring time-saving recipes. Some of them list the time required for preparation as well as for cooking, which is helpful to someone like you on a tight schedule.

As you start to incorporate new preparation ideas into your life, you will find that some things can be done in advance and some cannot. With breakfast, for example, you can mix the frozen orange juice the night before and leave it in the refrigerator in a well-sealed container. But you shouldn't put out bowls of cereal at that time, lest they attract dust, insects, or the cat. Nor should you cut open citrus fruits so far in advance, because they lose vitamins when exposed to the air.

Bagged lunch fare, on the other hand, can usually be made any time of the day or night and put into the freezer or fridge. You don't have to defrost the frozen items in advance, because sandwiches taken from the freezer at 8:00 A.M. are ready to be eaten by noon. Check with an up-to-date freezer cookbook, though, to be sure that all your ingredients lend themselves to this treatment. Put those that don't, such as shredded lettuce and sliced tomatoes, in the refrigerator for last-minute lunchbox additions.

When it comes to making dinner, many freezer manufacturers now advise their customers to cook many types of meat and fish while they're still completely or partially frozen. This method improves texture and nutrient retention and doesn't add as much cooking time as you might think. Nor should you defrost vegetables in advance, because doing so makes them soggy. Since starches are usually easy to make but somewhat tricky to reheat, we think of them as last-minute items too. But if you have too much rice or spaghetti left over to throw out in good conscience, steam it in a colander or run boiling water over it just before reusing.

Some of your best ideas for cutting down on preparation and clean-up time may come to you when you are already in the trenches. Thus, as you dirty a pan sautéing mushrooms, ask yourself what else you could sauté in it that same evening. You could cook three pot roasts in the same giant pot, for example, and do it in the same amount of time and with very little extra effort. You can freeze two of them, and then, when it comes time to serve them, you could vary their tastes by adding tomato sauce to one, Burgundy and onions to the second, and cabbage and beer to the third. You could also roast two chickens in the same pan, removing one early, storing it, and finishing it up quickly at some other time. Nor do all the foods cooked this way have to be multiples of the same item. While you've got the oil bubbling for french fries, why not put your deep-fat fryer to use making salmon croquettes and chicken tempura, too?

Some working mothers cook on an even grander scale than this. One woman we interviewed positively scorned the idea of making two and freezing one. If you have a full-sized freezer, she recommends going all the way and cooking ten. Then, by making four different main dishes in quantities of ten each, you have enough for forty meals, or the backbone of your weekly menus for the next four months! When a woman is getting that much return, she doesn't mind spending the extra few hours required to chop, slice, and brown additional ingredients. And once she's got the food into the oven, she has to wait no longer for 10 quarts than for 1. So, you may want to invest in a few very large pots (which need not be expensive), start to collect air-tight containers, and order your ingredients by the bushel. You could find large-quantity cooking a satisfying and richly rewarding experience.

Once you've got all this food made, you'll have to store it—a process requiring techniques of its own. One working mother recommends freezing the various dishes in packages 2 inches deep or less. If you make them any thicker than that, she cautions, reheating may burn the outside while leaving the inside ice-cold. She proceeds by lining her largest frying pan with heavy-duty aluminum foil and spooning in enough food for the entire family. Then she covers the top with another piece of foil and places the pan in the freezer. When the food is solid, she removes the frying pan and puts it back into circulation. Since all these giant frozen pancakes look alike, she makes sure to label them with masking tape. Then, when it comes time to heat one up, she removes the wrap, puts a tablespoon of water in the frying pan, puts in the food, clamps on a tight lid, and puts the burner on low. Twenty effortless minutes later, *voilà*—dinner is served.

But even if you're not organized enough yet for multiple-meal techniques, you'll be ahead of the game with anything at all that is cooked in advance. Therefore, when you think food, automatically think leftovers. Always buy a much larger roast or turkey than you need for Sunday dinner and count on utilizing it again. Variations on previously cooked food are endless and can be even more popular with your family than the original. Nor do you always have to reheat them before serving. Some leftovers gain fresh appeal when served cold or at room temperature, while their nutritive value stays exactly the same. Consider cooking double portions of other foods besides meat and poultry. Roast potatoes, for example, can reappear mashed atop shepherd's pie or sliced with onions in the form of home fries.

After the cooking comes the fun part—the eating—but after the eating, alas, comes the clean-up. Few of us like anything about this process except its results. However, a little organization applied to the end of a meal can help things go as smoothly as they did at its beginning. Work up an efficient after-dinner routine of your own, one that might go something like this: as soon as you finish eating, clear off the table and replace the centerpiece. Put all ingredients and leftovers away, scrape the dishes, put them in the dishwasher or, lacking that appliance, wash them and let them air dry. Wipe down the counters and then scrub, dry, and put away the pots. Try to keep your kitchen looking neat at every stage of the procedure. Then, if you have to dash off to a PTA meeting before you're all through, it will still have an orderly if not spic and span appearance.

When others are on kitchen duty—as they should be if you've cooked the meal—make sure they know how to clean up and are aware of where everything is stored. Nothing is more frustrating than having to search for the ladle when the soup is ready to be served. Label drawers if you think that might help and take all big and little helpers on an orientation tour of the kitchen. Be fair to the clean-up squad, though, by tidying up as you go along. You could even take your cue from one of our interviewees who keeps her ingredients on a tray to contain the mess. At a minimum get the pots soaking in water before you sit down to eat, even if it means putting the food over a warming light for a moment.

Armed with these hints, you should find cooking and cleaning up a breeze—or at least less painful then you ever thought it could be. Another way to streamline the process is to consider purchasing some of the super duper kitchen aids described below.

Take Advantage of Technology

Manufacturers are constantly coming up with new ideas to make life easier for you in the kitchen. In the last several years alone they've introduced or improved a host of useful items from electric knives and food processors to self-timing ovens. Since any potential time- or effort-saver merits your attention (not to mention your gratitude), we suggest that you keep abreast of culinary technology.

Many kitchen aids are a delight to own but one, in our opinion, is truly indispensable: the freezer. As one working mother said: "It's like having a cook in the house." A freezer saves you time by permitting you to cook big and follow through on other pre-preparation ideas. It saves you money by allowing you to stock up on sale items, buy economical large cuts of meat, and "order out" from your kitchen when you would otherwise go to a restaurant. In fact, if you use a freezer wisely, a dietician assured us, it can make up its purchase price within a year. We feel so strongly about this item that we urge you not to let cramped quarters deter you from buying it. Make room, as did one of our interviewees who keeps an upright in her bedroom and another who conceals a chest model beneath her kitchen table.

If you already have a freezer but keep forgetting to take the roast out of it, the microwave oven may be for you. It warms up frozen bread for lunchboxes without toasting the slices, reheats leftover meat so that it is still pink and juicy, and cuts down the cooking time of many foods by a third or more. The microwave oven has its limitations, notably its high price tag and the fact that many models do not cook food to a brown and crispy turn. However, the price is bound to start coming down and industry is constantly improving the oven's performance. So, before you dismiss it out of hand as an expensive gimmick, investigate. In view of your hectic schedule, the microwave oven could play a useful role in your life.

Another fast way to get food done is by broiling. In fact, it is the fastest conventional method of cooking steaks, chops, and chicken parts. But since oven broilers are hard to clean, it might be worth your while to add a free-standing version to your arsenal. The open electric units are smokeless, odorless, and almost totally immersible while the enclosed units are often self-cleaning. Either type will take enough business away from your regular broiler to keep your oven much cleaner, a lucky extra. The rotisseries that sometimes accompany these free-standing broilers could be a legitimate purchase for you, too. Not only do they produce a delicious bird or roast, but they do so one-third faster than an oven set on "bake."

It stands to reason that you can save time by cooking fast, but has it occurred to you that you can also save time by cooking slow? Slow electric cookers, often referred to as "crock pots," can work for you while you are out of the house. You simply throw the requisite ingredients into one of these inexpensive units before you leave for work, plug it in, and come home to a finished meal. Soups, stews, sauces, and other items that require or benefit from long simmering are particularly well suited to this method. Crock pots save you money too, because they enable you to utilize cheaper cuts of meat than those you would ordinarily put on the broiler. Some crock pots are attractive enough to be used as servers or food warmers and some have detachable heating units that can be used separately as hot plates.

The housewares industry has been mulling over the problem of clean-up as well as cooking, and it has come up with some valuable new shortcuts. You can now protect your oven from splatter with roasting bags and keep your pots stain-free with boilable ones. Or you can eliminate several pots altogether by making use of the freezer-to-oven-to-table cookware on the market. In addition, some working mothers swear by their self-cleaning ovens and others say they don't know how they got along without their trash compactors. But everyone agrees that the single most useful aid to cleaning up is still that all-in-one pot scrubber, plate scraper, glass washer, utensil dryer, and baby bottle sterilizer: the dishwasher. We heartily recommend that you buy one—right after you've saved up for your freezer—or hint loudly for it as a gift.

But you cannot raise a family, be a companion to your husband, hold down a job—and grind your own wheat and churn your own butter. Just as you depend on kitchen appliances to get you through the week, so you need the help of processed foods to enable you to survive it.

Convenience Foods

When someone says "processed foods," people automatically think of TV dinners and cheese spreads. But actually everything that is packaged in the supermarket has been processed to some degree. Indeed, it's hard to imagine an alternative to store-bought crackers, noodles, or bacon, yet your grandmother probably made these items from scratch. For her, even a chicken without its feathers would have been a convenience food.

For you, surrounded as you are by a plethora of packaged goods, the situation is entirely different. The problem becomes not whether to use commercially prepared products, but how to choose among them wisely. If you're an environmentalist or the sort who instinctively mistrusts the easier way, you may feel guilty about relying on commercial products. Don't. You can feed your family adequate amounts of protein, carbohydrate, fat, vitamins, and minerals using processed foods, and in some instances you can do it better with them than without.

Frozen vegetables are a good case in point. They often have a higher vitamin content than their unprocessed counterparts, which spend a substantial amount of time on a truck, at a distribution center, and in a store before reaching your home. Frozen vegetables endure no such arduous journey. The large growers station their processing machines right in the fields so that they can scoop up the vegetables the moment they hit their peak. As one authority put it, "The fastest trip in the world is from the field to the frozen food package."

Canned goods have their virtues, too. They enable you to serve a greater variety of food at lower cost and with greater ease than you could otherwise manage. And they allow you to keep food on hand for an almost indefinite amount of time.

When it comes to frozen dinners, though, our praise for the processed food industry diminishes greatly. For one thing, these dinners are not cheap. The more table-ready a product is, the more labor has been required to produce it and, therefore, the more it is going to cost relative to the value of its raw ingredients. For another thing, except for the "man-size" dinners, the portions are usually insufficient to satisfy anyone over the age of ten. And for a third thing, frozen dinners may contain more salt, calories, and non-nutritive additives than you would care to eat.

To choose wisely among processed foods, read the comparisons of different brands that appear periodically in magazines, newspapers, and *Consumer Reports*. Get into the habit of reading labels, too. Since ingredients are always listed in order of weight, a cereal that has sugar at the head of its lineup is obviously a no-no. And don't hesitate to supplement what the manufacturers have to offer. Beef up prepared soups with extra chicken, slip bran into pancake mixes, and put wheat germ into hot cereal. Use natural foods with "crunch" such as fruit to supply the valuable fiber that is so often processed out of commercial preparations.

As you educate yourself about nutrition, pass the good word on to your kids. It's amazing how fast they catch on. Even very little ones soon make the connection between drinking milk and building strong bones. In addition to your mini-lectures on good eating habits, keep a steady stream of fresh produce coming into the house. Otherwise, the processed version may taste "natural" to your children while the real thing tastes "unnatural."

Nowadays the convenience food process does not stop at your supermarket. Industry has carried it yet another step further, to the fast-food restaurants.

Is Ronald McDonald the Other Man in Your Life?

Feeding your family at a fast-food operation must be placed in perspective. The fare should not be compared to the culinary wonders of a regular restaurant or to the satisfying meals you make at home. In fact, food is not even the main attraction of these places—the service is. When used in moderation, fast-food restaurants have much to commend them to the working mother: no cooking, no clean-up, low cost, quick turn-around time, and a change of pace for the whole family. But moderation is hard to maintain. Like cigarettes and alcohol, fast-food restaurants are addictive, and without even realizing it you could be wending your way to the double yellow arches three times a week or more.

According to most standards, you would not be served junk

food once you got there. Almost all the major chains provide an adequate to generous complement of protein in their main dish—be it hamburger, chicken, fish, pizza, or roast beef sandwich. That is, by itself, this portion will fulfill at least one-third of a child's or adult's daily protein requirement. But the fast foods are often deficient in vitamins and minerals, while their lack of fiber or roughage spells bad news for the country's millions of hemorrhoid sufferers. Moreover, their overabundance of fats, calories, and sodium could lead to heart disease and obesity. Since the average male office worker should eat no more than 2,100 calories a day, it is easy to see how a steady diet of Big Macs (560 calories), shakes (317 calories), and fries (180 calories) would make your husband fat in no time. And they wouldn't do great things for you or your children's figures either.

In light of all this, you might want to get the fast-food habit under control by confining it to specific preplanned occasions such as Little League night. On the way over to the restaurant, pass out raw vegetables as a first course. Then, when you get there, encourage your family to order the plain double hamburgers, which usually have more meat and less calorie-packed window dressing than the specialties of the house. At fried-fish or fried-chicken restaurants, have them ask for the two-piece dinners. These are sufficiently high in protein yet lower in calories than the three-piece meals.

If your children insist on fries and cola, split an order between two individuals. But because the cola is composed of caffeine, sugar, calories, and nothing else, it would be good to avoid it altogether. Encourage the kids to order a shake instead or, even better, a container of milk. And if milk is not available, water must be. Get some salad or coleslaw on the table where it's available (admitting of course that it has to be eaten to do any good). Then, when you've finished eating, leave quickly before any of you succumbs to the restaurant's pastry. Back home offer fruit for dessert or, if that suggestion bombs, serve up some ice cream. The ice cream is more caloric than the fruit, but at least it is more nutritious than the pastry.

Since there is far more to eating than hamburger stands and pizza parlors, we'll conclude our chapter on food with a consideration of honest-to-goodness dining.

The Family Meal

According to many observers of the American scene, the family dinner may be going the way of the dinosaur and the dodo. The kids have extracurricular activities, Dad comes home late, Mom is too tired to cook, and everyone's attention is riveted on the TV. Under these circumstances it is little wonder that dinner often consists of a bite grabbed on the run.

Yet the communal meal should have an important place in family life. It provides a forum for the exchange of ideas and a vehicle for the transmission of values. It gives all the family members an opportunity, perhaps the only one of the day, to be together in the same place at the same time. And it conveys the sense that life is more than a struggle for survival.

For a working mother whose family time is limited, the communal meal has even greater potential. Indeed, eating with your children could become the most rewarding "quality" time of the day. Engaged in the mutually enjoyable activity of consuming food, freed for the moment of the pressures and distractions of the world, you can give the children your undivided attention and they can give you theirs. The meal itself need not be elaborate. Even the simplest fare taken together conveys your message: "Although I am gone most of the day, I feel that our home is a special place and that you are special people. We are a family."

A real family dinner can actually be a lot more fun than wolfing down a hamburger at a roadside stand. Instead of saving all your creativity for company, dress up your everyday table with a few fresh flowers, a paper hatchet on Washington's Birthday, and the children's colored eggs at Easter. Change the scene every so often, too: picnics in the park in good weather, trays in front of the fireplace on a cold night. Sometimes you may want to watch TV during dinner, which is fine on an occasional basis. But if your set is always blaring at mealtime, conversation will be hard to maintain and the real purpose of eating together will be virtually destroyed.

Of course, even without television the family meal could turn out to be a fiasco instead of an idyllic interlude. Throwing food, putting feet on the table, roughhousing, jumping up and down, and trading obscenities are standard operating procedure for children at many American dinner tables. If things start to get out of hand at your house, deal with the offender sternly. Eating with Mom and Dad is a privilege and one that must be earned with good manners.

Beyond the basics of decent human behavior, you may demand as much in the way of table manners as you have the strength for. Young children actually catch on fast to certain aspects of etiquette such as chewing with a closed mouth, putting the napkin on their lap, and keeping their elbows off the table. If you employ sign language, frowns, and a few gentle reminders (like a thousand), good manners should become habitual with them. And when they lapse by not saying "please" before asking you to pass the bread, try ignoring the request until they do.

In addition to how your children eat, what they eat—or, more usually what they don't eat—can turn the dinner table into a battlefield. Since harangues about starving to death and the world hunger problem do not stimulate appetites, save your breath. Instead, put a little of everything on the noneater's plate. Don't actively urge him to eat, but let it be known that he who does not sample does not get dessert. If, on the other hand, you have a child who eats so much that he is overweight, your job becomes one of helping him to cut down. Try giving him a big glass of water before meals, asking him to eat more slowly, and allowing him to leave the table as soon as he's done. Above all, do not heap fattening food on his plate and then berate him for eating it. Since no youngster can diet in a vacuum, you may have to modify everyone's menu to ensure his success. But in the long run, even the thin members of your family will benefit from eating lean, healthy meals.

The family dinner is a marvelous institution, but from time to time there is nothing nicer than the "un-family" dinner. To make it happen in your home, feed the children in the kitchen, then set the table for you and your husband in the dining area. Chill a bottle of wine, bring out the silver candlesticks, put on a romantic record, and forsake your blue jeans for a pretty hostess robe. Now you can sit down and enjoy the divine meal that *he* whipped up in the kitchen.

9

Pitch In!

Food preparation is just one of the reasons why you're always so tired. It can take as much as 105 hours a week or some 15 hours a day to work and care for a home and family without help. Using simple arithmetic, you can see why you race through each day like a character in some zany silent movie and why time to yourself is strictly pie in the sky. Yet like many working mothers you may not be tapping the one source that could bring you relief: your children.

Why do so many women martyr themselves rather than call upon their children for help? According to family counselors, it is because they think of the "good mother" as someone who is always taking care of everyone else. The good mother image is hard to shake off, partly because of cultural conditioning and partly because it satisfies the deepseated need to feel needed.

If you, too, are hung up on the good mother myth, you should realize that it consigns you to a permanent state of exhaustion. It also robs your children of a marvelous opportunity to acquire domestic skills, develop a sense of responsibility, and become part of a joint effort. Instead of you against them or them against you (as you are more likely to perceive it), you and your children can play on the same team. And if the tasks assigned them are truly important, the youngsters will experience the satisfaction of doing something for others rather than always having others do things for them. So stop feeling guilty and start handing out those household assignments today.

Orders of the Day

As you begin, try to imbue your youngsters with a sensible attitude toward housekeeping. Present it to them neither as something wonderful nor as something terrible, but merely as something that has to be done. Then introduce them to your new family motto—"Don't put it down, put it away"—and repeat it so often that it reverberates through their heads at night. Finally, link every action in the house to an immediate reaction. Have the children make their beds as soon as they wake up and have them rehang their towels as soon as they wipe their hands. If you establish this routine, the hope is that they will grow accustomed to straightening up as they go along.

Start the training program early by encouraging your very young child to feed himself in his high chair. Although his efforts will be clumsy and messy, don't stop him (and don't let your sitter stop him), because these are the first steps on the path to self-reliance. As the youngster advances through toddlerhood, laud his attempts to dress himself and put away his toys. Then by the time he is in nursery school, he should be capable not only of getting into and out of clothes, but also of making his bed, setting the table, sorting flatware, collecting laundry, and watering plants. By all means call upon him to do these tasks and to deliver messages and carry small parcels for you as well. With each new responsibility he will feel and become more grown up.

To enable your nursery-school-aged child to do his "jobs" more efficiently, give him whatever scaled-down equipment you can buy or make. Then divide up each chore into short, easy-to-follow steps. Demonstrate them with almost no talking because you want the child to concentrate fully on your motions, and then let him try them for himself. When he has finished, point out the telltale signs that a task was not properly done: crumbs on the table after wiping or tarnish on the silver after polishing. But since criticism inhibits youngsters from trying again, never downgrade his efforts. Instead, find something to praise and do so heartily. If you make housework a pleasurable way for a child to gain your approval, it could become his favorite game. And do encourage sitters and nursery-school teachers to reinforce your training with real-life domestic exercises.

After your children reach the age of six, the sky is the limit where self-maintenance is concerned. Under your supervision, they can start to do everything for themselves from washing their own hair to making their own breakfasts and keeping up their own rooms. In addition, from this age on they will quickly develop the motor skills and maturity to perform a wide range of household chores, including total meal preparation and babysitting. Indeed, in many simple societies around the world, children between the ages of seven and twelve have total responsibility for the house and younger siblings while their mothers are at work in the fields.

When showing your child the ropes, demonstrate each task, then have her do it with you, then without you but under your supervision. When you are satisfied that she knows what to do, even if she can't execute it too well, disappear. Where safety precautions have to be taken, as in cooking, review them thoroughly but calmly. Children have a healthy respect for potentially dangerous situations and they will not put themselves in jeopardy if forewarned. Of course, you will have to go through all the first aid remedies anyway, because accidents can happen.* And while you are playing instructor, be sure to stress the importance of putting equipment away. If your child makes it a practice to leave her supplies around, you could wind up spending inordinate amounts of time just picking up after her— which is not the idea at all.

When you are satisfied that your children can carry on without close supervision, hold a family council to assign tasks. Not only will the youngsters surprise you with their imaginative schemes, but they will be more likely to carry out plans they've

* See the first aid section, the emergency telephone list, and useful numbers at the back of the book.

made themselves than edicts handed down from on high. Some children have even been known to set penalties for chores left undone.

No matter what they come up with, though, you will need to make sure that all bases are covered. Give out assignments by the week or the month and switch around the most onerous jobs so that no one gets stuck two rotations in a row. But if Susie loves to dust, she could keep that job forever and if Doug still needs some supervision, he could team up with older sister Jenny. Just so long as everything gets done, we see no reason why family members should not be allowed to trade off from time to time or bend the schedule to suit themselves.

But a schedule is vital, and a written one works best, at least for the first few months. Try to attach the chores on it to certain days and/or times. Then, in exactly the same way that the "automatics" trigger something in your mind, so these standard procedures will get your kids into the habit of thinking, "Dinner is over, I must be taking out the garbage." Check-off lists also jog the memory and even spur some children into action. But many young people—like many older people—require more powerful stimuli to get them moving.

The Carrot . . .

All those smiling oven-scrubbers on TV notwithstanding, you probably don't love housework—and *you* can see the need for it. Little wonder, then, that your child, who is not bothered by mess at all, usually balks at pitching in. Anthropologists claim that the youngster would respond more positively if he were being asked to gather wood for the cookfire or draw water from the village well. Lacking both a cookfire and a well in middle-class America, you're reduced to having him remove specks of dust from furniture, which is obviously not as crucial to survival.

Not only is it hard for you to motivate your children through dramatic necessity, but you are bucking the trend of an entire culture when you try. American mothers demand less and get less in the way of juvenile assistance than women in almost every other part of the world. Moreover, they tend to look upon whatever help they do get as a lucky extra rather than an integral part of the household routine. In view of this, it is not surprising that American children too see their contribution to family life as a favor—a favor that can be granted or withheld at will.

The only way for you to start motivating your children in the face of these obstacles is through sheer force of personality. You've got to make up your mind that your home *will* run largely on kid power and that under no circumstances will it revert to the old source of energy—you. If you give children the out they will take it, but if you show them that you are absolutely determined to follow through on this, they will go along.

They'll even do so with a little enthusiasm if you offer tangible rewards for their efforts. Incentives work wonders in motivating people. And if the lure of a weekend in Miami can make a wealthy insurance agent hustle all year, think what the promise of an ice cream cone could do for your seven-year-old. As children get older, the incentives you offer have to be somewhat grander to get them to produce. But if the youngsters are made to understand that dinners out, weekend ski trips or even a family jaunt to Disneyworld are all possible when outside help is eliminated, you might just be inundated with volunteers.

We like incentives but we realize that they often come dangerously close to being bribes and that as far as children are concerned, the two are one and the same. When you offer an incentive, the underlying assumption is that the children still have to do their chores—you're just sugaring the pill. But when you bribe, you're begging a favor. Bribes quickly get out of hand as the price of favors escalates, and work starts to cost you more than it's worth. Bribes make children manipulative and, worst of all, they defeat that "we're all in this together" spirit which is the essence of cooperative housekeeping.

Allowances should not be thought of as incentives, either.

Children are entitled to some spending money that is not contingent upon performance of duties. However, if your daughter baby-sits or mows a lawn for you on weekends when she could be earning money elsewhere, you might consider paying her the going rate. And if your son puts in a great deal of time washing windows, something you would otherwise pay a professional to do, he also merits compensation. Since working for you may be your children's most viable way of earning money, why not check with them before going to an outside source? Chances are they'll be interested.

. . . and the Stick

Despite all your kind words of encouragement, all your cozy demonstrations, all your well-thought-out schedules, and all your delicious ice cream cones, your child may turn out to be a slob, and a recalcitrant slob at that. What's a working mother to do? First of all, resist the impulse to scream. Second of all, resist the impulse to nag. Did you ever do anything faster or better because you were nagged? And don't stew over it, either. Instead, count up to 175 and then embark upon a constructive course of action.

The first one that comes to mind is allowing your child to see—and suffer—the consequences of his noncompliance. If your son has not done yesterday's dishes, the sink will be full. If the sink is full, the chef won't be able to cook; and if the chef cannot cook, no one gets to eat. Above all, *Do not wash the dishes for him.* Instead, you might want to take the rest of the family out to dinner and leave the shirker at home. If you cannot manage anything quite that dramatic, you could take away some beloved privilege or, in extreme cases, even encourage the family to give him the cold shoulder. That should make him come around, because social ostracism is one of the hardest things for a person to bear.

If the trouble lies not with the way your child does his chores but with the way he keeps his room, you could try one of the following techniques developed by working mothers. One woman maintained a firm 9:00 P.M. bedtime in her household. However, if a child had set his room completely to rights while she was at the office, that youngster got to stay up until 9:30. Another mother, at her wits' end with a daughter who would get neither herself nor her room ready in the morning, finally refused to give the girl breakfast—or even to let her down the stairs—until both were presentable. A third mother took away her son's stereo after he had ignored several entreaties to straighten out his things. He became absolutely furious because he had always gotten away with delaying tactics before. But the next time he was asked to clean his room, he complied more quickly, if not more happily.

In addition to taking corrective measures such as these, it is a good idea to analyze what is really going on between you and your child in the battle of the bedroom. If your child procrastinates and procrastinates and then does such a sloppy job on his room that he seems to be baiting you, rest assured that he is. But do not rise to the bait. His passive-resistant behavior could very well be an attention-getting ploy. And the more you acknowledge what he is doing, even if you acknowledge it at the top of your lungs, the more you are rewarding him for the very behavior you are trying to change.

Institute a little passive-resistant behavior of your own instead. As far as possible, mentally remove the child's room from your house. Keep the door shut so you won't have to look at it and leave his laundry outside so you won't have to go into it. Don't even refer to the room in conversation if you can help it. Making believe that it doesn't exist might not get the room cleaned up, but at least you'll be less irritated by it. And once his living in a pigsty no longer merits your attention, your child just might weary of it himself. Of course, if you lack the fortitude to wait it out, you always have the option of going in and cleaning up the room yourself.

Are You a Good Boss?

The success of cooperative housekeeping depends in large measure on you. But since there are no guidelines for parent-employers, it is hard for you to judge your own performance. To help you evaluate how you are doing and zero in on possible trouble spots at the same time, we have compiled the following check list:

Are you apologetic? Despite all the benefits you now know accrue to your children from helping out, do you still feel in your heart of hearts that it is a "shame" they have to do housework? Nonsense! If *you* don't have a maid, why should they?

Are your standards too low? If you answered yes to the previous question, you may not be demanding enough of your children. They know when their work is not up to par even if they're not sure why, so don't demean their efforts by praising a shoddy job. Moreover, if they see that they can get away with once-over-lightly, they will have no incentive to improve.

Are your standards too high? They may be if you're not taking into account the age and nature of the child and the extent of his experience. If his experience is nil, tie your right hand behind your back and try to do one of his chores with your left. That's about how he feels when he does it.

Are you criticizing constructively? This is the most ticklish part of your job. But you will succeed at it if you focus discussion on the work, not the worker, and on how it can be improved, not on how badly it was done.

Are you explaining things clearly? You may find less to criticize if you take the time to go over each task step by step. Although housekeeping seems self-explanatory to you because you've been doing it for so long, it's all Greek to the novice. Better to err on the side of simplicity with children rather than obscurity.

Are you redoing the children's work? You may be if your standards are too high, and the temptation is great even if they're realistic. But try to live with the youngsters' efforts, no matter how clumsy, because the alternative makes the children feel superfluous and denies them the thrill of shouting, "Look, Ma, I did it myself!"

Do you really want to do it all yourself? If you are constantly redoing the children's work, it might be because you feel that no one can keep house in your house but you. Obviously, such proprietary feelings are incompatible with cooperative housekeeping and must be overcome.

Are you encouraging self-reliance? This is the main task of a parent-employer, yet you may like feeling needed so much that you're unconsciously encouraging the children to come to you for help. And they will if they find that this maintains your involvement in their lives. Unless you want to go on being the sole housekeeper forever, stop babying your assistants and start rewarding independent action.

Are you exploitative? You may be so burdened down with your own concerns that you're asking too much of your young assistants without realizing it. Children are entitled to participate in after-school programs and other social functions without quid pro quo stipulations. Make sure that you're not always placing your needs above theirs.

Are you considerate? Since the fastest way to lose the goodwill of your helpers is by being inflexible, try to look at things from their point of view. Allow reasonable delays and exceptions. The garbage can wait to be taken out until the commercial comes on TV, and a bed can go unmade when a school project needs full attention to meet the deadline.

Are you grateful? Children, like adults, need to feel appreciated. And though you are, indeed, "all in this together," a few kind words can go a long way toward dissipating the resentment of having to spend after-school time doing chores. Make your gratitude known because children bloom under praise.

Of course, no matter how ardent your thank you's, your children will probably not grab the broom from your hand and say, "Oh, please, let me!" And despite the most detailed of instructions, your home and cuisine will no longer be totally "you." However, the preservation of your good disposition and health is definitely worth the change in lifestyle—and the grumbling that accompanies it. So make up your mind that cooperative housekeeping is going to work. Do this by dwelling on the benefits all of you are receiving from it now, and think of how much better off your children will be as a result of it in the future. Indeed, they will be far better equipped to handle a home of their own than you were because they have a mother—and a working mother, at that—who refused to be a martyr.

10

Closing the
Communications Gap

At every point of interaction with your child—even while explaining about the vacuum cleaner—you'll want to contribute to a positive feeling between you. Since your time is limited, you may have to depend on odd places and odd times to grow closer, but that doesn't mean that you will be a less effective mother than the one who utilizes more conventional means of communication.

No one way to parent is any more valid than any other. Therefore, don't drive yourself crazy thinking you have to fit some ideal image of the 100 percent All-American Mom in order to do it right. You simply cannot be the sort Norman Rockwell made famous, the one who has six pies cooling on the windowsill, four craft projects laid out in the playroom, and two PTA committee meetings under her belt—all before noon. But let us state at the outset that food does not equal love; that your child wants you and not an arts and crafts counselor when you're around; and that there is absolutely no correlation between being a class mother and being a good mother.

In fact, your working has certain built-in advantages where your children are concerned. By being away a great deal of the time, you get some perspective on their behavior and can laugh at foibles that would send you up the wall if you were home all day. Moreover, since work adds another dimension to your life, you are not living solely for or through your children, and their successes or failures are probably not disproportionately important to you. Being absent much of the day, you cannot always be doing for your kids, or guiding, monitoring, and evaluating them. If you are the sort who has a tendency to take over, work saves you from smothering them. Like all living things, children need light and air and room in order to grow.

Quality Versus Quantity Time

"It's not the quantity of time you spend with your child, it's the quality." Or is it? This is *the* debate today for working mothers. But before we add our two cents' worth, we'd like to define the terms as we use them. To us "quantity" time refers to those mundane hours when you drag your child around on errands and chauffeur him from place to place. It includes the time you're sorting laundry and he's watching TV; the time you're talking on the phone and he's dribbling a basketball in your ear; and the time you're washing the windows in your room and he's drawing on them in his. In short, it's the time you and your child are in close proximity but not gazing soulfully into one another's eyes.

"Quality" time, on the other hand, consists of precious moments: those afternoons spent shopping together for a special party dress, having a hamburger by yourselves at McDonald's, or sharing a heart-to-heart talk after lights out. Like everyone else, we like one-on-one time. We think it affords a working mother the best opportunity to get to know her child without the distractions and distortions other personalities bring to a situation.

Quality time does not mean the most expensive time you can imagine, because a child is thrilled just to have a whole parent to himself. The idea is to pick a setting that's conducive to engendering positive feelings about each other. Occasionally, of course, you will want to arrange a "heavy date" and that will do no harm. But if you are always planning trips to the circus,

Disneyworld, or the movies during your quality time, you may actually be avoiding interaction with your child rather than fostering it. Or you may be trying to buy him off to compensate for the guilt you feel about working.

Quality time is meant simply for enjoying each other. If you're enjoying your child, he'll know it, and vice versa. But in order for it to work, you've got to make up your mind—no matter how much it hurts—not to mention table manners, posture, untied laces, and unmade beds even once. Nor does your child have to be learning something during this time—especially not with you as teacher. It is a long, slow process to get some kids to lower their guard, but it's only a matter of minutes before they can raise it up again.

How much quality time is enough? This is tricky. On an everyday basis, it might be fifteen minutes at bedtime. On a once-a-week basis, it might be an hour, and on a once-a-month basis it might be an afternoon. If you cut this special time too short or interrupt it with too many errands, it won't bring you and your child any closer. As Barbara Walters once put it, talking of her own busy schedule: "When I run in for ten minutes in between appointments [to see my daughter], how great can the quality be?" We recognize that large chunks of time are very hard to set aside, especially when there are other children in the family; but they can be found. And for the other children, this can become a special time with their father.

The advantages of quantity time are not as obvious as those of quality time, but they are very real nonetheless. During these periods you are providing your child with a role model of responsibility and adulthood, which he needs. You are supplementing the more intense aspects of your relationship with the leavening give-and-take of everyday family life, which he also needs. With all the other claims on your time it should be a relief to find out that you and your child don't have to be interacting "meaningfully" whenever you're within a football field of one another. Unfortunately, as you've probably already guessed, between the quality time and the quantity time and your job, there's almost no other time left. But we'll get to that in Chapter 15, "You."

Creating Time When There Is No Time

Finding quality time is a self-evident problem. But for the working mother even quantity time is hard to come by. As you well know, if you go alone you'll get the marketing done in half the time and at what seems like half the price without a child throwing his own treats into the basket. But if you take your child along, you can at least get some time to visit. (And there's always the chance that you'll meet someone you know who will say to herself, "She works and she's such a good mother, too.") Like everything else, you've got to compromise here. Sometimes, for the sake of efficiency, you should go alone. On other occasions, it's a good idea to take the children along. They like to get out, and even babies benefit from the stimulation of the supermarket and shoe repair shop.

You can build rapport with your child in odd moments if you seize the opportunity to turn quantity into quality time. You do this by keeping the radio and TV off, your ears open, and your emotions available. You can also do it by making the setting work for you. Although everyone agrees that a happy child is more important than a clean home and that love is more nourishing than food, these things are usually easier to say than to live with. But there is no reason why you can't accomplish both. While you're peeling potatoes or changing linens with your child, you can have just as good a talk as when you're out walking in the woods—and maybe a better one, because it might seem more spontaneous at home.

Chauffeuring presents another opportunity to create time where there is no time. One woman we interviewed put her child into a nursery school near her job instead of near her home so that she would be able to be alone with him during the half-hour drive to and from work. There seems to be something about the closed space, the droning engine, and the continuous motion of car travel that fosters intimacy, especially if the child is in the front seat with his mother. Some people sing or play guessing games. Even while taking the carpool you can avail yourself of the opportunity to learn about your child and the way he interacts with his peers if you keep your ears open.

Bedtime offers many of the same advantages as chauffeuring. You and your child are alone, in an intimate atmosphere free of the distractions of more active situations. Bedtime is particularly valuable for conversing with the very active child who is otherwise swinging from the rafters or beating up his little brother. The confined space of the bathtub can serve the same purpose.

After a while, of course, children are capable of putting themselves to bed and bathing alone. But you might want to continue participating in certain evening activities anyway, because they afford you extra opportunities to be with your children. A bedtime ritual, in particular, is good for children to be able to count on. It gives them a sense of security to know that they have you to themselves for some time at night and that they can unload emotionally during this period. This feeling may not be conscious on their part, but it is real. One mother we interviewed said she gets into bed with her children after lights out. In this way her kids get the benefit of her presence—and on their turf, which is important to children—while she gets the benefit of some rest. The only drawback to this scheme, she confided, is that she often falls asleep before they do!

When you are not physically present, the telephone can help you reinforce your relationship with your children. Some mothers have a set time to call home after school and they work their coffee break around it. Your children should know your office number and feel they can call you in an emergency or at a prearranged time. Talking on the phone is a treat for kids and even a three-year-old will be hurt if you always ask to speak to the sitter and not to him.

Just as there are many opportunities to create time where there is no time or turn quantity into quality moments, so the converse is true. When you're tired after a long day at work, giving your children an extra half hour of TV and a quick kiss in lieu of your standard bedtime routine can be very tempting. Sometimes you will do things like this because not doing them would seem like a punishment, which is counterproductive. But if you find that you are frequently substituting things for your personal attention, you may have hit upon one reason why you and your child are not as close as you'd like.

Recreation: Mine, Yours, Ours

One of the most effective ways to close the communications gap is by bringing a child into your world. If you're going to be doing setting-up exercises anyway, what's wrong with a little person grunting alongside, even if she can touch her toes and you can't? Take her along for company when you jog, and even buy matching warmup suits to make it official. If you're going to be taking a bath anyway, why not let your young daughter climb in with you? This can be a great timesaver (although it has short-lived usefulness unless your child stays very small or your tub grows very big).

You could also join your child's world as more than a spectator. You don't have to become "one of the guys," especially if you're not comfortable with that role, but you might find you really enjoy shooting fouls or riding a bicycle or playing Monopoly. The two of you might also embark on a new joint hobby. One mother we interviewed started a country and western record collection with her daughter. Another joined a bicycle club with her sons and the three of them now take to the road on Sunday mornings while the man of the house sleeps. Still another mother and daughter started out horseback riding together at a city stable and got into horse-trading as a joint venture! The possibilities are limitless.

But picking the right activity for you and your child can be a tricky proposition. Too often the project chosen is too sophisticated, and a parent becomes frustrated when the joint effort looks sloppy. You might want to try parallel play in these instances, making yourself available to your child but only as a consultant. Another danger, particularly in sports, is competing too strenuously with your child or, conversely, giving up in order to let him win. Neither approach builds friendship—or character, for that matter. Sometimes, in introducing a child to your favorite hobby, you may become anxious about his using your equipment. If you find that you are quaking every time he comes near your expensive photographic enlarger, maybe you'd better forget darkroom technique until he's more mature or you're more relaxed. Finally, to get away from the usual performance expectations, ask your child to teach you something for once. This role reversal will be a revelation to both of you.

Everyone loves a party and children are no exception. Let them help you set up and pass the canapés when your guests arrive—and then say goodnight. Let them help plan their own parties, too. Since you're away during the day, these will probably be dinner parties, but they don't have to be confined to birthdays. You could have a pre-Halloween dinner and then take the kids out for trick-or-treat. You could hold an Easter egg-rolling contest or celebrate Friday the 13th. Books that you can borrow from the library are filled with food and decoration ideas for events that can make your home a warm, "fun" place to be.

Encouraging a friendship with a family whose children are about the same age as your own can also lead to many happy adult-child recreation hours. Then, too, taking your children along to political rallies, church services, and community meetings enriches their lives while giving all of you a common fund of experience. Of course, if you find that you and your kids are always waving to one another across a crowded room, you may be overdoing a good thing.

All of which brings us to the ticklish subject of Togetherness. Togetherness is not for every family, yet the failure to achieve it often engenders as much frustration and guilt in mothers as working does. Anything less than a living Victorian family portrait—relatives of all ages scattered about the parlor idling away long, peaceful Sunday afternoons—seems to indicate a failure on our part. If we can't enjoy being together, what kind of family are we? A realistic one, we might answer. For one thing, a wide age spread among children may preclude many shared activities. For another, certain personalities just may not jibe, making family gatherings tense. And for a third, if some of the members would rather be off doing their own thing, a forced fun situation will be a dud. Part of the reason family outings often fail is that, as on New Year's Eve, we are *expected* to have fun. That in itself can be depressing.

Sometimes, though, family outings can be great, and should be investigated by the working mother as another route to achieving a closeness with her children. Getting into neutral surroundings often encourages new and positive feelings toward one another. At home the familiar battlegrounds too often trigger the familiar antagonisms. But in a holiday setting you should all be more relaxed, more receptive to each other, more willing to open up and be friends. Besides, who else will sit willingly through your vacation slide show, except your children who were there with you?

Since an outing has to be mutually satisfying to be of benefit, put in something for everyone. If your children want to go to the zoo, take care of that in the morning, go out to lunch at a restaurant you'll all enjoy—not the gold-tasseled-menu variety—and then stop by the museum you want to visit. Shared experiences are an invaluable aid to communication, but they should always be looked upon as the backdrop for intimacy, not a substitution for it.

A Word About Words

Many advice-givers place great faith in verbal communication with children. If only a mother would listen to what her kids are trying to tell her, they claim, everything would be grand. But it has been our experience that many children are about as communicative as the Great Wall of China. That old gag, "Where did you go? Out. What did you do? Nothing,'' is at least as true to life as the child who can't wait to tell all but finds no one willing to listen to him.

Verbal communication *is* important. Despite the ascendency of other means of communication and the decline of literacy, words still remain our primary tool for linking ourselves to other human beings. So it's little wonder you're disappointed when you ask your child what he's been up to all day and he says he can't remember. Chances are he can't, or is bored by the telling, or feels very proprietary about his personal experiences. And you should not press him to talk or he'll feel that you are trying to check up on him or to catch him in a lie. The good news is that your child-the-Sphinx is just like millions of other kids. His silence does not mean that he is harboring suicidal thoughts or punishing you for working. The bad news is that you still don't know what's going on in his head or in his life and you don't have all day to pry it out of him.

How to go about opening him up? You could try to get the conversational ball rolling by describing your own day. Fair is fair. Or you could hand on some news that might interest him about a neighbor or a child he knows. Everyone loves gossip, but few people ever think to tell it to children, even when it's clean. Another tack that seems to bring success is familiarizing yourself with your child's world so that you can ask him about it. Most children are not sophisticated conversationalists and they often need a concrete question to get them started. For example, "What did you do in school today?" often elicits only a noncommittal answer such as, "Worked." But, "How many rats did Noah the boa consume?" has been known to bring forth a five-minute monologue on the eating, sleeping, and mating habits of the South American boa constrictor. Which may be more about the boa than you care to know.

Another technique you might want to try is verbalizing some of your own negative feelings or emotional reactions. Once your children hear you bring your personal feelings out into the open, they will be encouraged to do the same. And as they talk about what is bothering them, their hostile feelings will seem less threatening to them and may even disappear. The more each of you cares about what you're discussing, the closer together it will bring you. From time to time you could also try asking your children for their opinion. This is not only very flattering to them, it can be a real help to you since children are often very original problem-solvers.

Finally, you will want to be the one to give your children bad news. They are going to overhear it anyway and by telling it to them yourself, you'll be sure they get the story straight. The fact is that there is nothing you *can't* discuss with children as long as you yourself are comfortable with the subject and you keep it on their level of understanding.

Some children are poor conversationalists because they are very young and have limited vocabularies. But they still have problems. If you think you know what is bothering your young child, you can try making up a story that includes all the elements of his problem in thin disguise. He may not get the point right away, but after a few recitations he will give you some sign that he understands what the story is about. That is your cue to bring his problem into the open. Sometimes the resolution of the story in itself will be enough to dissipate his anxiety.

A final word about words. Words are emotionally loaded and they don't always convey what the dictionary says, by rights, they ought to convey. Too often when you start to say something *to* a child, you end up saying something *about* him. If your comments are too negative, they may give him a bad self-image, and if they are too positive, too often, they may turn him into a praise junkie. Perhaps the best course to try to steer is that of neutrality. Of course, this kind of noncommittal response is the hardest thing for parents to achieve, because they tend to see their children as extensions and reflections of themselves. But it's worth working at, because a passive listener is an accepting listener as far as a child is concerned. Moreover, you will be encouraging him to do his own problem solving and independent thinking. Noncommittal responses keep the conversational ball in the child's court—where it belongs.

One of the ways to avoid the pitfalls of language is to bypass or supplement it with body language. A recent study reported that people around the world from Australian aborigines to Philadelphia physicists all reacted the same way to smiles, frowns, and looks of fear, surprise, grief, and joy. Undeniably, then, somatic messages are very effective and free of the ambiguity of words. Particularly where small children are concerned, actions do speak louder than words.

As a working mother you will want to employ body language, because it can maximize your efforts at communicating love to your offspring in the short amount of time you have together. Little children respond marvelously well to being held and spoken to in soft, intimate tones. Older children, too, can be greatly calmed and reassured by body contact. To facilitate this we recommend a rocker or a big, squashy chair to use frequently with a child on your lap. While reading a story you might try an arm around the youngster or a snuggle in bed after lights out. Boys may refuse this, especially when it comes from their mothers, and you too may feel self-conscious about it if physical intimacy is not easy for you. Try it anyway. If it doesn't work out, a warm smile, a squeeze of the hand, a tug of the braid can make the same unmistakable point: "I like you."

Discipline as Communication

Another unspoken but very clear form of communication is discipline. Discipline says to a child: "I care enough about you to be concerned about how you act and how you will turn out." Looked at this way, discipline becomes a form of love that strengthens, molds, corrects, and trains. Even while bucking its restraints, a child wants this guidance because it makes his world manageable and secure. Your own approach to discipline may be permissive or strict, but it must make clear that you're the ultimate authority. When you ask a child to set his own physical or behavioral limits, you are asking him to be parent to himself—and that no child should be expected to do.

Discipline manifests itself in rules that, when internalized, lead to self-discipline and the vindication of all your parenting efforts. Therefore, embrace rules: set them, stick to them, enforce them. Rules save you time because your thinking has already been done for you when a new situation arises. And they save you from saying yes in a weak or hectic moment when you should be saying no. Indeed, rules allow you to say one long, continuous no and yet not appear to be an ogress or a chronic criticizer. Finally, rules can guide the child who stays home alone, and can narrow the gap between a sitter's parenting techniques and yours.

How should you go about setting rules? Try to strike a balance between peer practice, your child's particular makeup, and what you can live with. Then regularly reexamine your decisions. Rules that safeguard a child at age nine may be excessively restrictive for him at age eleven. When you're together with your youngster, enforce the rules as consistently as possible. But when you're apart, accept the fact that you can't control his behavior. Nor can you count on the other adults in his life to control it, either. But persevere in your own training efforts anyway. Although you don't spend all day with him, you're the most important person in your child's world and as such your attitudes and actions are the crucial ones.

Finally, remember that all discipline is not negative. You may find yourself responding more often to bad behavior than good because the former is so much more conspicuous (or frequent) than the latter. But make a particular effort to comment on and reward your child for the good things he does. It will make the training process so much more pleasant—and effective.

Sometimes Things Go Wrong

Establishing a body of sensible rules within a matrix of loving discipline should minimize friction between you and your child. Still, there will be times when the two of you are just not on the same wavelength—indeed, when your only form of communication may be yelling at the top of your lungs. For some mothers even a slightly raised voice means the end of the world, perhaps because they were not permitted to show emotion as children. For other mothers unpleasant scenes were so common in their childhood that they think fighting is the norm. We'd like to think that the norm should be somewhere in between.

On the one hand, home can be a refuge from the big, bad world; on the other hand, to be valuable home has to be at least partially of the world. And in this world wherever there are people, especially people related to one another, there is bound to be conflict. Conflict is not only inevitable, it is not necessarily bad. In fact, constructively resolved, it is far healthier than the repression or denial of anger, because anger does not simply go away as it appears to. It goes underground to reappear in some other form. Therefore, if a child is allowed to experience conflict in the home, he will be better able to cope with it later on.

Conflict can be particularly threatening to you, the working mother, because you may immediately leap to the conclusion that it is somehow your fault. Let us assume that a child is upset and is acting out his anger. What are the possible reasons for it? He might be having a problem with his teacher, his baseball swing, his girlfriend, his developing body, his acne, his algebra, the color purple. In short, there are a million things that could be bothering him and none of them would have anything to do with you. Nor would they be resolved by your quitting work.

You can help a child to solve his problem by tactful prodding, by letting him know that you are on his side, and by assuring him that he is not alone in whatever is bothering him. But you cannot allow him to take out his unhappiness on the family. Nor should you be afraid to show him when his actions meet with your disapproval. In fact, it is important to display the anger, annoyance, or disappointment his behavior provokes. This display proves to the child that he, too, can get angry without jeopardizing your love. It also proves that his actions affect you and that, by extension, he is important to you. If you remain indifferent no matter what stunt he pulls, he can only conclude that he is unimportant and unloved.

How you handle your anger is of crucial importance, however. If you manifest it in sarcasm and character assassination, it could destroy your relationship with the child. And if you lash out with your hands, you're setting the worst possible example. A controlled spank is appropriate for a two-year-old who cannot be dealt with verbally, but hitting has no place in the discipline of an older child. Hitting communicates the message that adults cannot control themselves any more than children. If you want to use body language effectively in times of anger, ask your child to leave the room or physically vacate it yourself.

Often a child, especially a teen-ager, will fall back on the phrase, "But you don't understand me." When an argument does not stem from a lack of understanding but from incompatible points of view, you can make clear that you certainly do understand him, but that you don't *agree* with him. Hear a child out and then, if you still feel you are right, stick to your guns. Your confidence in yourself will be so reassuring to your youngster that it will more than make up for any single "wrong" decision you might make.

When the resolution of an argument or the response to misbehavior requires disciplinary measures, take them as soon as possible even if it means working through a surrogate. But whatever course of action you decide upon—isolation, deprivation, extra work—don't let the punishment exceed the crime and don't let it infringe upon your quality time together. That should be inviolable.

Because of your continuing efforts to get close to your child year in and year out, you need not be concerned that one argument or even ten arguments will destroy your relationship. The testimony of countless mothers in your situation is the best evidence that a good parent-child relationship can withstand your going to work and his growing pains without falling apart. As one woman described her relationship to her child in the book

Working Mothers: "Our love for each other was not made up of car pools, lunches, and rainy afternoons in the house. It was made of a kind of absolute assurance we both felt that no matter where we both were, we trusted that we were still important to each other."

11

Points of Contention

It's reassuring to know that a certain amount of friction is inevitable in family life and that it's not necessarily anyone's fault or failure. Still, you don't want to let every skirmish escalate into a major war. To achieve a somewhat peaceful coexistence, we suggest that you examine your pet peeves. Everyone has them, everyone overreacts to them, and everyone finds them lurking within her very own children.

Common Conflicts

Although we can't discuss all the everyday annoyances that send a mother up the wall, we have analyzed the most common parent-child conflicts and come up with suggestions for their resolution. In alphabetical order they are:

Bedtime: In some homes there's a tug of war every night over bedtime. The mother wants the children to go to bed at a reasonable hour so that she can be alone by herself or with her husband. The children want to stay up—and some of them truly can't fall asleep. If bedtime is a constant source of friction in your home, here's an effective way to proceed.

Decide upon a bedtime for each child, taking into account his total need for sleep, peer practice, the hour a younger or older sibling goes to bed, and your own convenience. Once you've established this time, stick to it. Every so often you may want to make an exception for a special event, but the very next night it should be bedtime as usual.

Then, as the moment approaches, start to slow down the pace. Allow the child to relax from the evening's excitement by turning off the TV, reading him a story, or having a quiet chat. Once the lights go out, however, your involvement with him ends. Under no circumstances should you spend your precious free time making endless trips to his room with water, cookies, and answers to unimportant questions.

Just as you must be firm about the time and ritual of going to bed, so you must be adamant about the place. You may allow a young child to fall asleep in your bed or on the living room couch "just this once." Unfortunately, "once" has a habit of turning into twice and thrice, and before you realize what's happening the child will sleep only when he's *not* in his own bed. Indeed, he'll wake up each time he's returned there. Since you cannot go into work bleary-eyed from such bedtime capers, you've got to put your foot down. There's only one place for a child to go to sleep—and that's in his own crib or bed.

You may be tempted to bend this rule if your young child seems to fear being alone in the dark. But in point of fact small children do not have enough imagination to be afraid of things that go bump in the night. So, if a two- or three-year-old tries to manipulate you with this routine, don't let him. He has simply learned a combination of words that he knows affects you and he's using them.

Sometimes a youngster under the age of three will start out in his own bed, but then he'll leave it to climb into yours. If your young child starts to play this game, keep your door shut or put a chain latch on his so that he can see out but can't leave. He will probably become furious at this turn of events, but once he's become convinced that you're unobtainable, he will fall asleep in his own bed and stay there.

"Sleep time" as a phenomenon is quite distinct from bedtime. It is important that you keep the two separate in your mind because, while you can control the latter, there is nothing you can do about the former. Fortunately, many children fall asleep shortly after they go to bed. But if your child is not one of them, do not hassle him about it. Rather, allow him to play, sing, talk, read, and listen to the radio. Do not allow him to leave his room, though, or watch TV (which is too stimulating), or monopolize your time. If you keep him away from the action, this child will conk out when he's fatigued. And in so doing, incidentally, he will get all the sleep he needs.

Run-of-the-mill sleep problems tend to decrease in children above the age of four or five no matter what course of action their mothers have followed. Occasionally, though, an older child will also have trouble falling asleep. His temporary insomnia might have been brought on by the beginning or end of school, setting the clocks ahead, or a bout of illness. And since sleep is a habit, it might take a few nights to reestablish the old pattern. If he continues to have trouble sleeping, you might try some of the techniques discussed above. If they don't work, then you might want to discuss the situation with your pediatrician. Not sleeping or at least complaining about not sleeping is rather common in children, but fatigue is not usually the result. Fatigue coupled with the inability to sleep and fatigue coupled with sleeping too much are combinations that should be checked out.

Clothes: Disagreements over clothing can begin disconcertingly early with your child's decision to wear a certain garment for two weeks in a row. Although you're horrified to see it on his back day after day, let him wear it—at least until it becomes hazardous to his health. This is a normal behavior pattern and one that he'll outgrow. Sometimes it's the nature of an outfit, not the repetition of it, that bothers you. But rather than get into a frustrating argument with a three-year-old about how purple clashes with red, try to live with it. His beloved outfit may be doing for him what your beloved outfits do for you: making him feel attractive and self-confident. Besides, purple and red could be the next "in" combination.

An older child's taste in clothing is more likely to be influenced by her peers. And no matter how much you may disapprove, if "everyone's" wearing something, she'll want to wear it too. Since it's not worth making an enemy for life to get your own way on this point, we suggest that you effect a compromise: Allow your daughter to dress as she sees fit when she goes out with her friends, but insist that she dress according to your standards when she goes out with you. A child of any age will sometimes fall in love with a garment in the store, insist that you buy it, and then refuse to put it on her back when she gets it home. In this instance we think you should be tough. Make it clear that either she wears the garment or does without. You can at least hope that she'll learn her lesson and be a more careful shopper the next time around.

The final and perhaps greatest bone mothers have to pick with their offspring about clothing relates to the instant aging process. It is uncanny how a child can put on a brand-new pair of pants and in no time at all have ripped or permanently stained them. The next time your youngster does in something new, take a deep breath and repeat fifteen times, "He did not do it on purpose." Actually, there's a gremlin in the dungaree factory who builds holes into the knees so that working mothers will have something to sew in their spare time. Since the same gremlin works on little girls' tights, we suggest that you store the good ones in your drawer until special occasions warrant their use.

Eating: A child's irritating eating patterns and poor table manners can ruin the family dinner. Instead of the pleasant "quality time" you used to look forward to after work, this meal becomes a battle royal—with you as the inevitable loser. To help you improve the situation we shall discuss six of the most common dinner table offenders. If your child is among them, bear in mind that it doesn't matter whether he developed his bad habits early in life or acquired them more recently. Either way the treatment is the same.

We'll start with the "Milkaholic." He's the one who is too lazy or too busy to do anything but drink huge quantities of milk. You cure him by setting a limit on his intake. Tape his name to a clear 2-pint pitcher, fill it with milk, and place it in the refrigerator. As he starts to consume the milk, let him know that when the bottom is reached, he will be restricted to water and a little juice until the following morning. This strategy works with the juiceaholic, too.

Our second offender is the "Snack King." He is never hungry at mealtimes because he eats so much in between. With him you've simply got to shut down the kitchen. Declare the cookie jar and bread box off-limits and even transfer their contents to the freezer, if necessary, to be used on an as-needed basis.

Our next case study is the "Short Order Kid." He likes so few foods that he always seems to require a separate menu— which is just what you don't need at 6:00 P.M. To shape him up, stop (pardon the pun) catering to his whims. You may offer him a substitute for one out of every ten foods served, but beyond that he either has to eat something from the meal's *one* set of dishes or go without. Eventually, he will get hungry enough to start sampling what the rest of the family eats.

The behavior of our fourth subject, "Mister Picky," is similar to that described above and so is its cure. Mister Picky usually has an aversion to a particular category of food, be it meat, vegetable, or fruit. Since you want him to get over that aversion, do not offer him substitutes. Rather, put a small serving on his plate without comment and then make a wide enough variety of foods available to him during the day so that he ends up having a balanced diet.

Now we come to our fifth case, the "Walking Gourmet." He is the child who takes a bite, runs around a bit, takes another bite, and then is off again. The only cure for this jack-in-the-box is to declare his meal over the first time he leaves the table. Denied access to his food, he'll quickly learn that in order to satisfy his hunger he must stay put.

Our sixth case is known as the "Slob." His antics range from the mildly irritating to the definitely disgusting, from the failure to use a napkin to the feeding of ears, nose, and floor. If the age for such gross misbehavior has long since past, do not put up with it. Remove your child's food as soon as he starts to play with it or banish him to a separate room where he will have to dine alone. Don't yell, don't spoil your own meal, but don't feed him yourself for the sake of neatness either. He won't learn anything from that except that being a slob brings him increased attention—which is just what he wants.

We end this section on eating with a short discussion of the "Overanxious Mother." Although not a juvenile offender, she contributes equally to the tension at the dining room table. This woman, who is herself a product of the clean-plate-club mentality, practically counts every morsel that goes down her child's throat. And if that child is by nature a small eater, the sparks inevitably fly. Don't be like her. First, convince yourself that your child will not starve himself to death. Second, plan appealing, nutritious meals, give the child a multivitamin with iron if you like, and then consider your job done. Ironically, the less concern you show, the more likely he is to eat. In this as in all the foregoing situations, you will get further if sitters and other temporary surrogates (named Grandma) back you up. But even if they don't, persevere in your approach when you are home.

Extracurricular Activities: Although many mothers take a prenatal vow not to let their offspring get over-committed, they find it hard to follow through on this pledge. Some communities provide such a tempting array of after-school and weekend activities that it's difficult to restrict a child's participation in them. Moreover, once they start to work, these very same mothers begin to look upon organized activities as a wholesome way to keep their children occupied (i.e., away from the TV and out of trouble) until they themselves get home. We think that you, too, should keep an open mind about extracurricular activities and even encourage your children to participate in them, though it might entail making complicated arrangements at the start.

Transportation is usually the rub. Promote activities that are held on the school premises right after school hours. If there's a late bus so much the better, but foot power is acceptable too, as long as the child is old enough and will walk home in all kinds of weather. If the extracurricular activity demands chauffeuring, you'll have to decide whether it means enough to either one of you to find substitute drivers and then owe them your life in paybacks. When the activity is held in the evening or on weekends, you will be in a position to drive—but should you? If it is very important to the child, a short-term proposition, not too inconvenient, and not just one of the slew of trips he's been committing you to lately, you probably won't mind. But if those conditions are not present, don't feel you automatically have to say yes. Make it clear at the start just how much chauffeuring you're going to do and then leave it up to the child to work within your requirements or find his own way. This approach should cut down on arguments over transportation.

Free Time: It may bug you to see your child waste his free time on frivolous pursuits. But as valuable as organized activities are, hanging around can sometimes be just as valuable and maybe even more so. Children need time to think, to be alone, to unwind, to fool around—just to be. They also need time to be bored. Many children today have scarce inner resources because so many of their waking hours have always been spent in purposeful activity. Looked at from this perspective, doing nothing is really doing something and something quite constructive at that. So the next time you find yourself haranguing your child about not putting his free time to best advantage, reconsider. Your feelings may be misguided.

Friends: From time to time you and your child may argue—heatedly—about her friends. You may disapprove of one youngster who seems to be leading her astray or bringing out the worst in her. Or it may be a whole clique to whom you object, because they are putting pressure on your daughter to join them in questionable activities.

Since friendship can be a volatile subject, you should approach it gingerly. If you come on too strong, your daughter might take great offense and even try to get in thicker with the object of your disapproval just to prove her independence. To avoid either occurrence, we suggest that you make your feelings known without hysteria and without demanding that she break off the relationship. Just ask her to give your line of reasoning some thought. Then, without making her aware of it, you could try to manipulate her activities so that she sees more of some children and less of others. You could also try to scrutinize her activities when you're around and make sure she attends only well-supervised functions when you're not.

Along the way, though, ask yourself why your child is seeking out this seemingly undesirable character: what is she getting out of the relationship and who is actually influencing whom? Also be candid with yourself about your real objections. If they amount to no more than an aversion to the youngster's style or that of his parents, you may be jeopardizing your relationship with your daughter over something very silly indeed.

The younger the child, the greater the control you can exert over her choice of companions. After she reaches a certain age, though, you will no more be able to censor her friendships than her reading material. But this is not all bad. We think youngsters have to get to know a variety of people in order to develop good judgment about them. After all, you won't be around to choose your child's friends forever.

Money: To keep money from becoming a point of contention, start giving it to your child early in the form of a small allowance. You decide how much the allowance will be, usually by asking around, and the child decides how he's going to spend it. You may point out the advantages of saving up for something special, but don't force the issue. If the allowance is to be a learning experience, you must allow the child to learn the hard way. Moreover, while some portion of it could be set aside for a general savings account, we feel that in general spending money should be spent.

As your child gets older and needs milk money, lunch money, and dues of various kinds, the concept of an allowance can be expanded to include all these small outlays. Some parents go even further. They sit down with their child and arrive at a weekly or monthly sum that includes everything from the church collection to school supplies. Then they turn this amount over to the child, who must practice real restraint if he is to live within his budget. Not only does this arrangement remove money as a frequent source of conflict between you and your youngster, but it provides him with invaluable training in fiscal responsibility as well.

In addition to their allowance, many teenagers earn substantial sums of money babysitting, mowing lawns, and working full time in the summer. If your child has this kind of independent income, you'll save yourself many arguments with him by making rules about it in advance. We think you should insist that a certain percentage be earmarked for savings, with or without a definite goal in mind. And you should also retain veto power over the money's ultimate disposition. If your child wants a motorcycle, for example, and you do not want him to have a motorcycle, you have the right to prevent him from buying one while he is living under your roof—and the fact that he can pay for it himself should not deter you from doing so.

Negativity: When a child is going through the Terrible Two's or some other negative stage of life, he may react to the world with just one word: NO. Once compliant and eager to go along with whatever you and his caretakers suggested, he now seems to balk at the simplest request. His negativity impedes progress. It also turns Mommy from a sunny sort into a shrieking witch.

If your child is currently living through a negative stage, we suggest that you never ask him a question when the answer you want is yes. Simply make the kind of positive declaration that assumes compliance, such as, "We're going to the market now." If that doesn't work, tell the child why he should do whatever it is you're requesting. You won't persuade him but he might change his mind while you're talking, and in the process you're satisfying your own need to deal with other human beings on a rational level.

There are a few other things you could try, too, depending on the situation. Where you have physical control, you could *make* the child do what you want, and under other circumstances—such as picking up his belongings—you could offer to help. Finally, you could withdraw your request. Sometimes it's better to let an issue drop than to face a showdown over it. You are not losing face here, because the decision is yours. Moreover, being in a perverse stage, your youngster may just decide to comply with your original request the moment you tell him to forget it.

Pets: The smart working mother avoids adding nonhuman creatures to her household for as long as possible. All of them require care, create messes, and cost money. Moreover, they may provoke animosity between mother and child, because the former expects the latter to be responsible for his pets and the latter so rarely comes through. For your own sake, then, stave off the child's requests (and your own craving) for a domesticated animal until the youngster is old enough to help care for it. You will also be doing the pet a favor, because very young children are a menace to animal life, as any veterinarian will tell you.

When you can put him off no longer, try to persuade your child to accept something that lives in a tank of water or a cage. If he won't go along with that, suggest a cat, and only as a very last resort a dog. But if a dog it is to be, bear in mind that all dogs are not created equal: small ones are easier than large ones, short-haired are better than long-haired, and large, long-haired dogs that slobber are the absolute worst. All those gorgeous Old English sheepdogs on television are owned by professional trainers, not working mothers, so don't get carried away into buying one. If you do, your at-home time will become one long session with the vacuum cleaner.

Possessions: Children's carelessness with possessions is a major bone of contention in many families. If it is in yours, expect—and train—them (even the smallest ones) to respect your property. What they do with their own possessions is another story. You may commiserate with the youngster who has ruined a watch, a bike, or an expensive dress, but you do not have to replace it for her. Stand firm. If you allow yourself to become a twenty-four-hour-a-day spare parts concession, your children will have no incentive to take better care of their things.

In fairness to young people, though, they cannot be expected to know automatically that expensive, sophisticated toys and equipment need care and maintenance. Many times a good bicycle is ruined because a child who is fully capable of riding it has not been taught or encouraged to maintain it. This is where you come in. Instead of blowing your stack after the fact, prevent ruination by showing the child how to care for his possessions, by giving him safe places to store them, and by providing the tools necessary for maintaining them.

Sometimes the sticking point with possessions is not their abuse but their use or, more accurately, their lack of use. Often a child will plead for some expensive item which, once granted, he tries out a few times and then consigns to the back of his closet. Before you spend a lot of money on another of these one-day wonders, try to borrow, rent, or buy it secondhand. This makes particularly good sense with a new hobby or sport that could involve a considerable outlay. If you start out low, you won't get (as) angry with your child when he drops out and blows your investment. Besides, you can always trade up later if the child demonstrates continued interest in or mastery of the activity.

Practicing: If your child is studying an instrument or taking some other kind of lesson, you may find yourself at loggerheads with him when he doesn't practice. Scolding and punishments may work for a while, but they are likely to engender hostility toward the activity. Instead of reprimanding him, join the child from time to time during practice sessions to offer moral support and companionship (never criticism!). You could also reschedule his rehearsals to take advantage of his energy cycle, even if it means your getting dressed to the screech of a violin. But if the child really does not seem to enjoy the activity, will never do it spontaneously, and does not improve with grudging practice—reconsider the whole enterprise. Perhaps you should save your money and your relationship by letting him quit. We're opposed to permitting a youngster to give up every time the going gets rough. Still, no one sticks with everything he's ever tried (surely you didn't), and it's possible that your child either has no aptitude for the field or is too young for it. Lessons dropped now can always be resumed at a later date when the motivation for taking them will be his—not yours—as will the responsibility for practicing.

Responsibility: Her children's inability to accept responsibility is the bane of many a working mother's existence. Because the youngsters are careless, forgetful, and immature, these women feel that they must do everything for them—and grow resentful in the process. If you and your child are also coming a cropper over his irresponsibility, start to remedy the situation by examining your own attitude. It is quite possible that you have been tacitly saying to the child, "Show me that you can do it and then I will let you do it." But responsibility must be given—it cannot be earned—and for the parent to wait to be shown before giving is to wait forever. The parent who *expects* a child to be able to handle a given situation more often than not has her expectations fulfilled. Of course, your child will still let you down from time to time, especially when the goals set for him are unrealistically high. But giving him the chance to try encourages him to become more grown up. And, what's just as important, it places the responsibility for his life where it belongs: on his own shoulders.

Sibling Arguments: You walk into the house at the end of the work day looking forward to bright tales of school and Cub Scouts. Instead, you are greeted with: "He pushed me into the wall!" "I did not!" "So I bit him and then he. . . ." Your first reaction (after the impulse to walk right out again) is to jump in and take sides. But lest you become part of the problem instead of the solution, do not even try to assign blame. You will be wrong at least half the time and will wind up punishing the responder instead of the instigator. In most instances there is no easily discernible right and wrong anyway—only action and reaction, thrust and parry, whine and scream.

If you can stand the noise and the two children are relatively evenly matched, leave them alone. Siblings have to arrive at a modus vivendi sometime and they'll probably arrive at it sooner if you stay out of the picture. Avoid imposing a settlement that automatically requires the older child—merely by virtue of his age—to give in to the "baby." However, when the noise starts to get on your nerves or one youngster has a sizable edge over the other, you should step in to the extent of sending each one to a separate room. In that way the punishment is equal—the children cannot play with each other—and you have been able to maintain the stance of a referee instead of a prosecuting attorney.

Sleeping: See "Bedtime" in this chapter.

Sloppiness: See Chapter 9, "Pitch In!"

Social Life: In our American mystique, the "good home" is the one that is the gathering place for all the neighborhood kids. The "good mom" is the one who's always in the kitchen with her apron on. She cheerfully invites the gang to stay for supper and she's delighted to put up a little guest for the night. You're not. You're dead tired from a long day of work and you're sick of having children underfoot, especially children who eat up all your food and drip ice cream on the rug you spent your last free day cleaning. You'd like to tell them all to clear out or at least clean up after themselves. But you're afraid to say a word because that would make you a "bad mom," and your self-image may already be more than a little shaky on that score.

You could try to strike a compromise, however, by working out a schedule with your children as to when they can feel free to have their friends over and when you'd prefer to be alone with the family. Like rules, a schedule gives you something to fall back on besides saying no. It also gives your children a graceful out with their friends. As for mess-makers, no compromise is called for. In your house everyone has to clean up after himself, period.

Studying: Your son's study habits may be sending you up the wall. You can't understand how he learns anything while listening to the stereo, watching TV, or talking on the telephone. Nor do you think that he puts in enough time on his assignments. In fact, though, your son may be learning a great deal and getting good grades. If this is the case, don't let his study habits trouble you. But if he is not doing well in school or could be doing a lot better, help him to get organized—and do it without lectures or criticism.

Attach homework to a time, such as the hour after dinner, and to a place, usually his desk. When the hour is up, check to see not *how* the work was done but that it was done. With long-term projects, help your child to gather his materials, spread them out in an out-of-the-way place, and set a timetable for progress. Then encourage him to keep pace with this timetable lest the last night find the two of you frantically assembling the pieces—just when you have work of your own to get ready for the morning.

It is also appropriate for you to advise your son on suitable topics for reports and to quiz him before a test. But beyond such generalized coaching, there is little you can do to improve his performance. To attempt to reteach what was presented in class is to invite a permanent state of war between you. Very few parents, including professional teachers, can teach their own children. Some parents get too emotionally involved and wind up fuming when a child seems unable to grasp the materials. They may also use methods that bear no relationship to the way the material was presented in school originally, thus confusing the youngster even more. Ultimately the responsibility for learning must rest with your son, both because it is rightfully his and because you have more than enough responsibilities of your own.

Telephone: What is more annoying to caller and callee than constant interruptions and even insistent screams from children when you are trying to carry on a conversation? If this goes on all the time in your house, instruct the children *not*—repeat, *not*—to disturb you when you are talking on the phone and to take their arguments elsewhere. To return the favor, do not answer your messages the moment you walk in the door or initiate long calls at that time. Such actions are extremely frustrating to children who have been bursting with news since three o'clock or earlier.

For their part, youngsters should not be allowed to hang on the phone ad infinitum, talk to callers during dinner, tie up the instrument when you need it, or dial long distance on a whim. A few simple rules about phone use will go far toward reducing household tension on this score. However, things do come up and you should expect to bend the rules to accommodate social crises and impossible homework assignments. At these times the telephone becomes a kind of lifeline for the young person.

Finally, you will be able to look more kindly upon your offspring if they stop answering the phone "Yah?" and start remembering who wanted to talk to you when you were out. In the first instance parental training and much follow-up correction should do the trick. In the second, you will have to get the little ones to turn the receiver over to the sitter or an older child. Instruct every person in your home over the age of six to write down all messages and to leave them next to the phone.

Television: If you feel that TV has gotten out of hand in your home, don't just stand there and fret, do something. Too many people feel that the television set has an independent life of its own. But remember that it doesn't: you control it just as you control so many other aspects of your home environment.

Your objections may center around the content of the shows your children watch. While TV can be instructional, entertaining, and an important shared experience, it can also teach violence and sexual stereotyping. Read advance reviews and watch some of your children's favorite programs with them. Then if you still feel that they are being exposed to undesirable fare, try to get them to switch to something else. With toddlers you do this simply by turning the dial. With older children, you've got to discuss your objections and apply moral suasion.

Chances are that you are even more concerned with *how much* your children watch than with what they watch—and for good reason. Used heavily, TV keeps youngsters from active pursuits; makes them cranky, passive, and unimaginative; and may even turn them into fearful individuals. All this seems a very high price to pay for their occupation while you're either working or desirous of a little peace and quiet. But berating your kids for becoming TV addicts without putting any restrictions on their viewing will produce nothing but hard feelings.

Instead, take a tip from those working mothers who have controlled the TV set by refusing to let it go on before 5:00 P.M., when a child has come over to play, or before a test. A few brave souls have banned it completely on school nights with reportedly fine results. A handful of mothers with preschoolers let TV precede lunch or bedtime but keep the cord unplugged the rest of the day. A number of other working mothers have set aside a specific hour or two in which their children may watch, while still others have allotted their youngsters a certain amount of viewing time to be used as the children see fit.

Of course, once you set up these kinds of rules, you've got to stick to them. If you keep making exceptions to suit your own convenience, the children won't take them seriously, nor will the sitter, whose cooperation is critical. Indeed, she's a key element in the plan. And if she keeps the TV on all day either to pacify the children or to provide herself with company, let her know in no uncertain terms that she can be replaced—by the very set she's watching.

Wanting Things: It is terribly annoying to have a child constantly ask—nay—beg, nag, wheedle, and whine for everything he lays his eyes on. After a while you begin to feel that he thinks of you as nothing more than a "buy me" machine and you grow resentful of it. Yet you're in for an unhappy time if you don't produce. No matter that the items in question are overpriced, poorly made, and of potentially short-lived interest—if you don't get them for him you're the bad guy and you're going to be punished with sulks and tantrums.

How did your child arrive at this depressing state? Partly through the medium of television. Thanks to the power of its commercials, TV has turned millions of children into insatiable wanters and your child is yet another victim of its seductive pitches. Since he cannot be expected to have any sales resistance, do not take your wrath out on him. But do turn the dial to a noncommercial station whenever possible—and leave it there.

Then, too, your own attitude has played a large role in shaping his. You may have been giving in to your child's whims or initiating the gift-giving process to compensate him for having a working mother. If you tried to "make it up to him" with material goods, you inadvertently encouraged him to expect instant, constant, and often expensive gratification. American parents—fathers and nonworking mothers among them—are notorious for trying to buy their children's affection with gifts, but it never works. One simply cannot build a successful parent-child relationship on a foundation of materialistic manipulation. Learn to say no without apologizing for it and your child will eventually get the message. In the process you will improve your mutual relationship and conserve your salary.

Wild After-School Behavior: Your child's teacher may tell you what a marvelously controlled and well-behaved youngster you have. But as you reflect upon the wild Indian who rockets about your home after school—to the great peril of everyone and everything in it—you wonder if she is talking about the right boy. She is. Your son has simply caught on to the kind of "good" behavior required of a student from nine o'clock to three and he is highly motivated to comply with it. But when the day is over he pays for that self-control by being loud, active, and "free" in both actions and words. Instead of trying to change his after-school behavior, understand that it is his safety valve. Give your sitter an idea of what to expect, and then help your son release his pent-up energy by steering him into active pursuits, especially those that will keep him out of doors.

Although you can experience conflict with children of all ages, the likelihood of it increases once your child becomes a teenager. Moreover, the disputes you have with him are apt to be more severe and require special handling. To help you keep the inevitable friction under control, we conclude this chapter with a consideration of that period of life every parent finds difficult: adolescence.

An Age of Contention

Your teenager is an adult-in-progress. This creates problems for you, because you've thought of him and treated him as a child all his life and now he no longer fits that description. It also creates problems for your offspring. Neither child nor adult, he is trying to come to grips with a rapidly expanding milieu. He is coming under great pressure to conform to peer standards that sometimes conflict with those at home. He is trying to cope with a developing body at the same time he is experiencing his first attraction to and for the opposite sex. And above all, he is working himself up to the psychological and physical break from the cozy family nest that has sheltered him throughout childhood.

No one can experience so many basic changes and face life with equanimity. As one psychologist said only half in jest, the normal emotional state of the adolescent is manic-depressive: high one minute, down in the dumps the next. But don't patronize or belittle either state, because to the young person experiencing them, the emotions involved are very real. Indeed, the teenager lives on the cutting edge of life. His elations and depressions, while often short-lived, are sometimes the most intense of his entire life. The events triggering these mood swings may seem inconsequential—meeting *the* girl, being cut from the team, facing an algebra exam, even watching a pimple bloom— yet they are of earth-shattering importance to the adolescent involved. You remember how it was.

While he is in one of his lows, your child may lash out at you for no apparent reason. Or you might start to pick on him simply because you're in a foul mood. But underlying these flare-ups there might exist a permanent state of tension, because you may have invested a great deal of hope and personal ambition in the life of your offspring. Although this is a natural parental tendency, any (subconscious) attempt to recoup on the investment is both destructive and doomed to failure. Your child cannot be expected to follow in your footsteps or to finish the things you left undone.

Nor should he be expected to agree with everything you believe in. Don't automatically consider him "wrong," "bad," or rejecting of you when he strikes out in another direction—he's merely trying to become his own person. Of course, if you try to cram your values down his throat, he may start to reject you. And if you try too hard to protect him from life, he may rebel; so save yourself the trouble. Besides, like the rest of us he will have to do a certain amount of learning the hard way in order to grow up. You can try to advise your child, but you cannot "give" him your experiences on which to build.

All of which points to the fact that it may be just as hard for you to wean yourself away from your youngster as it is for him to wean himself away from you. And many mothers never do manage it. Even when their children are grown up and have children of their own, these women are still trying to govern their offsprings' lives. Lest you fall into that pattern, start trying to relinquish control over your teenager now. Try to accept the fact that for better or worse the bulk of your training is done. Continue to make rules and set standards, but do so to advise rather than to bind the child to you.

Actually, we think that teenagers desperately need the right kind of parental guidance even if—or precisely because—they always seem to be challenging authority. Rules help them to steer a sensible course through the new, larger landscape that's opening up to them. Rules also give them a comfortable out with their peers. If your youngster feels uneasy about some venture his friends are cooking up, it is so much easier for him to blame you for his lack of participation than to decline on his own.

Setting rules with a teenager has to be done with finesse, however. If they're too exacting, he'll find himself permanently lodged in the doghouse, and if they're too numerous, he'll never develop any judgment of his own. Our advice is to concentrate on a few important areas and leave the rest to his discretion. Then when you do decide to take a stand, keep peer standards in mind. To demand that your son wear polyester slacks to school when everyone else is wearing dungarees is to invite a daily squabble and ultimate defiance. You don't have to give in every time your teenager wails: "Everyone else is allowed to do it!," but you can't expect him to deviate too far from the external norms either.

Having set a few key, unambiguous rules, be judicious about enforcing them. Within a framework of overall discipline, there's no reason why you can't make an exception now and then. Allowing some leeway about curfew time seems to us a cheap price to pay for your youngster's goodwill. It can be annoying to have your daughter phone from a party to ask if she can stay out later that night. But the very fact that she phoned shows that she respects the rules—and the person who set them.

Not only must the teenager be governed more sensitively than ever before, but now he must be *asked* in many situations where he was previously *told*. Your adolescent deserves to be consulted on important family matters such as vacations and relocation. And his okay should be obtained—in advance—for functions requiring his presence. It won't do any more to announce a Sunday visit to Grandma's on Saturday night, because the youngster may be unable to change his plans at that point. Nor should he necessarily be asked to. Even where his obligations or desires seem frivolous, you cannot always preempt them—at least not if you want to coexist more or less in peace. You could try to enlist his support for your plans, however, by reasoning with him in an intelligent, uncondescending manner. When approached this way, most teens will respond with remarkably mature and even self-denying behavior.

Of course, all your best intentions and psychologically sound tactics will not make living with an adolescent a breeze. Your teenager may interpret your silences as slights and your suggestions as criticisms—when he's around to hear them. Much of the time he seems so busy with outside interests that he only stops by when he wants to drop off dirty laundry or pick up a hot meal. And when he is in residence, he's likely to be closeted in his room. Sometimes he will favor you with his presence, but he may seem to be there more in body than in spirit. Indeed, the teenager can be so close-mouthed about his private life that he makes the Sphinx look like a stool pigeon. Since he needs to be involved with others, don't nag him to stay home with you. And since he needs privacy, don't pry into his desk or his thoughts—although the temptation to do so is great. Like his mood swings, this behavior is all part of the age.

The same could be said for his tendency to blow up the smallest disagreement into World War III. No sooner has the opening bell sounded than he's lost his temper, cursed, stomped around, and sulked like a three-year-old. We suggest that you try not to descend to his level: don't get off the subject and don't lose your cool. If you seize this opportunity to criticize his life in general and his friends in particular, you'll turn him off completely. If you overreact, you'll wind up arguing over the argument. And if you chase him up the stairs to get in the last word, you'll ultimately chase him out of the house. Let your adolescent retreat to his room and give him as much time as he needs to lick his wounds. When he returns to finish the "discussion," he'll be in a more rational frame of mind.

Fortunately for both of you, you work. This prevents you from brooding over an argument and encourages you to put it into perspective. Obtaining distance from the event should eventually get you to the point where you can laugh at it. Once you've done that, you've got it under control.

12

Major Childhood Problems

Many children manifest various kinds of misbehavior, mal-development, personality deviations, and psychologically created illnesses that are more serious than the irritants discussed in the last chapter. Indeed, at least 20 to 30 percent of all children have a major problem of one kind or another at some point in their lives. Though a mother might try to maintain some perspective about them, her child's troubles inevitably become her troubles. And though she might struggle valiantly to keep her family life in equilibrium, having a chronically unhappy person in the house inevitably makes everyone else unhappy.

If your child has a major problem, you probably find it exhausting to live with. Unable to leave it behind when you go to work, you find it preying upon your mind when you should be thinking of extra carbons, profit and loss statements, and continuing education. Moreover, your child's problem may be such that sitters quickly depart the scene and/or you cannot take advantage of the day-care centers, after-school activities, and camps that would make your life so much easier. Yes, having a troubled child is tough. Since you need a smoothly functioning family to make a go of your life, even a minor childhood problem becomes major—and what we're talking about here is often not minor.

Specific Complaints

If your child has a problem, it could be within your power to make the situation better or worse. You might make it worse if you blame yourself because, as we've pointed out so often in this book, guilt prevents affirmative action. Moreover, there's no reason for you to feel guilty. No study has ever demonstrated that the children of working mothers have more, worse, or different problems from the children of nonworking mothers. You might also make the situation worse if you hold out hope for some miracle cure instead of settling down for the long, hard pull. It is the rare human problem that is quickly resolved.

You will probably help matters if you can think concretely about the problem's possible causes and necessary solutions. Once you've done that, you should seek the best ways to bring it under control. To get you started we offer this rundown of the more common serious childhood complaints.

Aggressiveness: Excessive aggressiveness manifests itself in many ways. It can show up in continual fighting, in the ruination of property, or—turned inward—in self-destructive actions. This behavior springs from a variety of causes. It may be the result of a child's trying to master some difficult situation. It may be the result of parental overindulgence, overprotection, or overwhelming disorganization. It could even be the result of certain types of brain damage. Yet in the appropriate situations and to the appropriate degree, aggression is also a perfectly normal mode of behavior. In those instances it's your perception of it that would make it seem abnormal.

You may first notice aggressive behavior when your child is between the ages of one and two. He may attack all his playmates, taking their toys, hitting and biting them, and generally trying to bend them to his will. For most toddlers this is a normal reaction and has to do with their learning the rules of the "play with friends" game. You cannot explain these rules in any way that your toddler will comprehend, nor can you constantly supervise his play and act as a referee. But what you and your sitter could do is to bring your child together with others of the same bent. As he takes his lumps, he will come to understand that other individuals have rights too.

If your child is no longer a toddler, his aggressive behavior might be just a matter of his asserting his normal rights in an excessive manner. He may have to be taught that there are better ways to do this than by hitting, belittling, verbally abusing, or bullying others. Example plays its role in this, of course. If adults repeatedly hit the child in order to get him to comply with their wishes, he will tend to hit others. And if he hears adults verbally abusing one another when angry or threatened, he will use the same language in similar situations. Therefore, you will want to watch the family's responses and those of the sitter while at the same time letting your child know that there are better ways of persuasion than the angry ones.

If your son is displaying a great deal of aggression, he may also be responding to cultural conditioning. In our society boys are usually permitted to be more aggressive than girls, and in your particular subculture people may be tacitly encouraged to resolve disputes physically rather than verbally. Your child may also be responding to television. It has been asserted repeatedly by psychologists and social analysts that watching violent programs tends to increase the level of aggressive behavior on the part of the viewer and reduce his sensitivity to that violence. Try to cut down on the number of blood-and-guts programs your child watches and see if that helps.

Above all, you and your surrogates must send a firm, clearly understandable message to the child that his aggressive behavior is undesirable. You should try to talk to him calmly about the disadvantages of antisocial behavior and, finally, you will have to apply some reasonable punishments. If none of this seems to penetrate or if the aggressive behavior becomes law-breaking, self-destructive, and dangerous, you should seek professional help, starting with your child's doctor or school psychologist.

Passivity, Shyness, and Loneliness: If your young child is very passive, he was probably born that way and in time will outgrow it. But if you would like him to show more spunk, try the treatment we recommend for his opposite number, the aggressive child: get him together with other youngsters of a similar nature. Your son may simply need to find out how to exert his rights, a lesson best learned among children who do not constantly overwhelm him.

Once your child has left the toddler and nursery-school stage behind, an excessive degree of passivity could very well be cause for concern. We are referring here to the child to whom everything is always happening—through no discernible fault of his own. If your child always seems to be the innocent victim who is unduly oppressed by life, something is wrong. And when his passivity negatively influences his relationships with peers, adult authority figures, or his performance in school, you should have it checked out.

The infant who becomes shy of strangers late in his first year is showing a normal reaction having more to do with his emerging ties to his parents than to an avoidance of strangers. He will outgrow it. But the young child who tends to hang back and needs some time to become accustomed to new situations, especially those involving groups of children, is probably manifesting a normal inborn behavioral trait, one that he will have all his life. If your son is by nature shy, try to prepare him beforehand for new situations and don't push him into them too hard or too fast. Since time and encouragement will warm him up, inform your sitter and teachers that this is the way to proceed.

However, there does come a point where shyness must be considered extreme. No matter what the age of your daughter, her shyness should be considered abnormal when she avoids all new experiences regardless of how well you've prepared her; when she turns down invitations to go to friends' houses; when her life is narrowly circumscribed by her inability to leave home; and when she exhibits marked psychosomatic symptoms in new situations or as a means of avoiding them. Unless her behavior is related to some recent, obviously traumatic event and is in the process of improving, we suggest that you seek professional help.

Loneliness, which is often the outgrowth of either shyness or passivity, may be one of the most important indicators of emotional difficulties later on in life. The lonely child is the one without friends. He is neither liked nor disliked by his peers, but tends to be ignored by them. He hovers at the edge of activities rather than fully participating, and on the rare occasions he does attempt to join in, he doesn't seem to know what to do.

If you recognize your child from this description, take heart. He might actually be able to learn how to get along better with his peers. Although any suggestions you make along these lines will probably seem critical and punitive, your sitter, his teacher, or some other involved adult might be able to get him into activities requiring communication and cooperation. They might also be able to offer him specific suggestions for getting along with other kids—what to say and how to behave with them. Your part comes in helping him to develop his self-esteem to the point where he feels he does have something to offer a friend.

One note of caution: There are children with good friendship relationships who nevertheless often seek to be alone. If your child is one of them, don't jump to the conclusion that he has a problem—quite the opposite. He is the kind of self-sufficient, self-motivated person who will always be able to find something to do whether he has someone to do it with or not.

In evaluating your child's loneliness, look at his total behavior. Decide whether he is alone at his own choosing or because no one else wants to be with him. There is no law that says a child has to be popular. Nor is that even a valid goal for the youngster who is simply not cut out to be "one of the guys." But the absence of even one good friend should alert you to the possibility of a major personality problem.

Lying, Cheating, and Stealing: If your child manifests any traits of the "dishonesty syndrome," don't leap to the conclusion that he's a nogoodnik who is destined for a life of crime. While lying, cheating, or stealing can be symptomatic of a serious underlying problem, more often than not they are entirely within the bounds of normality.

When the three-year-old lies, for example, he is really doing some wishful thinking. The child is entering a very magical period in his life in which all sorts of imaginary playmates and supernatural phenomena occur. Your child's fantasizing becomes especially prominent when he has done something he was not supposed to do and it went wrong. He may say the dog did it or the man in the moon did it, even though he knows that you know that *he* did it. But according to three-year-old logic, if he wishes hard enough, maybe the wish will become the reality.

What should you do? What *not* to do is make the judgment that this child has told a lie. If you or your sitter know and not just suspect that the child is indeed responsible, then reinforce reality by pointing out to him that although he might wish it to be different, he did the deed. And if some disciplinary principle has been violated, then discipline him. But do not increase the punishment because the child has not come forward and, George Washington-like, told the truth. He never thought he was telling a lie.

The five-year-old, on the other hand, has the "sticky fingers" problem. Although his parents have spent years trying to get him to share his possessions, they are often mystified by their child's propensity to come home from school or from a friend's house with his pockets stuffed with things he "borrowed"— without the permission of the lender. Personal property concepts are confused at this age, and this sort of "borrowing" is not uncommon. Just return the objects in an unembarrassing but emphatic way and chalk up his behavior (which can still be seen in the seven-year-old) to the age.

When you know or even suspect that your older child has been dishonest, confront him with it straight out. Then set about to make immediate restitution of the thing taken, the idea "borrowed," or the advantage received from the lie. Help your child do this in the most dignified way possible, for your object is to teach him about the best in human relations. He'll get quite the opposite message if you set out to make a public spectacle of him. For example, go with him to the store and have him return the object taken or have him pay for it and apologize to the owner. Then give the child extra jobs to work off the cost of such restitution. Along the way avoid laying blame, lecturing, overreacting, and administering harsh punishments. Don't adopt the attitude that there is some deep character defect in your child—it might become a self-fulfilling prophecy. And don't insist that he make a clean breast of it either. When confronted with their dishonesty, most adults will deny, deny, deny—as we saw time and again during Watergate. Why should children be expected to be more noble?

When the dishonest act is no longer an isolated incident but part of a consistent pattern, you can take it as a sign that something is seriously wrong. Your child might be using this antisocial behavior to attract attention from peers and adults, he might be living up to what he thinks others expect of him, or he might be using it to maintain the appearance of success. If these or other serious underlying conditions are present, it will take a great deal of time and skilled professional help to straighten him out. On the other hand, he just might not know any better. If that is the case, you might be able to help him solve his problem simply by clearing up his confusion about sharing, borrowing, and ownership. But you will have to explain these concepts not only as they apply to material goods, but also as they pertain to other people's work and ideas.

Sibling Rivalry: Where there are two or more children in a family, they will automatically manifest some degree of that jealousy and competitive spirit we call sibling rivalry. It is your job to try to direct your children toward those activities in which they do well, to balance the achievements of one with those of the other, and to distribute praise and rewards as equally as possible. But it is beyond the ability of any parent to eliminate sibling rivalry completely.

Sibling jealousy usually manifests itself most intensely when children—especially those between the ages of two and four—are confronted with a new baby brother or sister. The older child's resentment is generally proportional to the amount of dependency he feels on his mother, but wherever sibling rivalry occurs, it is intense. Indeed, it can be equated to the outrage a woman would experience if her husband walked in one day with a new wife on his arm.

Your older child may manifest his resentment in negative comments, attacks on the baby, or veiled hostility such as kissing the infant very hard. He might also make demands on you each time you attend to the baby's needs. Since the older one is apt to revert to acting like a baby himself, don't be surprised if he takes up the bottle, crawls into the crib, and wets his pants. But do not indulge him in this immature behavior. Though he cries out to be babied, give him more privileges and responsibilities than ever before.

In handling sibling rivalry, try to find as much time as possible to be with your older child. Care for the baby out of sight if his reactions are extremely intense, or try to make him feel that this is "our" baby by encouraging him to help in its care. On the reverse side of the coin, don't ignore the newcomer because of the possible effect your attentions might have on the older child. Introduce the older one to the concept of cooperation and sharing toward you, his home, and even some of his possessions. If you go back to work soon after the new baby is born, your sitter must follow your lead. Tell her that you do not want the older one babied or ignored and direct her to play with both children. While not making too much of the older child's aggressive impulses, she must do everything in her power to keep the infant safe.

Fears: Fears are common and to a great extent normal in children as well as in adults. Moreover, they are necessary, because they both motivate much of our behavior and help protect us from harm. Fears may be objective (caused by things seen or heard) or subjective (caused by feelings). In childhood either type can be developmental. This means that unless they are excessive, fear of the dark, of water, of being lost, or of separation may be based more on limited comprehension than anything else. Such fears can be expected to decrease with advancing age and understanding.

Many fears are learned through encounters with frightening situations. Others are obtained by exposure to and imitation of the fears of adults. Still other fears are inculcated by parents and sitters when they want to warn their charges away from danger, discipline them, or keep the children dependent. Recent research would lead us to believe that excessive viewing of violence on TV is also fear-producing. The message youngsters internalize is that something bad will happen when they go outside, that various persons are trying to break into their homes, and that all strangers are bad. Finally, fears can result from unresolved feelings of hostility toward loved ones or emotional experiences beyond the child's ability to cope. They often occur at the beginning of new experiences, changed circumstances, or major alterations of a child's routine.

No matter what the initiating cause, deal with your child's fears when they begin to interfere with his life or impinge upon the actions of other members of the family. Keeping your own anxiety under control will help in this endeavor. Just talking to him about the fear and explaining the natural phenomena involved can be effective. Sometimes increasing his competence does the trick, as in teaching a child who is afraid of water how to swim. And many times exposure to the threatening situation causes its effect to decrease over time. Older children can often be taught certain techniques to help them overcome a fear. For example, you could tell the youngster to be a better friend to himself by reassuring himself just as he would reassure a pal. In addition, encourage him to stop scolding himself for being afraid. Tell him it's not his "fault." But do make your child understand that fears tend to get worse if no effort is made to combat them.

Do not attempt to criticize or belittle your child out of a fear.

That approach never works. Telling him that his fear is silly will only make him feel inadequate and will not banish the dread. But you should not give in to him when he seems to be manipulating you through his anxieties. Children quickly learn what brings them attention and special privilege, and they will wield this club skillfully in order to get their own way. If you sense that this is happening, treat the fear like any other bad habit that has to be curbed. Since you must work through a sitter or other surrogate some of the time, instruct her to handle your child's fears by simple reassurance, by distracting him with games or stories, and by resisting his manipulative attempts. Moreover, warn her against communicating her own anxieties or falling back on the "boogeyman" school of discipline.

Excessive fears that are the result of severe inner conflicts, that have gone on for long periods without decreasing, that do not respond to understanding and firm handling, or that border on phobias may need long and multidisciplinary treatment. Indeed, any fear that becomes unrealistic, paralyzing, and out of proportion to the stimulus requires professional attention.

Nightmares and Night Terrors: These phenomena often crop up during periods of stress and emotional strain as well as during times of excitement and overstimulation. Both of them are really fright reactions during sleep. In the nightmare the child awakes from a sound sleep in terror and can relate at least some of the content of the dream that both scared and woke him. He is oriented, can usually be calmed fairly easily, and can be put back to sleep within a short time.

Night terrors are different. The child may begin to scream or show a fright reaction but is still asleep when his parents rush to his bedside. He does not react to those around him and may engage in agitated, fearful, or peculiar behavior. The attack may subside spontaneously in a few minutes or you may have to forcibly wake the child to bring it to an end. If he is having a night terror, your child won't have any recollection of it or the fears that set it off.

Simple, infrequent occurrences of either nightmares or night terrors may need no more attention than decreased stimulation and excitement before bed. But where a persistent pattern seems to be developing, you should review—and try to ameliorate—the emotional and environmental factors that might be triggering it.

Tics and Habits: These are the unconscious repetitive mannerisms or actions that—despite your best efforts—you find so irritating in your own child. They include thumb sucking, nail biting, lip chewing, hair pulling or twirling, blinking, coughing and/or throat clearing, shoulder and/or neck twitches, rocking, and head banging. Although many tics and habits seem to have no particular cause, some of them may spring from an organic base. Thus, thumb sucking may grow out of the baby's normal need to suck, eye blinking may follow conjunctivitis, and coughing may begin with a cold or bronchitis. The action becomes a habit when the original reason for it has long since disappeared.

On the whole, tics and habits do not signify the presence of a deep problem, although many parents do note an increase in them during stressful situations. If your child has got something in this category, consider the stresses that are present, but in general the less attention you pay to it the better. Indeed, since tics and habits are largely unconscious, trying to punish, bribe, reward, or shame your child out of one will not work. If your youngster expresses a desire to give up his habit, he may be helped by some reminder such as a glove for the thumb sucker or a hat for the hair puller. However, an aid only works when the child himself is motivated to bring the habit to an end.

Once in a blue moon a child's repetitive motion is symptomatic of a rare disease. Just to be sure your child's is not, you might want to have your pediatrician check it out. If he can find no reason for that odd twitch—and he probably won't be able to—then consider it a habit and do your best to ignore it.

School Phobia: At some point in his school career, one out of every four children is going to experience school phobia. This can manifest itself in such conditions as headaches, stomachaches (with vomiting, cramps, and diarrhea at times), and pains in the arms and legs. The symptoms last for some time but they often disappear once the school year is well under way, possibly to recur after Christmas vacation or in the spring. Your child may experience his particular symptoms at the same or different times of the day, to such an extent that he is incapacitated, or with little more discomfort than a mild complaint. But great or small, the symptoms of school phobia are caused by muscle tension in the head, stomach, or limbs that results from internalized anxieties.

Many authorities consider school phobia to be the result of separation anxiety. But in some children it seems to be a consequence of the pressures generated by certain standards of performance. Thus school phobia occurs in good students as well as bad, and its symptoms frequently occur before such stressful or highly anticipated events as exams and important team games.

If your child exhibits the symptoms of school phobia, have him checked out by your physician. Follow through on the proper X-rays and lab studies where indicated. Then, once the presence of a serious illness has been eliminated, treat the symptoms with the care they deserve. This care could range from skillful neglect for the child with minimal symptoms to psychotherapy for the child whose life is constantly being affected by his stomach or his head. Just allowing the youngster some method of blowing off the accumulated daily steam could help. Try something, because research has shown that the complaints of school phobia do become chronic, indeed lifelong, if the afflicted child does not develop any better means of expressing his tension than by taking it out on his own body.

Learning Disabilities and Hyperactivity: We include these syndromes here because, no matter what they really are, they do affect a child's behavior. They may occur alone or in combination with one another.

By definition these two conditions are problems that interfere with the education of the child with average or better-than-average intelligence. The child who has a learning disability cannot seem to acquire the basic skills of reading, writing, math, or spelling, no matter how hard he tries. The hyperactive child cannot sit still long enough to learn or cannot focus on tasks long enough to do any constructive work. Although some parents seem to have an inkling that something's wrong before their child starts school, the problem usually surfaces when he comes under the scrutiny of a teacher.

If your child has a learning disability and/or is hyperactive, there are some critical facts that you must know. The first is that the cause of these problems is not known—repeat, *not known*. Despite the rash of articles and books blaming them on birth injury, food additives, psychogenic factors, television, and child-rearing practices, we don't yet have a clear idea of what the cause or causes are. The second critical fact is that the child who has these problems soon recognizes that he is different from his peers—that he has difficulty where they do not—and this lowers his self-esteem. The third critical fact and the one probably most difficult for you to deal with is that your child may start to display some secondary behavior problems. For example, the child who has great difficulty learning may turn the whole process off and not even make any attempt at new tasks. Not attempting means not having to face the failure that he has so often experienced. Or, alternatively, he may become the class cut-up, because this brings him the peer recognition that he cannot obtain through his school work.

In any event, once the question of a learning disability or hyperkinesis has been raised regarding your child, get it checked out with a reputable professional and then follow through on the recommended course of treatment. Wishing will not make these problems go away. On the contrary, if neglected they will become increasingly difficult to deal with, because they will be complicated both by your emotional reactions and by your child's behavioral defenses against his inability to measure up.

Enuresis or Bedwetting: This is one of the more distressing problems of childhood. It is particularly irksome for you, because it means you've got to face a soaked bed each morning while you're rushing to get ready for work. Not only does the bed need changing, but the sheets, pajamas, blankets, and child need washing as well.

Although some 50 to 60 percent of all three-year-olds are dry at night, repeated surveys have shown that up to one-quarter of all five-year-olds are still wetting their beds. Indeed, many authorities do not think that children under five with this problem should be included in the enuretic group.

The usual bedwetter has never been dry and his problem has been blamed on many causes. Over the years such things as urinary tract abnormalities, urinary infections, small bladders, deep sleep, and behavioral and psychiatric problems have all been implicated. Even the thought that the bedwetting is simply a prolongation of a bad habit has had its proponents.

Certainly the child who has been dry and then begins to wet the bed—as well as any other child with a history of bedwetting—should have his urine checked. However, the cause rarely lies there for the continuous wetter. The newer thinking tends to look at bedwetting as an example of a maturational delay (usually inherited), especially when it crops up in the child who has no other behavioral problems. This theory would seem to be borne out by the fact that only 2 or 3 percent of all twelve-year-olds continue to have the problem even when nothing is done about it.

And the fact is, very little can be done about it. Withholding fluids before bed, punishments, and most other methods that may have been passed down to you by your family will not work. Putting a child on the toilet in the middle of the night works with some children but not most. There are also a few medications or conditioning therapies your doctor may be able to suggest, but they can be used only after the youngster has reached a certain age and they, too, are far from foolproof. Instead of looking for a cure, we think that you would do better to count on time to rectify the situation and expend your energies on managing the extra laundry in the meantime. Getting that under control will lessen your resentment toward the bedwetter and get your day off to a smoother start.

Cover the mattress with a moisture-proof pad and buy all bleachable sheets and washable blankets. Then just strip the bed in the morning as a matter of course, dump everything into the washing machine, and remake the bed on the spot with a second set of linens. If you eliminate spread, blanket, and even sheets by using a comforter or light sleeping bag, you will speed up the process considerably. Some mothers find that using diapers at night for the child in the three-to-six age range is a mutually acceptable solution too.

Confusing the issue of bedwetting is the fact that your youngster may be dry when he spends the night elsewhere. This seems to prove that he could get his bedwetting under control if only he would try harder. Not so. Just as a man pinned under a car can somehow find the superhuman strength to lift the car off him, so the bedwetter can temporarily overcome his physical inability to stay dry when he sleeps at a friend's house for one night or several nights. But since, fortunately, your child does not live under that kind of "do or die" stress, you must expect him to relapse when he returns to more familiar surroundings. Lest you make him neurotic about something he can't control, try to keep bedwetting in perspective. It is almost always functional, it is almost never indicative of a serious psychological or organic deviation, and one day, when you're not looking, it *is* going to end.

Obesity: This is a kind of maldevelopment that stems from any of a number of causes. It could be inherited or come from long-term overeating. It might be the result of a personality disorder in which food satisfies some unfulfilled need or calms some inner anxiety. It might spring from self-destructive impulses, or it could simply be due to poor knowledge of nutrition. But for whatever reason they got that way, fat children in our society tend to be unpopular and unhappy and to develop secondary personality problems along the way. Helping your child to keep his weight down could rescue him from becoming one of those lonely and poorly adjusted fat ones.

Although he may not seem to consume a great deal of food, year after year your child may gain more than the normal amount of weight until it becomes obvious to all that something must give. And that something is a percentage of his intake. For the child who is growing normally in height, weight gain is a matter of too many calories. It doesn't take much overeating to eat too much. If a child's activity level is such that he eats as few as 50 calories a day more than he needs for growth or energy, at the end of a year's time he will have gained an excess of 5 pounds. Multiply this by two or three years and the eight-year-old whose height and build indicate a weight of 60 pounds is now 75 pounds or 25 percent overweight.

With most children the goal should not be one of weight loss but weight stabilization. This allows the child's normal growth in height to "catch up" to his weight. Often this can be accomplished by a minimal restriction of calories for if, as we just noted, it takes a measly 50 calories of unburned food a day to create a 5-pound excess weight gain in one year, eliminating that 50 calories (one cookie or equivalent) could stabilize the weight. Your first chores, then, are reading box tops to determine caloric content and obtaining a good calorie counter.

Highly restrictive diets are out in any case, because children need food containing important nutrients and they need proportionately more of it than adults to sustain growth. Also, few if any children under the teen years have the willpower or the concept of body image necessary to refuse the food that is offered to them. No child can be expected to sit at the table and watch his parents and siblings eat things he cannot. If a diet is too restrictive—if it eliminates all the goodies in life—he is likely to become a food thief who steals from his own kitchen or those of his friends. Therefore, the techniques that you use to get him to cut down must be largely unrecognizable.

Buy less and cook less. No one notices a 10 percent reduction in the size of his steak or minds a smaller potato. Also limit the number of cookies you buy each week. Once they are gone, they are gone and they won't be replenished until you go shopping on your next regular market day. Learn to cook low-calorie meals that end with fruit instead of rich desserts. Control the portions, too, by making up each plate individually instead of serving from a platter. Never ask who wants the extra chop or remaining potatoes. If no one realizes that they are left, simply dispose of them quietly. Finally, pack a lunchbox full of low-calorie foods for your youngster instead of having him buy the high-carbohydrate cafeteria meal.

A second set of techniques for reducing food consumption revolves around how the eater eats. Give your overweight child a glass of water before each meal and encourage him to take more of it at the table. Since many big eaters eat too fast, try to get him to put his fork down in between bites and to pause significantly before picking it up again. Allow him to leave the table as soon as he is finished and never cajole him into joining the clean plate club. On the other hand, don't keep nagging at him *not* to eat. You want to make him aware of the correspondence between what he eats and what it does to his body, but you don't want to make him crazy.

While dieting is difficult for adults (as you may know only too well), it is excruciating for children. And obesity clinics that treat young people all agree that the youngsters cannot do it alone: their families must cooperate fully. Therefore, if you have an overweight child, rid your larder of all junk foods (a process that won't do the rest of you any harm either). Limit the consumption of food to one place in the house and close down the kitchen between meals. Either eliminate snacks or pin them down to specific times and specific menus featuring fruit or crunchy vegetables instead of cookies. You've got to be very firm with your sitter on this point or she may bribe your child right into obesity plus.

If all these manipulative techniques are not getting your child to cut down, or if you suspect that his overeating may be symptomatic of some underlying physical or psychological problem, consult your physician.

Reactions to Change: Sometimes difficulties arise with a child but his mother has trouble pinpointing the problem. "He simply acts horrible," "She's become hard to handle," "We used to get along so well and now we're fighting all the time." These typical laments often describe the behavior that results from an upsetting change in the child's world. The change might be anything: parent or child illness; hospitalization; death; divorce; separation; remarriage; a different school; moving to a new community or even to a new house in the same community; the appearance of a new sibling; mother's going to work; mother's quitting work; or a change of jobs by either parent. In short, any change that occurs within his world may disrupt the carefully constructed equilibrium that the child has established. Since he now has a new set of circumstances with which to cope, he may react to the disorganization he feels with a behavioral change. It will take time for him to regain his balance.

Try to understand the change from your child's perspective. You have been through many experiences, but to him going to a new school or having to make new friends was totally without precedent. Therefore, the effect was much greater. No matter how well you may have prepared your child for the change and no matter how much he was truly looking forward to it, it had to be unsteadying.

Try to keep your guilt and sympathy under wraps, too, because they don't help the child cope any better. On the contrary, apologizing, commiserating, and blaming yourself may delay his coming to terms with the new situation—which he has to do eventually. To make it sooner rather than later, try to look at things in an optimistic light and count on your positive attitude to be contagious.

Finally, try to deal with causes, not results. View your child's misbehavior as a faulty means of coping with the new situation and a significant if disturbing means of telegraphing his distress. Reacting to the "noise" of that communication is like trying to hear what a radio announcer is saying by paying attention to the static. This is not to say that the behavior has to go unpunished, because you have the right to discourage any type of behavior of which you disapprove. But it is to say that your reaction must go beyond punishment to include an understanding of the cause. Punishment alone will not improve your child's behavior; in fact, it will probably make it worse.

Acting-Out Behavior: "Acting out" is the term applied to the kind of misbehavior that results from unresolved emotional conflicts. If your child starts to act out regularly, for whatever reason, apply some of the techniques we have just suggested. In particular, pay attention to his actions rather than his words. The words per se are meaningless—foul language he picked up on the school bus, sarcasms he adopted from adults, particular phrases he knows can get your goat. Ignore them all. Rather, respond to the actions he takes with some action of your own. If your child has a temper tantrum because he is frustrated by some minor problem, walk away from the tantrum. If he gets angry and throws an object or slams a door, remove loose objects and try to ignore the door. Trying to reason with him at the time he is angry doesn't work, nor does attempting to get him to verbalize that anger while he's in the midst of it. But meeting his response with yours at least serves to get you out of the acute situation. Then, when he's calmed down, you can try to get him to talk about it.

Finally, when dealing with a child who is acting out, try to characterize his behavior in neutral terms. If you start to think of him as "bad" and tell him so enough times, you could give him a negative self-image he might feel compelled to live up to. Moreover, since there's no way to change basic moral fiber, calling a child "bad" quickly brings you to an impasse over improving his behavior. Therefore, we suggest that you call his actions "excessive," "overenthusiastic," "misdirected," or "disruptive." This will help you to focus on the situation and to get started improving it.

Handling Acute Adjustment Reactions

In addition to the suggestions we've already made for handling specific behavior problems, we recommend a few other modes for helping a child cope with his anxieties. They are effective, simple, and can be utilized by you even though you work. The first is the story.

Since much of a child's misbehavior may be due to free-floating anxiety from a situational change, and since he may well have a hard time understanding and verbalizing this—you can do it for him. Think up a thinly disguised story about all the events in his life. Make the hero a child of the same age and in the same situation as he. Provide all the details and specifics that you think apply to your youngster. In other words, as they used to say in radio, the events are the same: only the names have been changed to protect the innocent. It is not necessary to make the story blacker than your child's real experiences. You are not out to make the point that there is always someone worse off. His own problems are bad enough for your youngster, and he couldn't care less that children in India are starving or that some children may have no shoes at all.

The idea behind storytelling is to give the child a peg on which to hang his anxieties. If it works, you may find that he wants to hear the story often. His questions and comments should reveal his concerns and open up areas to pursue. Even if he doesn't comment, just the fact of his wanting to hear the story lets you know that the method is working. Exposing fears and problems to the light of day always makes them seem so much less threatening than they were when they lurked under-cover.

If your child sees right through this ploy, if you don't feel clever enough to pull it off, or if the emotional content of the story is just as painful to you as it is to him—books can often serve the same cathartic purpose. There are books written on many levels dealing with real-life crises, and a children's librar-ian should be able to find one that fits your particular situation. Then, when you get the book home, you can either read it to your youngster or, if he's old enough, let him read it to himself. In the second instance, go through it first so that you'll be able to discuss the story with him when he finishes it.

Older children may be encouraged to write to friends or rela-tives about their feelings or they may be given a diary to confide in (for their eyes alone). The purpose is fulfilled when the emo-tion is expressed—no matter how it is expressed—and examined openly. It is the repressed feelings that come back to haunt us and the unspoken fears that grow into monsters too huge to handle. Admitting that he is afraid of the ghost in the closet is your youngster's first step toward being able to deal with it.

Sometimes the story is not even necessary. It might be suf-ficient just to confront your child with the problem straight out. Your youngster may have become frightened by his strong emo-tions or he may have thought that they would be so unaccept-able to you that he had to hide them. Merely by saying, "I know you don't like your new brother"; "I know you wish Daddy and Mommy were still living together"; or "I know that you are angry because Daddy got sick"—you may be able to open the floodgates of repressed emotion and clear the air. Even if your child denies that that's the way he feels, telling him that some children in his position do have these emotions may do the trick. He does not have to go so far as to admit to his hostile feelings in order to accept the fact that it's normal to have them.

Occasionally, telling your child how you really feel about life will help. Admitting that you do not like the new house or that you, too, have a sense of relief that Grandma's long, painful illness has ended in death will be a revelation to him. Your youngster may have been having great difficulty dealing with the disparity between how he was supposed to feel and how he really felt. Or he may have been unable to cope with ambivalence. Since children expect emotions to be black or white, you should try to help your child understand that in most instances they are either gray or striped. And that's okay.

Above all, make sure he knows that the negative, conflicting feelings he has are normal and that you understand the reasons for them. Let him know that your feelings for him will not change because of his feelings or new circumstances. You will still love him even if he doesn't like his brother. You will still care for him even though you don't love Daddy any longer. And lastly, tell him that his feelings will continue to change as time passes. They may get better or they may get worse, but they won't stand still.

After trying to work with and around your child's problem, you might want to consider it a bad habit that must be stopped without further ado. If the behavior does not seem to be associated either with stress or a change in his life, take a chance on this approach. Respond to the temper tantrum, the repeated fear, the repeated anxiety in the same way you would respond if your child walked around with his finger up his nose. Just tell him in no uncertain terms to cut it out: that you are disgusted with the habit and that you simply do not want to see it or hear about it any longer. Then consider the matter closed. When your child sees that his behavior no longer merits your attention, he just might stop it.

You also could try getting your child busy and keeping him that way. Plan activities, especially those involving other children his age. Try to limit the time he has to stew over his problems, the time he has to feel sorry for himself, the time that you and he spend reinforcing each other's sense of loss or anguish. There is certainly such a thing as being too busy, and too frantic a pace may cause fatigue. But just as you find that going to work or getting involved in extracurricular projects helps you over some rough spots, so activity helps a child to cope. Being busy enables him to make it through the bleak periods in his life. It engages his interest in the day-to-day process of living, and it forces him to look forward instead of back.

Finally, expect your child to regress and to require extra supervision until he has readjusted. This may necessitate a change in sitters or, where feasible, a temporary revision of your work schedule. With the older child the increased surveillance must be casual if not imperceptible, lest he resent you for hovering or—even worse—lest he permanently regress into an immature state.

Is It Time for Professional Help?

It is quite possible that at some point your child's problem will outstrip your ability to handle it through one of our suggested techniques. Any situation you can no longer abide or any behavior that has gotten out of hand merits consultation with a professional psychiatric worker. But when have things ''gotten out of hand''? We think it's when the problem has been constant or recurrent for at least three months and when your child does not seem to be improving either on his own or with your help. If you're still unsure, asking yourself the following questions should enable you to determine whether or not your child needs outside help:

How are the child's physiological functions? Have his sleeping patterns, eating habits, energy levels, bowel and bladder functions, or physical complaints changed? For example, the child who sleeps excessively long hours, is eating poorly, is constantly fatigued, and who complains of various aches and pains may be telling you that he is depressed.

What about his moods? Is he upset, unhappy, angry, or belligerent most of the time? Do his moods swing wildly? Are they appropriate to the situation? And most of all, are they different from what they used to be?

What are his behavioral symptoms? Setting fires, stealing,

having severe nightmares, having difficulty falling asleep and staying asleep, experiencing paralyzing fears, inability to separate from parents, and physically abusing smaller children or animals are only some of the symptoms that warrant immediate attention.

How is the child functioning in school? Have there been changes in the level of his school work and grades? Does he have a constant pattern of underachieving in his work when compared to his known abilities?

How are his relationships with other human beings—with the family members, peers, and other adult figures in his life? Is he constantly in conflict with people? Have his friends disappeared and is he becoming a loner? Does he shy away from contact with his teacher, camp counselors, and other adults?

Sometimes a child will show minor yet disturbing and persistent problems in most or all of the above categories, and sometimes he may show a particularly severe symptom in just one of them. Assuming that the symptoms are chronic, in both instances he needs professional help.

Although it is easier said than done, try to be optimistic and strong about your child's problem. Despite the fact that he may be resisting your help at every turn, he really is counting on you to see him through. And inwardly acknowledge but don't indulge the resentment you feel toward him. In many ways it is easier for a mother to deal with a child who has a physical handicap than with one who has an irritating habit or an emotional problem, but both young people are victims of circumstances beyond their control. If your child could be slim, popular, easygoing, honest, loving, happy, tic-free, and an A student—he would do anything to be just that. But for the moment at least he can't, and he's suffering tremendously because of it. So try not to think of your child as the enemy, no matter how miserable he's making your life. Withdrawing your love could be the final blow.

13

Of Pregnancy, Infancy, Family Planning, and Work

In our society male and female workers are treated very differently when they are about to become parents. The man is congratulated, kidded, or commiserated with, but his status at work remains unchanged. If anything, it is enhanced because employers tend to take fathers more seriously than they do bachelors or childless husbands. But while the father-to-be is being given consideration for a promotion, the mother-to-be is being asked when she's going to resign. Overnight she becomes the Invisible Man of the office, an employee sans status, sans security, sans future. In increasing numbers, though, women are contesting this fate by staying on the job during pregnancy and returning to work soon after delivery. If you plan to be among them, this is how we suggest you proceed.

Combat Criticism with Conviction

Once upon a time people just had babies. Nowadays the decision to do so often entails endless soul-searching, weighing of options, and rationalizing of fears and instincts. Then, when a woman does go ahead and become pregnant—worker or not— she is often put on the defensive. Her parents are usually thrilled, but many other people seem to have reservations. Their objections range from "overpopulation and world hunger" to "Do you know what it costs to send a kid to college today?"

and "You'll have to drop out of the ski house!" As the philosophy professor Michael Novak observed: "To choose to have a family used to be uninteresting. It is, today, an act of intelligence and courage."

If, on top of your decision to have a baby, you choose to continue working, you may encounter even more widespread disapproval. Despite the massive influx of married women into the job market, our society insists that the "real" mother stays at home, especially if she has an infant. Thus, when an advertising copywriter announced that she planned to return to work shortly after her baby was born, one co-worker asked indignantly why she didn't just get a stuffed animal, and another inquired snidely if she was going to stick her child in front of the TV from 9 to 5.

If you encounter a few such barbed criticisms among the "How Wonderful!"'s and "Congratulations!," try not to let them throw you. These comments usually stem from the critics' ignorance, unhappiness, or insecurity, and are therefore more of a reflection on their lives than yours. The co-worker who keeps telling you to quit is probably longing to do so herself and the superior who keeps urging you to leave for the sake of the fetus may very well feel threatened by your job performance.

To retain confidence in your plans, clarify your motives to yourself, then state them with conviction. Your firm stand will impress both you and your critics. For example, it is perfectly valid for any human being to state simply, "I want a baby because I want a baby." Since the desire for offspring is an emotional feeling, no intellectual explanation need be given. It is not a question of being programmed or bowing to parental pressure or fulfilling society's expectations, it is simply a matter of your desire to nurture.

While you feel that there is more to life than holding down a job, it is also perfectly valid for you to feel at the same time that there is more to life than having a baby. These two feelings do not have to be mutually exclusive in women—any more than they are mutually exclusive in men. Both sexes need the money, both need to see how far their abilities can take them, both need to be out among people, and both need a little human being to love. But since your husband probably won't be the principal caretaker, most of the burden of child rearing will be on your shoulders. Can you do both jobs and do them well? The experts say yes. According to research carried out separately by S. Thorsell and W. T. Farrell, evidence submitted at government hearings on discrimination against women, and informal employer opinion, mothers make as reliable and competent workers as anyone else. Moreover, from every study we've seen, mothers who work outside the home have as much chance of raising well-adjusted children as mothers who do no paid work at all.

High-Heeled and Pregnant

There are several advantages to working while pregnant. First, it makes the days go faster. Without something constructive to occupy one's time, nine months can seem like an eternity, as any ex-expectant mother will tell you. Secondly, working brings in money, a much-needed commodity at this point in your life. Thirdly, it provides you with a ready-made social life at a time when you belong neither to the mothers' coffee klatch nor the swinging singles. Finally, if you tend to be a worrier, work helps you to get your mind off the pregnancy and onto something else.

If one of your major worries is the wisdom of holding down a job at this time, let us set your mind at ease at once. Unless your job makes severe physical demands on you or is unsafe for the developing fetus for some specific reason, there is no medical imperative for you to quit. In fact, unless you feel unwell or complications set in, you can work right up to the time of delivery. You will not in any way be endangering the baby, because he is extremely well protected by insulating amniotic fluid. This fluid cushions him against jars, vibrations, and temperature changes as he rides around inside you in great comfort. Rest assured that you will not be more likely to miscarry or cause birth defects by going into an office than by staying home, no matter what your mother-in-law says. Nor will you be straining yourself unduly. After all, what is tapping on an electric typewriter compared to the child-chasing you'd be doing the second time around?

As your figure starts to blossom, you will have to pay special attention to your appearance on the job. Few pregnant women can get away with the tousled look. Comb your hair into a neat style, keep your nails manicured, and make sure your make-up is in place. Take a hard look at the clothes you will be wearing into the office too. The price may be right on Cousin Sue's old maternity wardrobe, but if it's been through two pregnancies already and dates back to the mini-skirt craze, perhaps you'd better reserve it for evenings at home. (Your husband always loved mini-skirts, anyway.) For the office buy a few washable mix-and-match separates to get you through the later months. You can even buy maternity uniforms, if uniforms are called for in your position. But if you want to look presentable in any of these clothes—do not eat, eat, eat. It is hard enough to get one's figure back after any pregnancy and an excessive weight gain will prolong the agonizing shape-up. Besides, who wants to make a triumphal return to the office still wearing maternity clothes?

Maternity Benefits

Early on in your pregnancy you should familiarize yourself with all the financial benefits—and liabilities—that come with your condition. Your personnel director, shop steward, and husband (if you are covered under his insurance policies) are good sources for this information. It's worth your while to wade through insurance policy jargon to become thoroughly acquainted with the coverage provided by your corporate and private health plans. In addition, find out if your company's sick leave can be used for maternity leave and whether you will be covered by disability insurance when the sick pay runs out. In 1976 the Supreme Court ruled that an employer does not have to compensate an employee for time lost due to pregnancy and childbirth, but some companies still do so as part of their fringe benefit package.

If you have expectations of working after the baby is born and you want to take advantage of all your benefits, you would be wise to continue working as long as you can. Don't stop until a complication of pregnancy or the actual birth forces you to stop. By leaving voluntarily before it is medically necessary, you might disqualify yourself for your company's health insurance, disability, and sick pay.* We have one final caveat to add to the above. Due dates are highly unreliable targets to shoot for. Some parents miscalculate, some doctors misjudge, and some babies seem to be in no hurry to vacate the premises. Therefore, even though you may not put your financial benefit package in jeopardy by staying home in your ninth month, you could end up using more maternity leave than you had counted on—before you're even a mother.

Office Strategy

It's best to avoid telling people at the office until you begin to show; otherwise the pregnancy will seem interminable to them. We recommend that you start out by telling your boss, because he might be miffed if he found out through the grapevine and thought he was the last to know. Be definite when you tell him. Name specific dates for leaving and returning—adding a disclaimer that Mother Nature often has ideas of her own. He will appreciate your giving him a concrete timetable so that he can line up a substitute well in advance. He will also think more highly of you, because you're going about the matter as befits a

*If you get fired at this time, bear in mind that the Unemployment Compensation Act of 1976 prohibits denial of unemployment benefits to female workers *solely* on the basis of pregnancy.

mature person who is concerned about both the organization and her career. As you proceed to tell your co-workers, always couple the announcement with the date of your expected return. So many people just assume that a pregnant woman is simply marking time at work until she can leave—if not for good then at least for a year—that you've got to disabuse them of that idea immediately. If you don't, you probably won't be taken seriously.

As time goes on your boss might become comfortable enough with your pregnancy to treat it as the natural phenomenon it is. Then again, he might not, because pregnancy makes some people nervous. If he's really a nasty soul, he might want you out of the way for some other reason and use your pregnancy as an excuse to get rid of you. If you feel that you are being unfairly pressured to leave your job, fight back. In 1974 the Supreme Court ruled that mandatory maternity leaves are unconstitutional under the Fourteenth Amendment. State laws, the 1964 Civil Rights Act, and government guidelines all prohibit pregnancy discrimination too. However, the application of these laws and rulings varies from occupation to occupation and from state to state. To determine just what your rights are, contact your state's human rights commission, a local chapter of the National Organization of Women (NOW), or the Civil Liberties Union. Not only will they tell you where you stand, but a phone call from any one of them might lead your employer quickly to reassess his attitude toward your pregnancy.

At the same time it wouldn't hurt for you to reassess *your* attitude. If you have been using your pregnancy to get out of unwanted work, you can't expect your employer to fling raises, titles, and greater responsibility into your lap. A person cannot have it both ways. If you want to continue up the career ladder or even hang on to the job you've got, try to seem as unpregnant as possible. Keep the conversation on business, not your due date, and keep the T-shirt emblazoned BABY at home. By going about your business with a minimum of fuss, you'll put co-workers, clients, and superiors at their ease. In time they may even begin to deal with you as Sue, Hillary, or Esther rather than The Pregnant Woman.

But society being what it is, you may still be first and foremost The Pregnant Woman around the office now. As such, be prepared for the endless question: "How do you feel?" The safest thing to answer is: "Fine." Then walk on or you'll be the recipient of every old wives' tale ever invented. For some reason the whole world, including bachelors and spinsters, feels compelled to give a pregnant woman advice. If someone has got you cornered in the cafeteria with horror stories that are turning you green, squelch her commentary with a sweet smile and the mild comment, "I've got a wonderful obstetrician. I'm sure he knows what to do." And since he does know what to do, take your problems to him rather than to the woman at the next desk, even if she once gave birth unattended and bit off the umbilical cord with her own teeth.

If you do plan to work throughout your pregnancy, inform your obstetrician of that decision as soon as you find out you are pregnant. He may have certain valid objections because of your particular job or medical history. But if he just has objections period, because he doesn't like pregnant women to work, he may not be the doctor for you. However, if he seems supportive of your plans, find out what accommodations he will make for you as a working woman. Even a phone call from his secretary to say that he is running late is helpful. It could enable you to work a half hour or more that you would otherwise spend cooling your heels in his office.

Although your obstetrician can help manage many pregnancy-related ills, he is not a miracle worker. At some point you may have to drop out temporarily or permanently. If you have morning sickness, for example, do not feel like a failure or a neurotic. Few people—male or female—can throw up at 7:00 A.M. and set off gaily for work at 8. If your symptoms are mild, you might be able to work around them by coming in a little later, lying down at lunch hour, or switching over to a more sedentary spot in the company. But if your symptoms are severe, you have no choice but to stay at home. By leaving before you exhaust the good nature of the people who have been covering for you, you'll find a warm welcome when you return.

Preparations

Whether you take time off or work up to the last minute, there are certain plans and purchases you'll be making during these nine months. One of the first decisions is where to stash the newcomer. The anthropologist Margaret Mead contends that a drawer could always be used to hold one small baby, and Dr. Spock gives directions for making a drawer into a crib by lining it with a blanket. But for some reason most American babies are not so easily accommodated. In fact, if you bought one of each item that's on the market for your infant, you'd have to buy the Palace of Versailles in order to house it all.

But even if you buy the minimum, which is what we recommend, baby equipment has a habit of oozing out and taking over the whole house. To avoid this, try to keep the baby and his accessories in one room. That room should not be yours, however, if you can help it. You need all the rest you can get, especially if you plan to return to work soon, and mothers and babies tend to wake each other up when sleeping in close proximity. Moreover, a baby can intrude upon private married life to an alarming degree just by being visible. Do not worry about missing his cry at night if he is next door or even down the hall. God gave infants a lusty set of lungs, as you will quickly find out. Moreover, he gave mothers special bionic ears which can detect a whimper through 3-foot stone walls, not to mention today's ¾-inch sheetrock.

If space is tight, you could put the baby in with an older sibling, provided the baby is a reasonable sleeper and his equipment does not displace that of the older child. You could convert a dining alcove into a nursery by closing off the opening with a screen. And you could renovate a large walk-in closet for the same purpose, provided it has adequate light and ventilation.

Faced with a one-bedroom apartment, some couples have simply moved into the living room and given the baby the bedroom. Although not perfect, this arrangement does permit the adults to socialize without constantly tripping over the playpen and diaper pail.

Now that you've blocked out space for the baby, what are you going to put in it? For you: a rocking chair to soothe your back when you come home from work and want to hold her. For her: a crib, chest of drawers, changing surface, an infant seat and, if you have someplace to use them, a car seat and carriage. Start with these essentials; you can always fill in later. Before you purchase anything, though, take a look at the *Guide to Buying for Babies,* which was compiled by the editors of *Consumer Reports.* The *Guide* will alert you to some brands with special advantages and warn you away from those with defects. This useful handbook plus *Consumer Reports'* update articles will help you spend your money wisely.

Whatever equipment you settle on, try to get it in bright colors. Studies show that babies are more stimulated by bright, intense primary colors than by the pastels with which they are usually surrounded. This is good news for those of you who want to get away from the sexist baby blue–light pink dichotomy or who simply like vibrant colors. Splash them on the nursery walls! Your child will be turned on and so will you, especially after spending eight hours in a dull green/gray office.

In between coats of paint, give some thought to child-care arrangements. Now is the best time for you to do your investigative leg work, especially if you plan an early return to the job. You will want to visit day-care facilities, interview sitters, and pick the brains of mothers—working and non—to see what caretakers are available in your neighborhood. At worst, you'll find the process educational. At best, you'll turn up the woman of your dreams who will have the coffee hot when you come home from the hospital and who will still be with you, packing the trunk, when "baby" goes off to college.*

*For a full discussion of the finding, training, and keeping of auxiliary help, see Chapter 3, "The Ins and Outs of Child Care."

There is one last activity we suggest toward the end of your pregnancy, and that is attending a clinic for expectant mothers. You should be able to locate one through your hospital, "Y," or other sponsoring organization. If you feel uneasy about the prospect of caring for a newborn, participating in a workshop (with your husband, if possible) will help to allay your fears. It will do more to bolster your self-confidence than any how-to book could, and it will provide a natural lead-in for that positive interaction with your newborn called bonding.

Early Bonding

Bonding is the process by which mother, father, and child become attached to one another. It is now being given considerable attention in child-development literature, because many experts feel it can set the stage for all future interpersonal involvement. Any expectant mother would do well to consider those techniques that promote bonding, but if you plan an early return to work, you should almost definitely use them. The positive, intimate "vibrations" you exchange with your baby soon after he is born can instantly transform you into the psychological parent. Moreover, they enable you to feel that despite long hours away from him, you have as close a relationship with your baby and as much influence on him as does the mother who stays home.

Natural childbirth can help you make a good start toward bonding. It is particularly valuable when the prospective father is included in the labor and delivery process. Taking care of the baby right from the start engenders a positive attitude toward the child and goes a long way toward making a mother feel competent. Some hospitals are encouraging this technique by offering a rooming-in plan. Under this arrangement the infant resides in the mother's room instead of the newborn nursery for all or a major portion of the day. The mother feeds, bathes, and changes the baby, sometimes with the father's assistance.

Breast-feeding is yet another way to achieve early mother-child interaction. Since physical closeness and relaxed one-to-one attention are part and parcel of the process, it can foster a lovely intimacy. You might want to consider breast-feeding even if you know you'll have to give it up once you start working. No harm will come of switching your baby over to the bottle, while much good may come of the few weeks you nurse.

There are certain factors that work against the bonding process, too, and one of these can be the baby nurse. Some baby nurses are wonderful. Some are terrible or, to be charitable, misguided. The latter category includes the woman who makes infant care into such a mysterious and elaborate ritual that the new mother is sure she will never learn it; the woman who won't let the mother near her child because she supposedly needs her rest, yet who refuses to help out by cooking or cleaning; and the woman who picks up the infant at the first sign of fussing. When this last species of nurse leaves and the child lets out its first substantial bellow, the mother panics. She is sure she's doing something terribly wrong, because "The baby was so good when the nurse was here!" To avoid falling victim to any of the above, try to find a woman who will let you care for the infant as much as you want and who will pitch in around the house. If you don't get this impression about the available baby nurses when you speak with their references, spend your money on someone to take over with the house while you take over with the newborn.

Leaving Your Baby

Establishing an early rapport with your baby should enable you to go back to work feeling good about yourself, but in reality no mother leaves a very young child without experiencing guilt pangs. The old myth concerning a mother's place dies hard, perhaps because it is constantly being reinforced by psychologists who assign to mothers the awesome—and impossible—responsibility for everything their babies are and will become. To which we say faddle. Babies are not shapeless lumps of clay waiting to be molded by Mother's expert hands.

Your baby comes equipped with his own personality, which will remain essentially the same whether you go to work or stay at home.

Your baby also comes equipped with his own individual timetable for development, and hanging over his crib from 9 to 5 will not make him walk, talk, or cut his teeth any earlier. Children simply cannot be rushed. Stop worrying because the little girl down the block is already spewing forth sentences while your daughter, who is two months older, hasn't gotten beyond "mama" and "dada." She's not holding back to spite you, as one anxious mother told us was the case with her daughter. It just isn't her time to talk yet.

Not only will your baby be very much her own person and develop at her own pace whether or not you're home all day, but she'll love you just the same. Recent studies of infant attachment indicate that your baby will recognize you as the most important person in her life whether you're working or not. Dr. T. Berry Brazelton, who works extensively with very young infants, has found that a normal baby develops three reaction systems: two positive ones to the mother and father and a negative one to strangers. An infant who has a part-time parent substitute quickly develops a fourth system. Like those directed toward the parents, this system is positive, but it in no way diminishes, competes with, or changes the baby's feelings toward her parents. This means that your infant will develop her primary tie to you no matter how many sitters she has or how close she gets to any of them.

Writing in the journal of the American Academy of Pediatrics, Dr. Mary C. Howell (herself the mother of eight) concludes that the "strength of the infant's attachment to the mother is not related to the presence or absence of multiple caretakers, but to the total amount of attention the infant receives from all caretakers." That holds true for infants left in day-care centers, too. As some researchers point out, multiple attachments are common even within the nuclear family in which the mother does not work. Moreover, they feel that multiple attachments may be indicative of the ability to form strong or healthy bonds, whereas a single attachment may signal the tendency to form weak or unhealthy bonds.

If you have a choice, will it make any difference to the baby when you go back to work? Frankly, no one knows. Some authorities are now saying that a mother who plans to return to work early might just as well do so in the first month or two of the baby's life, thus sparing him the need to adjust to a new arrangement. We feel that if you're going to resume work rather quickly, the fourth month is about the best. By then the baby has made his initial attachments, outgrown any "colic" reaction he might have had, and has settled down to a regular routine. We agree with the opinion of most experts that the one time to avoid starting a job if you can help it is between nine and twenty-four months. This is the age when children are traditionally most fearful of losing their mothers. But even if you do go back then, your child can probably accustom himself to the new situation quickly, because most babies are adaptable and resilient creatures.

In this as in all things, though, your child will take his cue from you. If you are confident and optimistic about leaving him, he will be too. But if you are tentative and fearful, he'll cling for dear life. To make parting less traumatic for you and your baby, try to feel good about the situation. Think positively about the affectionate and attentive care he will be getting while you're gone. Concentrate on the benefits he'll receive from exposure to others, and remind yourself of all the good points we've made above. Thus armed, you should be able to wear a smile as you leave, a smile both of you can believe in.

Do take into account your own sense of timing in scheduling your return to work. Although you may have set your return date before the blessed event, you can't always know in advance when the right moment will be. You might have thought you'd want to go back right away, but the baby's fussing at night, your postpartum blues and physical difficulties, or just the sheer effort of caring for a newborn may have changed your mind. Or, compared to the excitement of having a brand-new baby, the office may now seem pretty dull. Therefore we urge you to keep your options open as much as you can. You won't be opting out if you decide to stay home longer than planned, nor will you be a failure as a working mother. The decision to stay home with the baby—just like the decision to have him in the first place—is a personal one.

Hassle-Free Baby Care

If you do decide to go back to work soon after the baby is born, you may find yourself carrying a load that would make even Wonder Woman burst into tears. Yet despite the fact that your situation is no longer unique, almost all of the advice available to you assumes that you must be home twenty-four hours a day. To read some of these elaborate how-to ideas, one would think that the hardest way is always the best and that all other ways are wrong. But we feel that as far as the working mother is concerned, what's easiest is best and whatever works is automatically right. Therefore, we suggest that you start looking around for products and persons that can simplify your life, a quest you might embark upon right at home.

Getting your husband interested in child care from the start has the highest priority. Not only will his involvement help to neutralize any jealousy he might feel toward the baby, but it will enable him to get comfortable with her fast. Just as you only learned to mother by mothering, so he'll only experience a closeness to his child by taking care of her. Moreover, you simply cannot do it all without his help. If your husband does not take to child care like a duck to water—and many men don't, despite all the recent publicity to the contrary—ease him into it by demonstrating, then supervising the routine. If he still resists, you may have to make him go cold turkey. Make an appointment some Saturday afternoon and leave him alone with the baby. Faced with the reality of a dirty diaper, he'll probably change it.

In addition to getting your husband involved, help yourself by cutting all the corners you can. Your baby will not know the difference if you take shortcuts with her maintenance, but you will: you'll feel much more relaxed as soon as you stop trying to live up to yesterday's rigid and often unnecessary protocols. Thus, if you are too busy to give your baby a full bath some days, just wipe off the dirtiest or most odoriferous parts, sprinkle on a bit of powder, and pronounce her bathed. Cleanliness is definitely not next to godliness in your situation. Likewise, if you find yourself too rushed to take her out, simply place the carriage or crib next to an open window. The air's the same (or maybe even a little cleaner) up on the twelfth floor as it is down on the street. Finally, if you received a gift of a baby dress that needs ironing, send it back to the store by return mail, give it to an enemy, or save it for one very, very special occasion (and ask the donor to iron it).

When it comes to feeding, choose between breast milk and formula on the basis of what's right for *you*. Many mothers like to breast-feed for the convenience and psychological satisfaction they receive from it. Some are even able to keep it up when they go back to work. But if you cannot synchronize breast-feeding and work schedules, are physically unable to nurse, or simply have no desire to do so—don't let the breast-feeding advocates make you feel that you are any the less maternal. "Good" mothers have been using substitutes since ancient times. Moreover, no one has yet proved that children are calmer, less neurotic, or more attached to their mothers as a result of breast-feeding. Millions of infants have developed perfectly on modern, modified cow's milk formula and your baby will too, if that's what you decide to feed him.

If you do choose the bottle, investigate all the shortcuts for its use. Some formulas come in premixed, premeasured, and disposable containers, which are expensive but could be a godsend when you're rushed. In addition, some pediatricians have relaxed the rules on sterilization. Check with yours to see if you can skip the procedure altogether or have your dishwasher do it for you. You can also save time by taking the bottle out of the fridge and popping it right into the baby's mouth. No intermediate stop at the hot water faucet is necessary, because milk is equally digestible ice-cold or warm and your baby will accept it either way. However, if you simply cannot bring yourself to give the child a frosty drink, at least spare yourself the trouble of warming the bottle until it's hot. Almost all hospitals now feed their newborns formula that is room temperature, so there's no need for you to take it any further than that.

By all means, embrace ready-made baby foods with a joyous heart. There is absolutely no reason for you to start from scratch when someone has already put nutritious, sterile, varied, and inexpensive meals into little jars. In fact, processed baby foods are now better than ever. Over the past few years manufacturers have ceased adding nitrites, nitrates, and other possibly unwholesome chemicals and have eliminated or drastically reduced the amount of added sugar, salt, and starch in their products. Since some of the jars contain more valuable nutrition than others, read the ingredient lists carefully. But after a long day at the office, is it not a blessing to be able to feed your child without cooking or cleaning up? Of course, it's not a great hardship to run table foods through a blender or processor either. But as a general rule, we'd rather see you spend the limited time you have with your baby fondling and enjoying her rather than grinding out her pap.

Kid or Kids?

Before you know it your baby will no longer be a baby and you will start to ask yourself whether you should begin on another one. If population trends are any indication, your answer may very well be no. In recent years the number of children in the typical American family has dropped from 2.3 to 1.9, and one out of every six American youngsters is now a singleton. In several respects having just one child makes good sense for the working woman. It enables her to partake of the child-rearing experience and gives her an entry into the world of families, yet it does so with a minimum of time lost from her career. Moreover, having an only child cuts down on the number and cost of caretaker arrangements and offers great flexibility in choosing a lifestyle.

On the other hand, unless a career woman can accept only-childom as a normal, healthy state of affairs, she may find herself tacitly apologizing to her youngster for his lack of siblings as well as for her working. If she's the type who would feel guilty leaving two children, she'll feel twice as guilty leaving one. Somehow, even if two children are far apart in age and/or have nothing in common, a mother can always rationalize her being away from them on the grounds that "they have each other." Lacking the second offspring, she may feel constantly pressured to provide companions or organized activities to fill up her youngster's day.

Having another child solves these problems for a woman, just as it provides her with another dimension in mothering. A second child could also serve to take the heat off the first, because the parents' hopes would no longer be invested solely in him. Then, too, a sibling traditionally brings the firstborn down to earth, teaches him to share, and offers live-in companionship.

However, logistical problems, emotional wear and tear, and sheer noise level all increase geometrically when another child is added to the family. For some reason their combined total is always far greater than the sum of their parts. The mother of two has to deal not only with her relationship to each one but with their relationship to each other. As one woman said of her family, "I have three children, really: Priscilla, Evan, and something called 'interaction.' " All too often the mother finds herself feeling like a referee or, when the children vie for her attention, like the rope in a tug of war. After a long day at the office that's not how she wants to feel.

When a woman shoots for three or four, she can take all the aforementioned pluses and minuses and multiply them accordingly. The large family may work well for the woman who has only limited career aspirations. But if she has a yen to become president of General Motors, she'd better have (a) a small family, (b) a great deal of energy, (c) picture-perfect children, or (d) full-time help.

From all of the above you may have gathered that there is no perfect solution to the family planning dilemma. Nor can you know in advance how any one choice will turn out, because individual personalities and luck play such a large part in the results. When trying to arrive at a decision, you will have to consider your professional aspirations, husband's predilections, known energy levels, and high or low thresholds of aggravation. Then forget about all of them and rely on gut feeling— which is what it would have boiled down to anyway.

The In-Between Years

Perhaps you thought you'd be returning to work as soon as the umbilical cord was clipped. But then you found out how extraordinarily difficult and expensive it is to obtain good child care and how much fun it is to do it yourself, and you decided not to return for a while. Like many other women you are now facing what we call the In-Between Years. This can be a time of happy self-discovery or it can be a time of miserable frustration. It's all what you make of it.

We suggest that you make much of it. Use this interlude between jobs to develop new facets of your being. Give full vent to your maternal drives, nesting instincts, and creative forces. Succumb to a secret passion for belly dancing and indulge your long-suppressed mania for jigsaw puzzles. Sleep late, set a lazy pace, and revel in your new-found freedom. Try to bring out the underachiever in your soul. Even Madame Curie, a compulsive worker if there ever was one, took off a full year early in her career and spent it reading junky novels.

The In-Between Years are also a good time to become active in the preschool PTA, civic affairs, and charitable organizations. In addition to doing your bit for society, this volunteer work will familiarize you with the workings of your community and introduce you to some of the people in it. Remember, you can do more as a volunteer than stuff envelopes. You may be able to apply your vocational skills to meaningful tasks or, conversely, you may acquire vocational skills in the course of volunteering that will help you advance your career later on.

Although you may be exploring new avocations during this period, there is no reason for you to abandon your vocation either. If you want to return to work someday, it makes good sense to keep up with professional developments and maintain your contacts in the field. One way to do both is by seeking part-time, freelance, or temporary employment; another is by doing volunteer work in the same or an allied field. Many women find that the perspective they gain from the In-Between Years leads them to switch professions entirely. They use this time to go back to school to get the specialized training and university degrees that will enable them to make a second start. By making the most of the In-Between Years, you too can eventually return to work refreshed and—if you must say so yourself—better than ever.

14

Single Parent, Double Duty

When a woman loses her husband through divorce or death, she experiences a number of conflicting emotions: remorse, anger, loss, relief, guilt, self-pity. She needs time to sort these feelings out, yet she has no time. She must cope with financial tangles, but she may never have seen a balance sheet. She may have to take a job right away, but often she has no marketable skills, or she might like to quit the job she has, but what used to be a lark is now a financial necessity. Because of all this, she craves peace at home as never before, yet her children may have started to behave in disturbing ways. If any of these dilemmas are yours, we suggest you take a deep breath and read on.

First Things First

The first thing you should do is do nothing. When you are close to a traumatic event, it is difficult to assess your own situation correctly. Clarity of vision comes only with time, so give yourself as much time as you can before making any major moves. Then, when you do act, try to incorporate changes singly rather than in wholesale lots. In your situation the temptation is great to make sweeping changes, as though by severing all connections with the past one could sever all the hurts too. But it doesn't work that way. Memories can rarely be put aside at will, while new opportunities present their own set of problems, problems that you might find extremely stressful at this point in your life.

Ideally, any immediate commitments you do make should be neither overwhelming nor binding. If you are already working when the separation or loss occurs, try not to undertake any new, high-powered projects for a while. If you go job hunting, try to find something that is absorbing (and will pay the bills), but won't do you in. If you return to school, start with one or two courses rather than a full academic load. And if you move—rent, don't buy. Moreover, when tempted to walk down the aisle, remind yourself of that old saw, "Marry in haste, repent at leisure," because quick remarriages are inherently risky.

The go-slow dictum is particularly applicable when it comes to changing residences. Familiar surroundings spell emotional comfort to people of all ages, so do not be quick to leave town. If you must move for financial reasons, try to relocate in the same neighborhood or, if your children are of school age, in the same school district. In any case, try to relocate someplace where you think you'll stay a while. Although children do adapt quickly, they may find changes upsetting after a divorce or death. Moreover, with you off at work a great part of each day, they will have to find new friends on their own. This is no mean feat. The new kid on the block has to break into established cliques and prove himself from scratch. If you can remember back to your own childhood, you'll recall what an uncomfortable process that is.

Children's Reactions

A child will make new friends and he will adjust to a home life without Daddy. But like you, he will have to work through a welter of confusing emotions first. Preoccupied with your own emotions and the thousand and one details attendant upon a divorce or death—all the while holding down a job and running a household!—you might easily misjudge your child's reactions. His outwardly normal or even better-than-normal behavior could lull you into thinking that he is taking things in stride. Don't be fooled. Even very young children are sensitive to loss and no youngster emerges from a familial trauma totally unscathed. Though delayed, repressed, or peculiarly channeled, his strong reactions are there and they are giving him some degree of trouble.

One of the most common reactions a child has to divorce or death is the feeling that somehow he caused it. All children occasionally wish a parent ill. And if a child is going through that stage in which fantasy plays a large role in his life, he may see a concrete, causal relationship between his wish and his father's removal. Moreover, in many pre-divorce situations parents fight over everything, including the children. A child overhearing these fights could gain reinforcement for his theory that he is the reason Daddy left. Convinced that his bad behavior was at fault, he may try to be extra good so his father will come back home.

More often, however, his anxiety and confusion are manifested in offensive behavior. Although your first impulse may be to clamp down on your temporarily obnoxious child, you should allow him to "let it all hang out." Bottled-up emotions tend to surface later in even more bizarre or antisocial ways, so get them out in the open as soon as possible. Lest your child get the impression that it is somehow more noble not to cry, don't tacitly request that he keep a stiff upper lip and act like "a little man." Rather, encourage him to express his emotions openly by expressing yours and by letting him mourn with you. Don't hold back. Even if you cry each time you mention your ex-husband's name, make a point of mentioning it. Otherwise, you might be creating a taboo that both of you will have to wrestle with for years to come.

Supposing you do everything right, your child will still feel terribly vulnerable when her father moves out or dies. It may not be so much her father's disappearance that is bothering her as the realization that, having lost one parent, she could lose another and then would be totally alone. You will have to assure her that you will never abandon her. Even if that assurance is excessive and unrealistic, she needs to hear it at this time.

Feeling so insecure, she may object strenuously to your leaving the house to go to work—or to drop off the laundry, for that matter. You must go, but try to alleviate her fears by making your comings and goings as regular as possible. If your job does not permit you to follow a set routine, at least try to call home at the same time each day. This will reassure her that you are well and still interested in her. If possible give your social life a routine, too. Pick a time such as Friday night, declare it Mother's night off, then leave the house as advertised. Some evenings you may have to take in a movie by yourself, but it is still important that you go. Not only does this regular night off give you a much-needed respite, but it gives your daughter something else she can count on. Moreover, the routine relieves you of some of the hassle preceding departure. Now, instead of reciting a lengthy litany in your defense, you can retreat behind the short, neutral statement, "If this is Friday, I must be going out."

When all is said and done your child will take her cue from you in this as in every other situation. If you show that you are worried sick about money, she will be too. And if you dwell on hypothetical disasters such as losing your job, she will dwell on them too. So, unless you want to produce a genuine neurotic, soft-pedal your fears in front of the youngster. And don't wring your hands over her future. The chances are excellent that she will rebound satisfactorily from the trauma—especially if you don't allow either of you to wallow in self-pity. Rather, seize every opportunity to talk up the positive aspects of the situation as Lynn Caine, the author of *Widow*, did with her children. "Look," she told them, "you have one terrific parent. Some kids have two yukky parents. So stop feeling sorry for yourselves."

Count Your Pennies

One of the greatest shocks accompanying divorce or death is the realization that not only have you lost a husband, but you've lost your financial underpinning as well. Even if you've always worked, having access to your husband's income provided you with many material goods and a great sense of security. Now all of that is gone. True, the deceased may have left life insurance, but its benefits often prove inadequate in the face of today's raging inflation. Or the divorced husband might be required to provide alimony and child support, but these payments are usually disappointingly small—if they are honored at all. It's little wonder, then, that many middle-class women suddenly find themselves in serious financial straits when they are widowed or divorced.

The bright spot in all this is the concrete nature of finances. In contrast to the emotional upheaval you and your children are experiencing and about which you can *do* very little because time has to take its course, here at least is a problem you can tackle with pencil and paper. And the sooner you begin the better. Even if you've never filled in a check stub, we suggest that you start in on your finances now. You'll get better as you go along.

Your first job will probably be to discover where your money goes. To find out, carry a purse-sized notebook with you and enter in it every cash transaction you make. Then, in a larger budget ledger (which you can buy ready-made), account for the bills that you pay by check. The petty cash notations combined with the ledger information should give you a complete picture of how you are spending your money.

If you find that you are spending more than you are taking in—a very common state of affairs—you might want to try a hot new technique called Zero Based Budgeting (ZBB). Recently taken up by the federal government and many major corporations, ZBB demands that you justify all outlays over and above those needed to survive. You can go about doing this by listing each expenditure you have and its less expensive alternatives on a 3 by 5 card. When you have everything written down, arrange the cards in order of importance. As you go through the deck, you should be able to spot those items that could be eliminated and those that could be replaced by something cheaper.

For more sophisticated, long-range planning you will need the help of professionals. Accountants, attorneys, insurance agents/estate planners, stockbrokers, and investment bankers all know a "better way," no matter how small the income or how paltry the estate. If you are fortunate enough to have access to a women's center, you may be able to get much of the guidance you need at low cost. But even if you must spend precious money garnering expert financial opinion, consider it money well spent. Left to your own devices, you might make serious and very costly errors. However, since the good client is the educated client, we don't recommend leaving your finances totally in the hands of the professionals either. You can learn more about money management through articles and books, many of which are directed toward women in just your situation.*

One of the first topics the experts will take up with you is taxes. Find out what you can expect to pay on April 15 and start putting away the money for it *now*. To help your accountant prepare your income tax statement and to protect yourself in case of an audit, keep evidence of all charitable contributions and other tax-deductible items.† Another point the experts are sure to raise is that of a savings account. A rainy day fund equivalent to two months' salary is the generally recommended cushion for disaster. Finally, if becoming a divorcée or widow has put you into debt, the experts may tell you to shred your credit cards and close down your charge accounts. Painful as these remedies are, they will put you on the road to financial solvency, which is where, as a single working mother, you want to be.

Blessings in Disguise

After meeting with the financial experts, your head will probably be spinning from all the options and contingencies that you

* See the Bibliography for suggested reading on this topic.
† See the Appendix for an example of a home filing system.

have to take into account. How will you ever manage it, you ask yourself. For that matter, how will you ever manage being a single working mother? Self-pity (and/or panic) overwhelms you and you feel like taking the first plane out of town, leaving job and family far behind. Yet, ironically, it is just these responsibilities that should prove to be your salvation in the long run.

Like many women who have just experienced a separation or loss, you may feel so tired that you can hardly drag yourself through the day. The last thing you feel like doing is getting dressed and going out to work. Yet even if you don't need the money, this is probably the best thing you can do for yourself. The demands of work are such that for several hours each day you must think about something else besides yourself and your troubles. And because it gets you out among people, work also brings with it a reprieve from loneliness. You may feel out of it in other social situations, but on your job, at least, you can feel you belong.

Working has other advantages, too. The fact of making money relieves tension, while the act of doing so strengthens a shaky ego. Working also imposes a regularity on your life. It gives you a place to go and a set time to be there. But perhaps most important of all, working makes you function, and as you function you slowly knit yourself back into one piece. No wonder so many divorcées and widows attribute their survival to holding down a job. As Lynn Caine expressed it: "I am convinced that having to go to work every day and act as if I were fine and on an even emotional keel helped me back to normality. When I was working, I had a respite from my fears, whether real or fantasy."

Having to care for children imposes the same time out from self-concern and the same goad to normality. Between packing lunches, buying Brownie uniforms, arranging sleepover dates, and checking homework, what mother could find time to brood? Moreover, children demand that life go on. Although you might like nothing more at this point than to pull up your drawbridge to the world, they force you to interact with others. Above all, though, children provide love, a focus for your life, even a reason to go on living. Yes, you're probably better off now with children than without. But you may have to remind yourself of this rather frequently, especially when the kids are hassling you through one of their "games."

Everyone Plays but No One Wins

Loss of a father through divorce or death inevitably disrupts the delicate equilibrium of family life. Until a new balance is achieved, both mother and children usually find themselves testing out new lines of authority, new frontiers of privilege, and new ways to manipulate one another. If you are unhappy with the way you and your children are interacting, you might all be caught up in one of the following common but harmful "games":

"We'll Go On Just As We Always Have": Being a worker, a parent, and a single woman, you face tremendous new strains in day-to-day living. You should be cutting every corner you can. But if you are like many women in your situation, you may be trying to carry on as if nothing had happened: working all day, cooking and cleaning at night, and refusing to ask your children to "suffer" any more than they already have by sharing the burden. What is the inevitable outcome of such heroic efforts? In his book *Creative Divorce,* Mel Krantzler cites one woman who collapsed under the strain. "I was so tired and irritable all the time," she confessed. "I couldn't give [my children] the kind of support and attention they really needed. I was hung up on preserving the externals." You can't fool your children just by serving dinner punctually at the old hour. They know it's a new ball game now, so what better time to institute new rules? Refer to our chapter on getting kids to pitch in and keep telling yourself that they'll be better people for it—which they will.

"I'll Make It Up to You": Another common way divorcées and widows assuage their guilt is by indulging their children in ex-

travagant presents and outings which they can ill afford and which the children little appreciate. All fathers and mothers, divorced or not, working or not, try to buy their youngsters' affection from time to time. But it never works. Affection can't be bought, children can't "show" gratitude, and neither side gets any real satisfaction from these exchanges. Besides, they can turn kids into manipulative, present-grabbing monsters. If you feel yourself falling into the "buy me" trap—and you are particularly vulnerable to it right now—realize that guilt is behind your acquiescence. Stop apologizing for what you've done to your children and you'll find it easier to stop buying.

"It's Okay with Me": Still a third way the single working mother tries to compensate her child for the loss of his father is by giving in on matters of discipline. She thinks her across-the-board acquiescence will make him feel happy and loved. Yet ironically her permissiveness often telegraphs the opposite message. Whereas discipline would prove to the youngster that she is involved in his life, letting him run wild—on top of her long absences—may leave him in doubt. A child who needs to know where he stands will test his mother with outrageous behavior in order to find out. When a mother cries in exasperation, "He's just asking for it!" she's right. For even as he is screaming and resisting control, the child is gaining emotional reassurance from being disciplined. So, establish some basic rules and try to get your child to adhere to them. If he doesn't, hand out the punishment he so richly deserves—and needs.

"You're the Man of the House Now": In this dangerous game single mothers elevate their sons to the place Father once held, a place the young boys cannot possibly fill. Divorced fathers make a similar mistake when they turn their daughters into girlfriends and visitation days into dates. Playing with the Oedipal complex this way is playing with fire, so be alert to any signs that you might unconsciously be creating such a situation to fulfill your own social needs. Without realizing it, you might also be instigating a related game we call "Best Friends." Here,

single parents abandon the authority structure of the parent-child relationship in a bid for intimacy. In trying to get down to their child's level, however, they make him terribly uncomfortable and confused. For if the roles are not clearly delineated, how is the youngster to know who is the parent and who is the child?

"Woe Is Me": In another distortion of the parent-child relationship, a troubled parent may unload more problems onto a child than the youngster can handle. While open communication is a good thing, it can also be overdone. If you suspect that your underlying motive for speaking intimately with your child is a desire to elicit his pity or support, cease and desist. You may be attempting to shift the burden of parenting to him. Instead, confide in a therapist or a supportive friend. If you can't obtain a live listener, you might want to try spilling it into a tape recorder, which has also been shown to bring tremendous relief.

"Getting Even": In this game a divorcée tries to strike back at her ex-husband through the children, purposely hanging him up on plans for visitation days and threatening to withhold the youngsters until he produces the alimony check. At other times she may not so subtly ask the children to spy on their father and report back on his new way of life. Inevitably, she has a sarcastic comment on all she is told. These tactics place a great strain on the already-conflicted youngsters, who are being told, in effect, to choose sides. If you are thinking of initiating a round of "Getting Even," think again. This is a vicious game in which everyone loses, especially the children.

"Perfect Parent": This may be your ex-husband's way of getting even with you while he assuages his own guilty conscience. For a few hours each week he gaily builds cardboard forts, tours city parks, and wines and dines the kids at their favorite watering holes. Then he leaves—until the next visiting day when the carnival starts all over again. In the meantime you've got to play the heavy by disciplining, criticizing, and laying down the

rules. Fortunately, most fathers peter out as playmate-cum-tour guide and with longer visits at vacation time they shed the role altogether. When voices start to get raised and behinds start to get whacked, you can assume that things are back to normal. Until that occurs, however, you'll just have to accept being second banana.

"Divide and Conquer": Children often initiate games of their own and this is one of their favorites. When their father was living at home, it was easy to check out their outrageous demands backed up by the argument, "But Daddy said we could." Now that he has digs of his own, their claims are more difficult to verify. Don't even try. It is very possible that your former husband did promise the kids the moon, but you're not obligated to give it to them. What you'll have to make clear to the children is that there are two sets of rules now and they'll have to respect both of them. Moreover, since they may not be above pitting you against their father to obtain certain goods and privileges, you'll have to squelch your competitive urge. Be strong—resist the temptation to play.

"But Daddy Would Have Let Me": In this variation of the foregoing game, children who have lost a father often invoke his image to manipulate their mother. In real life the man may have been a tyrant but, when it suits the children's purposes, he suddenly becomes the most permissive and open-handed figure that ever lived. This maneuver can be devastatingly effective. To combat it you will have to point out gently but firmly that no one knows what Daddy would do in any given situation if he were here. And since he's not here, your children will have to deal with the reality of you now instead of fantasizing about what might have happened "if."

Sometimes harassed working widows also invoke the name of their dead husband, but they use him as a disciplinarian or setter of goals. "If your father were here he would . . ." is a phrase they fall back on when they want their children to behave in a certain way that they themselves cannot enforce. While the effectiveness of this ploy is doubtful, its destructiveness is certain: it increases the children's guilt and fears. If you hear yourself calling upon your late husband to play the heavy, stop in mid-sentence and try another approach.

"Make Mommy Mad": Children have a special radar system that enables them to pinpoint their mother's weak spot and hone in on it with uncanny accuracy. In the post-trauma period especially, if a mother is neat, her children may become super-slobs. If she hates dirty language, they may swear like drill sergeants. Some of this behavior may stem from a developmental stage through which they are passing, but much of it may be a cry for attention. If your children are a study in perversity right now, it's probably because they are wrestling with their feelings of abandonment, guilt, anger, disbelief, and denial. Be as supportive as possible, but set limits on repugnant behavior. As with all limits, these will bolster their sense of security while at the same time ensuring your survival. If your children go beyond perversity to cruelty, goading you to tears by the use of certain key emotional phrases, you may have to separate yourself from them—fast. Let them know that you know what they are up to, then leave the room. Isolation may prove so uncomfortable that they'll quickly abandon their vicious new game, "Make Mommy Cry."

The two main remedies we suggest in the preceding paragraph can really be applied to all the games in this section: don't overreact to negative behavior, but do pour on the extra T.L.C. Since games should properly be viewed as faulty communication, not as battles to be won, you should concentrate on finding out *why* you and your children are playing them instead of trying to come out on top. After all, you want to bind up wounds right now, not open them. Hopefully, the trauma you've all experienced will ultimately draw you closer. Then one day when the smoke clears, you may be able to perceive a new and possibly even stronger family arising from the ashes of the old.

The Real American Family

Perhaps one of the greatest impediments to your forging this new family unit is that none of you believes it can be done. You and your children may be close, caring, and vitally involved with one another, but without a man in the house you may have trouble thinking of yourselves as a "real family." The Great American Family has not varied much from the Dick and Jane readers of your childhood to the TV sitcoms of your children's childhood. It invariably consists of a father who goes off to work, a mother who does not, and a boy and girl who are followed by their good dog Spot as they gambol about their neat green yard. Any other grouping in any other setting seems inadequate and atypical.

Yet, in fact, it is the Great American Family that is atypical today. According to the U.S. government, only 7 out of every 100 households in America now consists of a father, a nonworking mother, and children. Moreover, one out of every six children in America lives in a single-parent household. But old stereotypes die hard and many divorcées and widows get so hung up on depriving their children of a "real" family that they lose sight of what their family was really like when it was intact. To make this point, Mel Krantzler cites the case of one ten-year-old who was told by his mother that divorce was imminent. "Does that mean you and Daddy won't be fighting all the time?" the child asked.

To assume that only a reconciliation, resurrection, or brand-new male could make you into a real family again is self-defeating. You are as much a family as you think you are. Therefore, start thinking of yourself and the children as a complete living unit and, once you've convinced yourself, do a selling job on the kids. Refer to the two, three, or four of you as "the family." Observe a certain amount of tradition at holiday and birthday time, keeping certain celebrations just for "the family." Adhere to a regular dinner hour if possible and sit down together—as a family. Shared experiences will contribute to the spirit of togetherness you are trying to create and a warm, welcoming hearth will provide a rallying point for it.

It is also good for your children to feel that they belong to something larger than just your nuclear unit. Therefore, make an effort to get together with aunts and uncles, cousins, siblings, parents, and grandparents—that whole loose network called the extended family. And if it's feasible, keep in touch with your former husband's relatives too.

Many divorcées and widows also try to hook up with married couples who have children about the same ages as theirs. Families with fathers can provide role models and a sense of rootedness, just as the extended family does. But you will probably have to take the initiative in these situations, because many married women will either feel uneasy about your single status or will assume that you're not interested in them. If you have been reluctant to approach married couples out of a fear of being a third wheel, we can only urge you to give them a try. They may be as eager to make friends as you are. Moreover, by not seeking out the companionship of two-parent families, you would be confining yourself to other divorcées, widows, and their children. Not only could this depress you terribly, but it would present your kids with a skewed view of the world.

Since the one thing your own household cannot supply is a man, you might want to investigate a Big Brother program for your fatherless son. While not a replacement for Dad, the Big Brother volunteer can provide your child with the older male companionship he may sorely need. If your ex-husband is anywhere to be found, you will probably want to encourage his active involvement with the children too. He's the only father they've got, after all, no matter what you may think of him. In addition to which, the more people with whom your children are in positive contact, the stronger they and your family life will be.

Along with the myth of the Great American Family, we all cling to our belief in the Happy Childhood. This ideal seems innocent enough, yet it is actually harmful, instilling guilt in the single working mother and inhibiting her ability to parent.

The Happy Childhood

Like the Great American Family, the Happy Childhood has been a mainstay of our culture for generations. Some seventy-five years ago Kate Douglass Wiggins, the author of *Rebecca of Sunnybrook Farm,* articulated our deepseated belief in it when she declared that every child "has a right to a genuine, free, serene, healthy, bread-and-butter childhood"—on the farm, no less. Few American parents can deliver the farm today, but they try their darndest to give their children all the rest. Yet they may be setting themselves an impossible task. After studying childhood down through the ages, we are not sure that the Happy Childhood ever existed outside the nostalgic musings of writers who haven't been kids themselves for a good many years. Moreover, we don't think it is within a mother's power to "give" a happy childhood to her offspring, even if it did exist.

All children, even those who come from Great American Families, find growing up an uncomfortable process. Arithmetic, unpopularity, the inability to palm a basketball, and a thousand other serious and not-so-serious miseries befall them before they reach adulthood. Nor is home necessarily the great refuge from it all. Mother may nag, father may drink, sister may taunt, and brother may bully. Yet in spite of and probably because of all this, everyone grows up. Indeed, we feel that unhappiness should be viewed as an inevitable and positive concomitant to maturity instead of an aberration, because it contributes so substantially to the maturing process.

Yet even if you accept this premise and remember only too well the lows you experienced as a youngster, you may feel terribly threatened when your own child is unhappy. And no wonder. In America people consider a child's unhappiness an affront, an accusation that his parents have done something wrong. Adults feel that a cause must be found, a finger must be pointed, and the situation must immediately be rectified. The divorced or widowed working mother is conditioned to believe that the finger can only point to her, since she alone is responsible for the child. On top of this guilty acknowledgment, the divorcée may be suffering from a damaged self-image. Having failed with her husband, she dreads but does not doubt that she might fail with her child. To prevent this, she gives in to him at every turn—thus becoming the loser in the "I'll make it up to you" game.

Just as many a single working mother feels that she can give her youngsters a Happy Childhood by gratifying their every wish, so she may try to accomplish the same end by devoting every spare minute to them. While family time is an admirable thing, there comes a point where a single mother will want a social life of her own too. And we feel she should have it. Otherwise, a woman will come to resent her children and they will come to feel that the whole burden of her happiness rests on their shoulders. Still, when she goes out at night after working all day, she is likely to feel that she is running out on her youngsters. As one woman reported to Carole Klein in *The Single Parent Experience:* "I feel terribly torn about it. Here I am getting all dressed up, leaving him alone again after he's been without me so much already. He always cries when I leave. Always. It's not exactly the music to go out dancing by."

Of course, young children with two parents in residence and a mother who is home all day also tend to protest when they are left behind, but the married woman is in a better position to slough off these protests because of her traditional home life. If you are divorced or widowed and working besides, you have no such comforting prop to shore up your resolve. Moreover, since you are the one parent the child can relate to—and therefore be deprived of—pleas to stay home affect you even more keenly than they would a married woman.

Any sitter will tell you that five minutes after you are out the door (and usually sooner), your youngster is usually so absorbed in a game or TV show that he hardly notices your absence. But if you want to spare yourself the upsetting histrionics that accompany a nighttime parting, try to arrange something special for your child. Have a friend sleep over or hire a favorite sitter who will actually play with as well as mind him. If your child can go out at the same time you do, to a friend's house or to Grandma's, so much the better. He may even push you out the door on those evenings when it means going out himself.

When your children enter the preteen and teen-age stages, a whole new situation arises relative to your social life. The good news is that you don't feel as guilty when you go out, nor are you dependent on babysitters any more. The bad news is that you can't go off at will because your youngsters are beginning to have a social life of their own and you've got to chaperone and carpool. While we don't believe in giving up everything "for the sake of the children," we do feel that they are entitled to attend evening functions at school and have friends over at night. And for everyone's peace of mind, you'll probably want to stick around when they do. With some compromise and a lot of elaborate arranging, you'll eventually forge a working agreement. If your kids have reached this stage of independence, rejoice. Your responsibility for them is almost over.

15

You

It is no accident that it took us fourteen chapters of discussing your children, your husband, your job, your meals, and even storage for your vacuum cleaner to arrive at a consideration of *You*. No doubt you also wind up last in any allocation you make of your time and resources. This is not a situation unique to the mother who works: the mother who stays home also puts herself at the bottom of the list. But she at least has the possibility of getting to the bottom, whereas you seem to owe every second of your time to other people and other things. We think that this is wrong. We think you're too important to be a mere drudge, and in this chapter we'd like to help you put yourself—if not at the head of the list—then at least way up there among your top priorities.

The Pursuit of Happiness

So many working mothers have been so earnest about keeping their nose to the grindstone and their shoulder to the wheel that, when we asked them what would make them feel good, they had trouble coming up with anything except sleeping. (Fantasies such as having an affair with Robert Redford and spending a month on the Riviera were not allowed.) In our culture the average man would not have this problem. He would be able to name sixteen things right off the bat that would make him feel good. That's because he's accustomed to having leisure time, to feeling that he deserves leisure time, and to indulging himself in that leisure time.

You should feel the same way. Since you work hard too, you also deserve to indulge yourself. But since you may be new to this game, you may first have to identify what really makes you happy—not what you think should make you happy or what others have designated as worthy pleasures. In your circle, for example, it might be perfectly acceptable to get your hair done once a week, but if you spent the same amount of money on a massage, you might be considered wildly extravagant. By the same token, you might be commended if you took up needle-point, but thought of as a weirdo if you got your pilot's license. Happiness is a very personal thing, however, and what turns you on might not turn your friends on or even be particularly constructive. And that's okay.

Sometimes the pursuit of happiness will require some advance planning. Send away for a cooking-school catalogue, sign up for that flower-arranging course, get your belly-dancing costume, or buy a new easel. If you like to read but never seem to get around to it, try setting your alarm clock a half hour earlier two or three days a week. Put an electric coffee pot on a timer near your bed and keep yesterday's unread newspaper or a good book on your night table. What a delicious way to start the day! If you love the theater but never remember to buy tickets, subscribe to a repertory company or make a bimonthly date with another couple to go to a show. Make these commitments to yourself as binding as they would be if you made them to another person.

Sometimes it's nice to pursue happiness on the spur of the moment. One of the greatest drawbacks to being a working mother is the feeling that nothing can happen to you unexpectedly, at least nothing good. You get so locked into your routine that life takes on a very predictable pattern. The only solution to this problem is to look for little ways to break up the monotony. Save up a vacation day or a sick day and spend it on yourself when you really feel down. Making the necessary arrangements to free yourself for a whole day might seem so formidable that you dismiss the thought out of hand, but we promise you the effort will be worth it.

Stay in bed all day if the children are not home and read a sexy novel or watch soap operas on TV. Eat nothing but chocolate-covered marshmallows, chocolate-covered peanuts, and chocolate-covered raisins. Or go out and see a movie, browse through the stores, call up a friend for lunch, explore an unfamiliar part of the city. This kind of day could set you up for months to come.

In identifying the things that make you happy, don't overlook things themselves. Contrary to what the Puritans would have had you believe, material goods do bring happiness as does the very act of purchasing them. Yet many mothers have trouble spending money on anything but an absolute necessity, even if they earned the money themselves. If you, too, become conscience-stricken at the point of purchase, start out by indulging yourself in small, inexpensive, semi-useful ways. You can always use another nail polish, for example, or another lipstick. This kind of little present will give you a lift without breaking your bank account or causing you to suffer pangs of self-recrimination. Gradually you can move on to bigger and better things.

And, finally, don't overlook doing things the easy way in your pursuit of pleasure. There is no reason to feel guilty about using a cleaning service, caterer, or tailor just because you could conceivably do the job yourself. If they're affordable, you should consider these people your legitimate support troops. And stop feeling that the hardest way is always the best or the most noble (frankly, my dear, no one gives a damn). Remember how all work and no play made Jack a dull boy? It could do the same to you and make you very, very depressed, besides.

A Time and a Place for Everything—Even You

You can only focus on what makes you happy and then go to it if you set aside time to yourself. Yet most working mothers are too self-denying to do this. In response to our question:

"How do you find time to yourself?" the women we polled said: "I don't," "When the children are asleep," "When I'm in the bathroom," and "When I'm asleep." Not one had an hour or even a half hour in the day to call her own.

Admittedly, discretionary time is as hard to come by as discretionary income, but you'll have to create it somehow. If you don't, whole weeks can go by in which you literally don't have a moment to yourself. When the pursuit of happiness takes place outside the home, you may have to leave your briefcase in the office, serve a frozen pizza, or opt out of a family activity to squeeze it in. When "happiness" lies right at your own doorstep, you'll have to get tough.

Decide what constitutes your prime time for privacy and make it clear to the children that you are unavailable to them then. If you're adamant about it, they should come to respect your time alone. Hopefully, the children will go to bed at the same time you go off duty, so the house will be quiet. And hopefully, too, you'll get your second wind so that you can still get some mileage out of the evening. But even if the house is noisy, the children are still running around, and you're flat out, try to do something nice for yourself before you sink into oblivion—even if it's only throwing a little cream on your face.

Time to yourself works best when you have a place to yourself. The mother's dilemma has always been having a whole house to oversee and no room to call her own. (Father at least usually gets a chair.) Since the bedroom is probably the closest you'll come to adult turf, we suggest that you jealously guard its sanctity. Be strict about making the children knock, and then let them enter only after you've invited them in. Whenever possible, communicate through the door. Sound carries perfectly through wood (as you know so well), and matters demanding your immediate, urgent, life or death, personal attention often resolve themselves by themselves if you simply decline to emerge. Alone at last, you can have a shot at getting dressed on time, doing your exercises straight through, making a civilized phone call, or taking a quiet bath.

Sometimes you will need another place of your own to pursue

a hobby. Since you want to spend the precious free time you have doing the activity instead of setting it up and taking it down, try to find a permanent base of operations somewhere. Commandeer a corner of one room and make it off limits to everyone else. If an invisible barrier is not enough to keep your children out, put up a folding screen or suspend a giant shade from the ceiling. One working mother turned a walk-in closet into a mini-office, workroom, and gift-wrap center. Another working mother converted a standard-sized closet into a combination sewing center/greenhouse. And still another put her sculpting supplies in a roll-away cabinet. Try to carve out a place for yourself even if you don't have a specific interest you want to pursue. Psychologically, having a place to oneself leads to making time for oneself and to thinking of oneself as a priority item.

Mrs. Goodbody

Treating yourself as a priority item includes taking care of your body, because people who are in good physical shape tend to feel better. But what working mother do you know—present company included—who feels tiptop? Dragged out is probably a more accurate description. And no wonder. You're constantly moving at top speed with rarely a minute out to relax. You're prey to every contagious disease your children bring home from school as well as those floating around your office. Moreover, you're probably under a great deal of pressure. Like most people, you may need a certain amount of pressure in order to produce, but you may be punishing your body in the process. That is the conclusion of doctors who have been studying women business executives, those in the vanguard of the "libbing" of America. According to a recent article in the *Wall Street Journal*: "The special burdens of being an isolated female, plus the normal tensions of middle management; often combine to place tremendous emotional stress on women executives. Consequently, physicians report, they are starting to fall prey to such traditionally male stress-related diseases as heart attacks, ulcers and high blood pressure.''*

Even if you're not an executive, being a working mother can be emotionally stressful, so pay attention to what your body is telling you. If you start to experience mysterious aches and pains and find you're irritable, fatigued, and distracted all the time, you may be living under too much stress. Ignore these warnings and you may find yourself suffering from more serious conditions such as colitis and ulcers. No two people have an identical tolerance for stress, so don't compare yourself to Mrs. Doitall across the street. She may be able to cope with more than you naturally—or she may be popping Valium like crazy when no one is looking.

A large component of feeling good is getting enough sleep. True, you might be able to accomplish more by sleeping only four hours a night, but you'd soon get so rundown that you wouldn't be able to cope at all. You can't compare your resiliency to what it was when you used to stay up all night doing term papers. You were younger then, you bounced back faster, and you could sleep right through the following day. Now you've got to be back in harness early the next morning. And when you don't recoup your lost sleep within twenty-four hours, it's lost forever.

If you have to get up early and your husband insists on watching the eleven o'clock news in bed, get him a TV set with an earplug and a long cord. If he snores, you get the earplugs. And if he gets up earlier than you do, have him lay out his clothes the night before. Resort to eyeshades, blackout curtains, and threatening notes if the sun and your own little early birds are conspiring to get you up at the crack of dawn. Finally, invest in a firm mattress to ensure a good night's sleep and to avoid backaches upon arising.

Exercise is another key ingredient in the recipe for good

---

*You don't have to be part of management to be aggravated. According to the National Institute for Occupational Safety and Health, the second most stressful job in America is that of secretary.

health. You may need to set aside more time for it now that you're working, because your job may not keep you as active as full-time housework did. But since you probably have neither the time nor the inclination for an elaborate exercise routine, think of ways to sneak in a little body movement here and there. While standing in line for a bus or waiting for a telephone call to go through, for example, you could rotate your neck, contract your buttocks, or do some stomach holds. Schedule a weekly hour of exercise too, in which you do something you enjoy such as tennis, dancing, or ice skating. Look for activities you can do with the children that will enable you to be with them and become physically fit at the same time. This might take the form of some spontaneous exercise over the weekend. And don't forget that walking is exercise, perhaps the best exercise there is. It's great for your heart, great for your figure, and great for your nerves. If you take a brisk walk in lieu of a big lunch, you may find that you're less sleepy in the afternoon.

When you start to work, you may not only exercise less but also eat more or worse. The daily confrontations with the coffee wagon, business lunch, and lounge room candy machines could overpower anyone. Moreover, there's something about sitting at a desk all day that seems to lead to a craving for sweets. Before you know it, all those extra little snacks can cause you to gain unwanted pounds. From both a medical and cosmetic standpoint, overweight is undesirable, so try to counteract the office situations that trigger your eating. Also try to choose foods that are low in calories and high in fiber and nutritional content. This isn't easy when you're out in the world all day, because packaged and fast-food fare tends to be just the opposite. One rarely finds a raw carrot in a vending machine. If you want to eat well to maintain a trim figure, good health, and optimum energy, you may have to bring at least some of your food from home.

Finally, there are some simple preventive steps that you should be taking for the sake of your health, such as visiting the eye doctor once a year and the dentist twice a year. Moreover, you should check your breasts once a month for lumps. The likelihood of your developing breast cancer is one in twelve, but you can impressively increase your chances of containing the disease by early detection. So don't be an ostrich—examine. In addition, see your gynecologist once a year if you are under thirty-five and twice a year if you are over thirty-five, taking contraceptive pills or using an I.U.D. (If your general practitioner examines your breasts and takes a Pap smear, a separate visit to the gynecologist may not be necessary.)

Many informed people are now saying that yearly general physicals are a waste of time and money, because they rarely turn up anything significantly wrong with the body. If you go by statistics, these commentators are correct. However, regular checkups provide baseline data that are valuable for comparison purposes when something does go wrong. They can help bring emotional problems out into the open. And they can help you establish a rapport with a doctor whom you may need to call in the middle of the night for an emergency or deal with over the phone for less serious ailments. For these reasons, we think you should get a checkup once a year.

Truly, this is an age of medical miracles when it comes to preventing and curing diseases. But when it comes to feeling good on a day-to-day basis, you hold all the cards. You have it in your power to be healthier or at least to feel better by sleeping enough, exercising regularly, eating and drinking in moderation, and not smoking. This a regimen without gimmicks. Its success will depend largely on how important you are to yourself. You should be important enough so that you'll think as much about maintaining your health as you do about maintaining your home.

Now that we've gotten you to focus on the inner woman, we'd like you to turn your attention to the outer one.

Threads

Looking good on the outside can make you feel better on the inside. Knowing that you're well dressed can boost your morale at home, give you confidence on the job, and just plain make you happier wherever you are. Unfortunately, you don't have much time to devote to your wardrobe; but approaching it in a methodical manner should see you through.

First of all, review every stitch of clothing you own. Give yourself enough lead time for repairs and replacements so that by the time the new season is ready to start, you will be too. Set certain automatic target dates such as:

Labor Day:	review winter wardrobe
Columbus Day:	add to winter wardrobe, take advantage of sales
New Year's Day:	final addition to winter clothes, shop sales
Valentine's Day:	review spring clothes
Easter:	take summer clothes out of storage, review
Memorial Day:	send last of winter clothes to be cleaned and stored

Arrange to be alone during your closet reviews. Fix yourself a cup of coffee, put on some music, and get into a very self-centered mood. Then try on everything you own. Even though you put a dress away just four months ago, it may have shrunk in the last cleaning, you may have expanded in the interim, or a hem may have fallen. Do you have the right shoes, bag, coat, and jewelry to complete the outfit? Try them on too. Very helpful in these closet reviews are a good light, a good full-length mirror and a fold-up coat rack. Costing less than $25, the coat rack comes in handy for parties, cleaning closets, and packing for trips, as well as for going through your clothes.

Scrutinize every garment carefully. If you don't like the way it looks in your mirror, give it away. If it has faded, lost its shape, collected snags, stains, pills, and frays, or just gotten the general blahs—give it away. And if you didn't wear it at all last year, out it goes. Accessories are the exception to this rule, because they rarely go out of style and are expensive to replace. But adhere to the major tenet of organization and give away 20 percent of everything else.

Now that you know just what you have, you can start to think about what you need. In addition to your working wardrobe, which we discussed in Chapter 5, "The 'Real World,' " you'll want to have the appropriate clothes for movies, dinner parties, entertaining, and sports. Think about what you'll want to wear for upcoming events such as Thanksgiving or your annual trip to the mountains. And don't overlook something to put on after work. While you don't have to "dress" for dinner, the family deserves something better than your old stained bathrobe every night.

In allocating your clothes budget, try to cover every category of your life, but plan to spend the most on things you wear most often. You'll make your money go further and be better dressed too if you work around one or two basic colors that are compatible with your everyday coat. You don't have to look as though you've been wiped down with a paint roller every time you step out the door, but color coordination does help to make one look well organized.

Subdued colors, classic styles, and mix-and-match separates will stretch your budget, as will clothes that are sturdy. Look for garments that say "wash and dry" or at least that give promise of spending more time on your premises than the dry cleaner's. Some jobs do demand particularly durable clothing, but that doesn't mean they have to be dreary. While on field trips to such remote places as Bali and New Guinea, Margaret Mead made it a point to wear pretty, brightly colored dresses because the native children were so taken with them.

Now you know what you have, what you need, and the sort of clothes to look for. But don't be in a hurry to buy. Browse around first to get the feel of this season's look without committing yourself to clothes that could quickly become a cliché. Moreover, by starting out slow, you'll still have money to spend when you're ready for a pick-me-up. On the other hand, don't wait too long. The stores are stocking clothes further and further in advance of the season, as anyone who has tried to buy a bathing suit in July well knows.

When you do sally forth to buy, look for matching pieces first. If you can find a blue sweater to go with your blue skirt, you will have a whole new outfit for the price of that one top. But do take the skirt with you, as well as high heels, a slip, and anything else you'll need for this excursion. What is more ludicrous than trying on a business suit in Hush Puppies and socks? And never, ever go shopping without a list to guide you. "You can always use it," the saleslady says. Except that you don't use it, because it doesn't go with anything else in your closet. So develop sales resistance to the extra mauve blouse—even if it is "you." In addition, concentrate on those stores that seem to buy with you in mind and those manufacturers that seem to cut to your figure. By following these suggestions and some of the others we've made above, you should save both time and money on clothes and be happier with your purchases.

Friendships

Sometimes in their selfless drive to be everything to everybody, working mothers forgo all their personal friendships. They don't have time for friends, they say, and besides, they feel they should be spending every spare moment with their families. In our opinion this is a mistake. No matter how mature children are, they cannot take the place of adult companions, nor should one's husband be the only bridge to the grown-up world. A working mother needs the emotional support and social give and take only her peers can give. As you start to focus on yourself and what makes you happy, we urge you to consider friends. They humanize what could otherwise become a very robot-like existence.

Unfortunately, some of your old cronies may have counted you out once you started to work. Don't be paranoid about this. It doesn't necessarily mean that you've become an object of envy, resentment, or disapproval. More likely, you have simply ceased to exist as far as they are concerned. If your acquaintanceship was based on a daytime activity such as bowling league or reciprocal babysitting, once that connection was severed, so essentially was the relationship. Your feelings may be hurt because these women no longer ask you to join them in the old activities, but since you know and they know you're going to have to decline their invitations anyway, you can't expect to have it both ways.

Moreover, from where they sit it may look as though you've dropped *them*. And, indeed, you may have gotten too busy to keep up with your old friends once you started to work, or when you did get together, something in your attitude may have said, "I've gone on to bigger and better things." You may truly feel more of an affinity now for the woman who works or goes to school, but the stay-at-home woman still can have a lot to offer even if, on the surface, she's not "doing anything with herself." However, you may have to make the initial overtures. In this day of women's lib, the stay-at-home may have such an inferiority complex or feel so threatened by you that she wouldn't dream you'd be interested in her friendship.

Make the overture. Seek out a stay-at-home mother in your neighborhood and develop a good working relationship with her. Things do come up and you need at least one person close by whom you can count on in an emergency. In addition to looking for this "best friend," cultivate the goodwill of other mothers in your community. If you want them to include your children in various activities, make it clear that you will participate to whatever extent you can. Or return their favors by taking their children to nighttime or weekend events, or by inviting the youngsters to stay at your home for a few days so that their parents can go on vacation. You could also show helpful mothers your appreciation by buying a doll house enthusiast a miniature rocker, taking a gourmet out for a fancy French meal, or picking things up in town for the woman who is stuck at home. Even if you can't repay in kind, showing your appreciation in some way will ensure that you and your children don't get shut out.

Unfortunately, many working mothers find themselves in just

that position. They blame it on the housewives' bias against women who work; while this can be a factor, the working mother's attitude often doesn't help much either. Burdened with the concerns of office and home, some working mothers simply expect housewives to do them endless favors out of the goodness of their hearts. Or they expect the stay-at-homes to pitch in because "they have nothing else to do with their time."

If you find yourself thinking this way, remember that the housewife's time is just as valuable to her as yours is to you. Nor is she under any special obligation to help you out just because she's there and you're not. So thank the other women profusely for whatever they do—be it running a Brownie troop, organizing a school fair, or carpooling your child—and think of all the ways you can to help them out. As the old maxim goes, "The only way to have a friend is to be one."

Entertaining

One way to be a friend is to invite people to your home. What could be nicer than relaxing, sharing ideas, and catching up on all the latest gossip in the comfort of your own living room? So far, so good, but at some point your guests will expect you to offer them something to eat, and that's when the trouble begins. Entertaining can be a creative outlet, one that is often cultivated in the pursuit of pleasure. However, women who viewed it that way all their lives tend to see it as a chore once they start to work. If you too grow faint-hearted at the thought of having people over, bear in mind these few basic do's and don't's.

Do make it simple: Put together a few of the frozen dishes you've packaged for your family, add a garnish here and there, and—*voilà*—you've got a meal fit for company. Or serve a simple roast, which many people love but rarely get to eat any more because hostesses are so intent upon displaying their culinary skills.

Do make it buffet: By setting the food out and letting the

guests help themselves, you free yourself from having to serve. Buffet also has the advantage of giving guests something to do with themselves and allowing them to choose what and how much they are going to eat.

Do make it lap service: This is acceptable today for everything from a hootenanny to a black tie affair. The advantage of lap service is that it eliminates the time-consuming chore of setting the table. The drawback to it is that, due to impromptu seating arrangements, someone may feel left out or get stuck with just one other guest all evening. To prevent this, divide up the guests into seating groups or have them do it themselves by picking out of a hat.

Do make it communal: When each person brings a dish, you obviously will have less to prepare. Moreover, you may have less need to play hostess too, because the participants will feel a greater stake in making the party a success. Instead of sitting back and adopting an "entertain me" attitude, they're more likely to make an effort to mingle and see that everyone is attended to.

Do make it outdoors: Outdoor cooking practically dictates a simple menu and one that can be prepared in advance or put on the grill at the last minute. If they're combined with some physical activity, picnics or barbecues can be held even in very nippy weather. And either one is ideal when children are involved.

Or, don't make it at all: Let the local deli do the work. Everyone enjoys a six-foot hero or a wine and cheese party in which the cheeses are labeled and the wines are not. These novelty repasts also have the advantage of being conversation pieces and, because they are cold, of having a long life span on the buffet table. If it is a make-your-own-sandwich or make-your-own-sundae party, the guests get to add their own creative dimension to the festivities.

Don't build the party around food: Eating does not have to be the focal point of every gathering. You could have friends over to watch a TV special, for example, or to play cards or backgammon. A sandwich and a glass of beer—all that is required for this kind of evening—is something even the working mother could swing during the week.

Don't always use your china: Nowadays disposable table settings are all but expected at informal and large gatherings. Not only are these paper and plastic products a great convenience, but they can be wonderfully attractive as well. Sometimes an imaginative touch such as serving chicken in individual baskets positively makes the meal. Entertaining is illusion and no one can resist a bit of show biz when he sits down to eat.

Don't feel locked into dinner: Other times of the day may be more convenient for you to entertain now that you're working. Sunday brunch is a prime example of this. Not only are you well rested then, but the menu requirements are simple and universally well liked. After-dinner entertaining may also work out well if you have small children to tuck into bed before the guests arrive.

Don't feel you have to go it alone: Using a catering service or buying ready-made party dishes at a gourmet shop may be within your budget if you compare it to the combined cost of the ingredients and the value of your time. Also consider hiring teenagers to help you serve and clean up. Your high school employment bureau may be able to furnish you with bright and reasonably priced waitresses and bartenders. If you're entertaining certain business associates, you may be able to deduct a portion of your costs as a legitimate business expense or your company may pay for it all. Certainly check out these possibilities before you start to slave over a hot stove.

Don't keep reinventing the wheel: You don't have to come up with an original menu for every gathering. Indeed, some working mothers serve a single company recipe for an entire year or until they invite their guests back. Others keep a log of what they served to avoid repetition and to remind them of their successes and failures.

Some working mothers feel they have to prove something when they entertain. They want to show the world that they are as feminine, creative, and domestic as the woman who stays home. As a result, their parties become Twentieth Century Fox extravaganzas—except that the star is missing, because she has to keep track of all those bubbling pots in the kitchen. Lest you too miss out on all the fun of your own gatherings, make them as work-free as possible. But if you find you can't be a relaxed hostess no matter what you do, take your friends out for a pizza. If they're true friends, they'll love you anyway.

Family

Although often your greatest source of satisfaction, your family can sometimes appear to be the major barrier between you and the realization of yourself as an individual. When it does, you may wish you were a single girl again, a hippie, or a nun. But in point of fact, you are probably realizing more of your human potential by living within the context of a family than by living alone. And you are probably emotionally healthier too. Statistics would seem to indicate that family life is generally less stressful than being on one's own.

Part of your disillusionment with your family may stem from preconceived notions of how it should be. Subconsciously, you may have always assumed that *your* family would be perfect. It would look a lot like the Brady Bunch, in fact. In this ideal family the siblings are always supportive of one another, the parents are always tenderly amused, the children are always respectful—full of the devil perhaps, but never "bad." The greatest crisis to confound their existence is Marcia's accepting two dates for the prom.

Statistically, this family is one of a small minority, because of the rise in working mothers and in single-parent and single-child households. Realistically, this family is nonexistent, because no group of individuals can live under the same roof without experiencing times of intense conflict. But emotionally this family is all too real. It presents an absolute standard that you may try to attain, yet never do. Your children cannot be beautiful enough, you cannot be detached enough, your house isn't clean enough and, for some reason, your problems don't resolve themselves in the half hour allotted to a situation comedy.

Try to detach yourself from that impossible dream. Family life was and always will be a struggle. In some ways that struggle has been intensified in modern-day America because there are fewer hands to help with the housework, babysitting, and other chores. Moreover, all the satisfactions have to be derived from a smaller number of individuals. With fewer people in a smaller physical space, the relationships may be more intense too. Raising children and maintaining a good relationship with one's spouse takes a lot of hard work, and no one ever does it perfectly (the Brady Bunch notwithstanding)—even if she stays home all day trying.

But there are tremendous satisfactions to be derived from family life as well as burdens to be assumed. What could do more for a woman's ego than being the most important person in her household, for example? And when a child needs extra T.L.C., a husband needs a sounding board, and a room requires a woman's touch—you're *it*. Although you might go further, faster, in your career if you didn't have a family, then again you might not. And though you might not have dishpan hands, rings under your eyes, and a sore throat from yelling, you might also find yourself without the range of loving relationships your family provides. So stop thinking that irresponsible bachelorhood would bring out the essential You. As far as we're concerned, family life is "where it's at."

You, You, You

When you can think about You as distinct from your roles as worker, housekeeper, and mother, you're well on the way to being a successful working mother. For only someone with a strong sense of self will be able to carry off so many different and sometimes conflicting roles without getting lost in the shuffle. And only someone who is in touch with her emotions and how she's feeling physically can work up to capacity, yet not get so carried away that she dangerously overextends herself.

These may or may not be the best years of your life, but they are certainly the most taxing. You and the other working mothers in America are putting tremendous demands upon yourselves, and you're doing it without the support of the society in which you live. Under the circumstances, we think you're coping remarkably well. But we do look forward to the day when business, school, and home life will be responsive to your particular needs. Hopefully, by the time your daughters are grown up they will have it so much easier that they will look back upon your pioneering efforts in wonder. "Mother, how did you do it?" they will ask. You probably won't know yourself. "I just did it, that's all," you'll reply. And that will be the truth.

Appendix

THE TOOLS OF ORGANIZATION

You'll be far more efficient if you equip a drawer in your
kitchen and the desk in your home office with the following
supplies:

Kitchen Control Center

pens, pencils
stationery for school notes
pins for affixing notes to jackets
pads for notes and lists
box of lunch money
masking tape, transparent tape, rubber bands, and paper clips
scissors and small sewing kit for last-minute repairs
telephone directories, personal and public
bulletin board/blackboard

Your Desk

address book/public phone book
personalized stationery, postcards, and extra envelopes
personalized stickers and/or name stamp
stamps

pens, pencils
scratch pads
stapler with extra staples
scissors
transparent tape, rubber bands, paper clips
typewriter (if you use one)
adding machine or calculator (makes everything easier)
checkbook

HOME FILING SYSTEM

In order to get your household papers in order, clear out a file drawer or buy a large cardboard box and fill it with manila folders in alphabetical order labeled as follows:

Bills: File them with the oldest first. If you make partial payments, indicate the amount outstanding on the inside of the folder along with the due dates of regular payments.

Canceled Checks: Keep canceled checks and old stubs in chronological order. You'll want them to use as proof of payment in disputes with stores and for verification in case of an Internal Revenue Service audit.

Car: This folder contains all records of repairs and replacements and a schedule of maintenance work. Such records are good to have when you try to sell your car, because they provide proof of upkeep. They also come in handy when you want to confer with a garage mechanic.

Charities: Put solicitation letters here with their return envelopes. If you keep saying, "I just gave to that," you are probably right. Charities work from so many lists that your name is bound to come up more than once a year. To avoid going through all your checks each time you are solicited, keep a running list of when and how much you contributed.

Committee Work: If you belong to an organization, keep all the information relating to it here. Then on meeting night, you can just grab this folder and run.

Entertainment: After entering the date and time of a show in your calendar, file the tickets here. You might also want to keep restaurant reviews, entertaining tips, and ideas for family excursions in this folder.

Estimates: Business cards and estimate sheets for paint jobs, re-upholstering, and household services should be contained here. They help you compare costs from artisan to artisan and from year to year.

F.Y.I. (*"For Your Information"*): This contains important papers requiring action: questionnaires to be filled out, school permission slips to be signed, courses to be registered for. Go through it often.

Hobbies: Anything written about a favorite pastime goes here. That includes special-interest catalogues, magazine articles, notices of meetings, and ads.

IRS: Put everything here you'll need for April 15: acknowl-edgments of charitable contributions; business expense receipts; W-2 forms; social security records if you employ a housekeeper; loan payment statements; etc. Check with your accountant to find out what is relevant in your particular situation.

Miscellaneous: These papers don't require action and don't fit any particular category, but somehow you can't throw them away. Let them age gracefully. If they sit here long enough, you'll forget why you wanted to keep them in the first place and find it easier to get rid of them.

Sales Receipts and Credit Slips: These come in handy for re-turns and straightening out accounts. File them with the oldest toward the front and discard them after three months.

Special Projects: This is the place to organize a one-shot event. When it is over, discard the material and recycle the folder.

Travel: This is the place for advertisements, brochures, and articles about spots you'd like to visit.

Warranties and Instructions: Gather all those little booklets that have been cluttering up your kitchen drawers for years and put them in here. Add to the pile with each new gadget or appliance.

USEFUL TELEPHONE NUMBERS

	Name & Telephone
Plumber	_____
Electrician	_____
Appliance repair: refrigerator	_____
washer-dryer	_____
stove-oven	_____
furnace	_____
air conditioner	_____
water heater	_____
Car repair	_____
Oil delivery	_____
Utility company (gas-electric)	_____
Water company	_____
Garbage-removal company	_____
Snow-removal service	_____
Telephone Co: emergency repair	_____
business office	_____
Septic tank service	_____
Insurance agent (house, car)	_____
Railroad station	_____
Bus station	_____
Apartment house superintendent	_____
Apartment house manager	_____
City housing authority	_____
Other	_____

ILLNESS CHECK LIST

Refer to the following list of questions when discussing your child's condition with the sitter or pediatrician:

Respiratory Illnesses

Fever: Length of time? Steady or fluctuating?
Cough: Extent? Sounds like? Chest pain?
Breathing: Labored? Noisy? Rapid?
Throat: Sore? Redness? Trouble swallowing? Neck glands?
Earache: Fussy? Pulling at ears? Discharge?
Eyes: Red? Discharge? Tearing?
Headache: Complaint of? Holding head?
Vomiting: Alone or after coughing?
Appetite: Fluid intake in last several hours? Food?
Sleeping: Sleeping well, too much, not at all?

Gastrointestinal Upsets

Fever: Length of time? Steady or fluctuating?
Stomach pain: Where? Steady or crampy? Intensity? With BM or without? Length of time?
Vomiting: Frequency? Amount? Appearance?
Fluid intake: How much in last several hours?
Urine: Amount? Frequency?
Food being fed: Type? Being accepted?
Bowel movements: Consistency? Amount? Frequency?
Appearance of child: Looks sick? Mouth dry?
Activity level: Is child moving or still? Any problem walking?

FIRST AID

In lieu of a full-fledged first aid course—which every member of your family and "staff" should take at some point—we offer a rundown of basic procedures to be followed when emergencies arise.

Breathing Difficulties: Any difficulty in breathing, any stoppage of respiration, any excessively shallow, noisy, or rapid breathing constitutes an emergency of the greatest magnitude. Although it is beyond the scope of this section to teach the techniques, all parents—indeed, all adults—should learn cardiopulmonary resuscitation (CPR) and the newly described method for prevention of choking, Heimlich's Maneuver. Remember, if breathing has stopped, you only have five minutes at best during which it can be reestablished before brain damage or death occurs. You have somewhat more leeway in the case of noisy, rapid, shallow, or other breathing difficulties, but they too can be dangerous. Therefore, you must calm the patient, immediately call your physician, and/or quickly transport your child to the nearest emergency room.

Broken Bones: Immobilize the part you think is broken or have the emergency rescue team do it, then transport your child to the hospital.

Burns: The best first aid for all burns is the immediate application of ice or cold water. This treatment not only relieves pain, but it may actually minimize the extent of the injury. Next, cover the burned area with some sort of nonstick covering such as Telfa pads or even Saran wrap and then call your physician. Under no circumstances should you cover the burn with butter, first aid cream, petroleum jelly, or some home remedy, nor break any blisters that have formed. If clothes or other materials are stuck to the burn, leave them alone.

Cuts (Large) That Leave a Gaping Hole and/or Bleed Profusely:
Without exception, bleeding should be controlled by the application of pressure directly to the cut. Use a dry compress of gauze pads, clean towels, clean clothing, or even paper towels. A tourniquet is not needed. In all but the most unusual circumstances, bleeding will stop in twenty minutes or less when pressure is applied, at which point the child should be taken to his physician or a hospital emergency room.

Cuts (Small), Scrapes, and Similar Injuries: Wash with soap and water, cover with clean bandages, and keep clean.

Dental Emergencies: Whether the injured tooth is primary or secondary ("baby" or "permanent"), call your dentist when trauma occurs. If the tooth has been completely knocked out, find it if you can, wash it off, and put it in clean water, because your dentist may want to try to replant it. If the tooth has been knocked loose, there are other procedures he may try in order to save it. In most instances, injury to a tooth also means soft tissue damage and swelling. Use ice on the afflicted area unless the nerve of the open tooth screams *No* to the cold.

Electric Shock: Severe electric shocks can cause heart stoppage and respiratory arrest, requiring cardiopulmonary resuscitation, but more commonly they result in burns. These can be treated with ice like any other burns. However, *they should be seen by a physician as soon as possible,* because electrical burns that look minor can be very deep and potentially serious.

Head Injuries: A child who has banged his head but has not knocked himself out may vomit once, complain of a headache, feel dizzy, and want to fall asleep—all of which is normal. Giving him an aspirin or an ice pack for the pain is all right, because it will not obscure any important developing symptoms; but don't give him any other medication. Permit him to sleep, but wake him every hour or so for at least the first six to eight hours after the injury. Ask him if he knows who he is, where he is, who you are, and what is going on. As long as he remains oriented, can walk with good balance and rhythm, and does not develop any symptoms other than those we've mentioned, he will probably be okay. But if your child has lost consciousness, can't recall the events leading up to his fall, or starts to develop other suspicious symptoms, contact his physician.

Insect Stings: Unless your child has an allergic reaction to a sting, applying ice to it is all that is necessary. The swelling that appears within the next day or so is not an allergic reaction, whether it appears around the site of the sting or even up and down a limb. An allergic reaction consists of generalized symptoms that usually occur within minutes of the sting. These may be any type of rash, especially hives, any problem with breathing, or any change in consciousness. If your child exhibits an allergic reaction, he needs prompt medical attention.

Lumps, Bumps, Strains, Sprains, Twists, Muscle Pulls, etc.: Always apply ice at first to decrease the swelling and control the discomfort. Then after eight to twelve hours, use heat in the form of a heating pad, hot water bottle, or hot baths to overcome stiffness and assist the healing process. If the child is not using the injured part reasonably well after 24 hours, he should be seen by a doctor.

Nose Bleeds: These are more common in children than broken bones or severe lacerations. The nose will often spout a large amount of blood either spontaneously or from minimal trauma. For the most part simply pinching the nostrils will control the bleeding in the same manner as putting direct pressure on a cut. Do not put the child's head back (he will simply swallow the blood, which will then irritate his stomach and cause him to vomit). And do not apply ice to his nose, forehead, or back of his neck, because it won't do him any good.

Poisoning: This refers to the ingestion of such toxic material as medicines, household products, plant material, cosmetics, and petroleum products. If the material ingested is nonpetroleum and noncaustic, induce vomiting by giving the appropriate dose of Syrup of Ipecac. But if, according to the label, the material contains petroleum distillates in any form or is caustic, do not induce vomiting. In either case, try to determine the amount of material swallowed, relay the information to a poison control center or physician, then follow instructions. If you are directed to a medical facility, take a container of the toxic matter with you.

Splinters: Remove splinters with a clean, sharp needle or tweezers. If they do not come out easily or are buried deeply, call the physician. Do not soak wooden splinters unless advised to, because soaking softens the wood and may make their removal more difficult.

Swallowing Solid Foreign Objects: Unless your child is coughing, gagging, or choking from the ingestion of coins, small toys, marbles, etc., there is NO EMERGENCY. If the object gets into the stomach, it will usually be passed without a problem. But if there are any signs of respiratory difficulties such as coughing or if the child has any trouble swallowing, take him to the nearest emergency room where he may have to undergo X-ray studies of the lungs and esophagus.

Unconsciousness: A loss of consciousness is often very serious. But since it is only a symptom and not a disease, the seriousness of it cannot be determined until the underlying cause is known. Until it is, make sure that the victim is breathing, that his mouth is clear of all foreign material, that he is in a comfortable position, and that he is kept warm until he can be moved to a hospital. Loosen all tight clothing, check for bleeding, but—*unless you know that he could not have possibly hurt his neck*—*DO NOT MOVE HIM UNTIL TRAINED HELP ARRIVES.*

EMERGENCY TELEPHONE LIST

Children's doctor   Name _____

                             Telephone_____

Parents' doctor   Name_____

                             Telephone_____

Family dentist   Name_____

                             Telephone_____

Pharmacy   Name_____

                             Telephone_____

Hospital Emergency Room   Telephone_____

Poison Control Center   Telephone_____

Police   Telephone_____

Ambulance   Telephone_____

Fire Department   Telephone_____

Taxi   Telephone_____

Neighbors   Name_____

                             Telephone_____

                             Name_____

                             Telephone_____

Mother at work   Telephone_____

Father at work   Telephone_____

Children's Schools   Name of child_____

                             Name of school_____

                             Telephone_____

                             Name of child_____

                             Name of school_____

                             Telephone_____

Other   Telephone_____

The phone number here is   _____

This apartment's address   near_____

RESOURCES

Camp Information

American Camping Association
225 Park Avenue South
New York, N.Y. 10003

Association of Private Camps, Inc.
55 West 42nd Street
New York, N.Y. 10019

Camp Advisory Service
500 Fifth Avenue
New York, N.Y. 10017

Child Safety

American Academy of Pediatrics
Box 1034
Evanston, Ill. 60204
Write for their child safety suggestions sets, which are available at nominal cost.

American National Red Cross
17th and D Streets NW
Washington, D.C. 20006
Publishers of the standard first aid manual and other worthwhile materials to help safeguard your child. These materials are also available through local chapters.

Bicycle Institute of America, Inc.
122 East 42nd Street
New York, N.Y. 10017
Send for their free publication, *Bike Quiz Guide,* and test your child.

Health and Welfare Division
Metropolitan Life Insurance Company
1 Madison Avenue

New York, N.Y. 10010
Ask for their booklet, *Your Child's Safety.*

Day Care

American Academy of Pediatrics
Box 1034
Evanston, Ill. 60204
Write for its publication, *Recommendations for Day Care Centers for Infants and Children.*

Child Care Resource Center
187 Hampshire Street
Cambridge, Mass. 02139
Write for its list of publications, including *How to Select a Child Care Center.*

Child Welfare League of America
44 East 23rd Street
New York, N.Y. 10010
Write for general information and publications.

National Association for Child Development and Education
500 12 Street SW
Washington, D.C. 20024
Send a stamped self-addressed envelope to receive information regarding profit making day-care centers.

Education and Career Counseling

American Association of University Women
2401 Virginia Avenue NW
Washington, D.C. 20037
The AAUW acts as a clearinghouse for information regarding women's educational opportunities. Write for its fact sheets.

Catalyst
14 E. 60th Street
New York, N.Y. 10022

This organization aids women all over the country with its career planning, job placement, and educational advisory services. It also prepares useful publications, such as *Your Job Campaign*. Write for complete information.

International Association of Counseling Services
1607 New Hampshire Avenue NW
Washington, D.C. 20009
Its *Directory of Approved Counseling Agencies* lists types of services, hours, and charges for counselors in the United States and Canada.

National Organization for Women (NOW)
5 S. Wabash
Suite 1615
Chicago, Ill. 60603
Its 800 local chapters provide employment seminars, legal advice, and referral services.

Women's Bureau
U.S. Department of Labor
14th Street and Constitution Avenue NW
Washington, D.C. 20210
The Women's Bureau issues an enormous amount of information on occupational opportunities, educational programs, and in-service training courses, as well as research on other topics of interest to working mothers such as child care.

Also investigate the career and continuing education counseling services of your local school system, women's center, YWCA/YMCA, and other community organizations. And don't overlook the guidance given by professional organizations, trade associations, labor unions, and colleges.

Help for Family and Childhood Problems

American Association of Marriage and Family Counselors, Inc.
225 Yale Avenue

Claremont, Calif. 91711
Write for a list of certified counselors in your area.

Child Study Association of America
Wel-Met, Inc.
50 Madison Avenue
New York, N.Y. 10010
Write for a list of their publications giving advice on various childhood stress situations, such as *What to Tell Your Child about Sex* and *Helping Your Child Understand Death*.

Family Service Association of America
44 East 23rd Street
New York, N.Y. 10010
This organization can provide you with the names of local family service agencies that provide counseling for emotional problems, child-care placement, and other family needs all over America.

National Association of Social Workers
1425 H Street NW
Suite 600
Washington, D.C. 20005
Check first with the NASW office in the closest large city or your state capital for their *Register of Clinical Social Workers*. If you can't locate such an office, check with the national headquarters listed here.

Selected Bibliography:
Helpful Books for Working Mothers

Abarbanel, Karin, and Siegel, Gonnie McClung. *Woman's Work Book.* New York: Praeger, 1975.

Adams, Charlotte. *Teen-Ager's Menu Cookbook.* New York: Dodd, Mead & Co., 1969.

Adams, Jane. *Sex and the Single Parent.* East Rutherford, N.J.: Coward, McCann & Geoghegan, 1978.

Bel Geddes, Joan. *How to Parent Alone: A Guide for Single Parents.* Somers, Conn.: Seabury Press, 1974.

Berman, Eleanor. *The Cooperating Family.* Englewood Cliffs, N.J.: Prentice-Hall, 1977.

Bird, Caroline. *Everything a Woman Needs to Know to Get Paid What She's Worth.* New York: David McKay Co., 1973.

Boston Children's Medical Center and Elizabeth M. Gregg. *What to Do When "There's Nothing to Do."* New York: Delacorte Press, 1967.

Bracken, Peg. *The I Hate to Cook Book.* New York: Fawcett World Library, 1976.

——. *The I Hate to Housekeep Book.* New York: Fawcett World Library, 1974.

Brazelton, T. Berry. *Doctor and Child.* New York: Delacorte Press, 1976.

——. *Infants and Mothers.* New York: Delacorte Press, 1969.

———. *Toddlers and Parents.* New York: Delacorte Press, 1974.

Brinkley, J. H., et al. *Teen Guide to Homemaking.* New York: Mc-Graw-Hill, 1976.

Burros, Marian Fox, and Levine, Lois. *The Elegant but Easy Cookbook.* New York: Macmillan, 1967.

Caine, Lynn. *Widow.* New York: Bantam Books, 1975.

Cardozo, Peter. *The Second Whole Kids Catalog.* New York: Bantam Books, 1977. Activity ideas.

Carson, Byrta R., and Ramee, Marue C. *How You Plan and Prepare Meals.* New York: McGraw-Hill, 1968. For teenagers.

Chess, Stella; Thomas, Alexander; and Birch, Herbert G. *Your Child Is a Person.* New York: The Viking Press, 1965.

Cooper, Joseph D. *A Woman's Guide to Part-Time Jobs.* Garden City, N.Y.: Doubleday, 1963.

Crocker, Betty. *Betty Crocker's Cookbook for Boys and Girls.* Racine, Wis.: Western Publishing Co., 1975.

———. *Betty Crocker's Family Dinners in a Hurry.* Racine, Wis.: Western Publishing Co., 1970.

Dyer, Ceil. *The After Work Entertaining Cookbook.* New York: David McKay Co., 1976.

Eimers, Robert, and Aitchison, Robert. *Effective Parents/Responsible Children.* New York: McGraw-Hill, 1978.

Flach, Frederick. *A New Marriage, A New Life.* New York: McGraw-Hill, 1978.

Galinsky, Ellen, and Hooks, William H. *The New Extended Family: Day Care That Works.* Boston: Houghton Mifflin Co., 1977.

Ginott, Haim. *Between Parent and Child.* New York: Avon Books, 1973.

———. *Between Parent and Teenager.* New York: Avon Books, 1973.

Glickman, Beatrice M., and Springer, Nesha B. *Choices in Child Care.* New York: Schocken Books, 1978.

Green, Martin I. *A Sigh of Relief.* New York: Bantam Books, 1976. Child safety and first aid procedures.

Hautzig, Esther. *Life with Working Parents.* New York: Macmillan, 1976. For children.

Hawke, Sharryl, and Knox, David. *One Child by Choice*. Englewood Cliffs, N.J.: Prentice-Hall, 1977.

Heloise. *Heloise's Hints for the Working Woman*. New York: Pocket Books, 1971.

Hennig, Margaret, and Jardim, Anne. *The Managerial Woman*. Garden City, N.Y.: Doubleday, 1977.

Hewitt, Geof. *Working for Yourself: How to Be Successfully Self-Employed*. Emmaus, Pa.: Rodale Press, 1977.

Hope, Karol, and Young, Nancy. *Momma Handbook: The Source Book for Single Mothers*. New York: New American Library, 1976.

Klein, Norma. *Girls Can Be Anything*. New York: E. P. Dutton & Co., 1973. For young children.

Klimo, Joan F. *What Can I Do Today?* New York: Pantheon Books, 1971. Craft ideas for children.

Kraft, W. R. *When Teenagers Take Care of Children*. Philadelphia: Macrae Smith Co., 1965.

Krantzler, Mel. *Creative Divorce*. New York: M. Evans & Co., 1973.

Laird, Jean E. *Hundreds of Hints for Harassed Homemakers*. St. Meinrad, Ind.: Abbey Press, 1971.

Lakein, Alan. *How to Get Control of Your Time and Your Life*. New York: New American Library, 1974.

Lenz, Elinor, and Shaevitz, Marjorie H. *So You Want to Go Back to School: Facing the Realities of Reentry*. New York: McGraw-Hill, 1977.

Liebert, Robert M.; Neale, John M.; and Davidson, Emily S. *The Early Window: Effects of Television on Children and Youth*. New York: Pergamon Press, 1973.

Love, Sandra. *But What About Me?* New York: Harcourt Brace Jovanovich, 1976. Positive presentation of reentry as it affects an only daughter; for children.

Lundell, Margaretta. *Mothercraft*. New York: Simon & Schuster, 1975. Stories and activities for children.

Moore, Alma C. *How to Clean Everything*. New York: Simon & Schuster, 1971.

Nelson, Paula. *The Joy of Money: A Contemporary Woman's Guide to Financial Freedom*. New York: Bantam Books, 1977.

O'Neill, Nena, and O'Neill, George. *Open Marriage: A New Life Style for Couples.* New York: Avon Books, 1973.

Paul, Aileen. *Kids Cooking Complete Meals: Menus, Recipes, Instructions.* Garden City, N.Y.: Doubleday, 1975.

Pogrebin, Letty Cottin. *Getting Yours.* New York: David McKay Co., 1975. How to overcome common problems women face on the job.

Princeton Center for Infancy and Early Childhood. *Parents' Yellow Pages.* Garden City, N.Y.: Anchor Press, 1978. A source book for everything from day-care centers to musical instruments.

Rossman, Isadore. *Two Children by Choice: The Why and How of the Two Child Family.* New York: Parents Magazine Press, 1976.

Selye, Hans. *The Stress of Life.* 2d rev. ed., New York: McGraw-Hill, 1978.

Shaevitz, Marjorie, and Shaevitz, Morton. *The New Working Couple.* New York: McGraw-Hill, 1978.

Spock, Benjamin. *Baby and Child Care.* New rev. ed., New York: Pocket Books, 1976.

Steinfels, Margaret O'Brien. *Who's Minding the Children? The History and Politics of Day Care in America.* New York: Simon & Schuster, 1973.

Sweeney, Karen. *Every Woman's Guide to Family Finances.* New York: Major Books, 1976.

Index